WINSTON CHURCHILL
IN THE TWENTY-FIRST
CENTURY

DA

Published by the Press Syndicate of the University of Cambridge
The Pitt Building, Trumpington Street, Cambridge CB2 1RP, United Kingdom
The Edinburgh Building, Cambridge CB2 2RU, United Kingdom
40 West 20th Street, New York, NY 10011-4211, USA
477 Williamstown Road, Port Melbourne, VIC 3207, Australia
Ruiz de Alarcón 13, 28104 Madrid, Spain

© Royal Historical Society 2004

A catalogue record for this book is available from the British Library

Library of Congress Cataloguing-in-Publication Data applied for

ISBN 0 521 84590 4 (paperback)

First published 2004

Printed in the United Kingdom at the University Press, Cambridge

A politician's character and position are measured in his day by party standards. When he is dead, all that he achieved in the name of party is at an end. The eulogies and censures of partisans are powerless to affect his ultimate reputation. The scales wherein he was weighed are broken. The years to come bring weights and measures of their own.

(Winston S. Churchill, *Lord Randolph Churchill* (1907), p. 823)

It is not given to human beings, happily for them, to foresee or to predict to any large extent the unfolding course of events. In one phase men seem to have been right; in another they seem to have been wrong. Then again, when the perspective of time has lengthened, all stands in a different setting. There is a new proportion, there is another scale of values.

(Winston S. Churchill, *The Unrelenting Struggle* (1942), pp. 1–2)

CONTENTS

vi

NOTES ON CONTRIBUTORS

Paul Addison is Director of the Centre for Second World War Studies in the School of History and Classics at the University of Edinburgh. He is the author of *The Road to 1945: British Politics and the Second World War* (1975) and *Churchill on the Home Front 1900–1955* (1992).

Stuart Ball is Reader in the School of Historical Studies at the University of Leicester. His publications include *Baldwin and the Conservative Party* (1988), *The Conservative Party and British Politics 1902–1951* (1995) and the short biography *Winston Churchill* (2003).

David Cannadine FBA is the Queen Elizabeth the Queen Mother Professor of British History at the Institute of Historical Research, where he was previously Director. Among his many books are *The Decline and Fall of the British Aristocracy* (1990), *G. M. Trevelyan: A Life in History* (1992), *Class in Britain* (1998), *Ornamentalism: How the British Saw their Empire* (2001) and *In Churchill's Shadow* (2002).

David Carlton is Senior Lecturer in International Studies at the University of Warwick. He is author of *MacDonald versus Henderson* (1970), *Anthony Eden: A Biography* (1981), *Britain and the Suez Crisis* (1988), *Churchill and the Soviet Union* (2000) and numerous academic articles. He has also co-edited twenty-one further books.

John Charmley is Professor of Modern History and Dean of the School of History at the University of East Anglia. He is the author of a number of monographs, most notably *Churchill: The End of Glory* (1993), *Churchill's Grand Alliance* (1996) and *Splendid Isolation?* (1999).

Peter Hennessy FBA is Attlee Professor of Contemporary British History at Queen Mary University of London. He was a journalist for twenty years with spells on *The Times* as a leader writer and Whitehall Correspondent, *The Financial Times* as its Lobby Correspondent at Westminster and *The Economist*. In 1986 he was a co-founder of the Institute of Contemporary British History. His books include *Cabinet* (1986), *Whitehall* (1989), *Never again: Britain 1945–51* (1992), *The Hidden Wiring: Unearthing the British Constitution* (1995) and *The Prime Minister: The Office and its Holders since 1945* (2000).

Roland Quinault is Reader in History at London Metropolitan University and a former Honorary Secretary of the Royal Historical Society. He is the author of numerous studies on modern British politicians including several members of the Churchill family. He co-edited *Anglo-American Attitudes* (2000) and is currently completing a book on British prime ministers and democracy from Galdstone to Blair.

David Reynolds is Professor of International History at Cambridge University. He is the author or editor of nine books, most recently a study of Churchill's war memoirs entitled *In Command of History: Churchill Fighting and Writing The Second World War* (2004).

Chris Wrigley has been Professor of Modern History at Nottingham University since 1991. He was President of the Historical Association, 1996–9. His books include *David Lloyd George and the British Labour Movement* (1976), *Lloyd George and the Challenge of Labour* (1990), *Arthur Henderson* (1990), *Lloyd George* (1992), *British Trade Unions since 1933* (2002) and *Winston Churchill: A Biographical Companion* (2002).

John W. Young holds the Chair of International History at the University of Nottingham. His books include *Winston Churchill's Last Campaign: Britain and the Cold War, 1951–55* (1996), *Britain and European Unity, 1945–99* (2000) and *The Labour Government's International Policy, 1964–70 (2004).*

ACKNOWLEDGEMENTS

This book originated as a conference held early in 2001 to mark the centenary of Winston Churchill's maiden speech in the House of Commons on 18 February 1901. We are most grateful to all the participants for converting their original papers into publishable essays, and to Tony Benn, Lord Carrington, Lord Deedes and Lady Soames for their reminiscences and recollections. The conference was held at the Institute of Historical Research, which co-sponsored it with the Royal Historical Society. We happily record our thanks for all the help and support which they both provided, and we are especially indebted to Aled Jones for his advice and assistance in the preparation of this volume, and to Jinty Nelson and Kenneth Fincham for preparing the index.

DNC
RQ

PROLOGUE: CHURCHILL FROM MEMORY TO HISTORY

By David Cannadine

When Winston Churchill suffered his landslide defeat in the general election of 1945, having been brutally 'dismissed by the British electorate from all further conduct of their affairs', it stimulated David Low to one of his most memorable and moving cartoons, by turns favourable and critical, sympathetic and realistic.[1] He constructed it around the notion of the split personality of 'The Two Churchills': one of them was 'The Leader of Humanity', the great man who had defied tyranny and masterminded victory during the Second World War; the other was 'The Party Leader', an altogether lesser and more boorish figure, who had berated and insulted his Labour opponents in the recent campaign, and had been summarily rejected by the voters. In his cartoon, Low placed Churchill the leader of humanity serenely atop a vast podium, receiving the homage and acclaim of the free world, whose liberties he had defended, and whose honour he had saved. By contrast, Churchill the party leader lurks and sulks far below, by turns bad-tempered, cast aside, bewildered, unhappy and forlorn. And Churchill the leader of humanity offers these words of comfort and consolation (and criticism) to Churchill the party leader: 'Cheer up! They will forget *you*, but they will remember *me* always.'[2]

But 'always' is supposedly forever, whereas for Churchill this version of 'always' is already almost over. In the middle of the first decade of the twenty-first century, there are few people still alive who can remember (or forget) Churchill's greatness (or shortcomings) in the immediate, contemporary sense that Low was describing, and their number diminishes inexorably, year on year. Anyone who can recall Churchill's speeches as originally delivered in 1940 must be at least in their seventies today. It is almost sixty years since the Second World War ended, and the surviving servicemen and -women will hold no more reunions after VE Day and VJ Day are marked for the last time in 2005. And there is now scarcely a handful of people alive

---

[1] W. S. Churchill, *The Second World War*, I: *The Gathering Storm* (1948), p. 526.

[2] 'The Two Churchills', Evening Standard, 31 July 1945. Reprinted by kind permission of Solo Syndication.

who can personally remember Churchill in his time and in his prime. Among them are Tony Benn (whose family knew Churchill well, and who overlapped with him in the Commons for fifteen years), Lord Carrington and Lord Deedes (who both served in Churchill's last peace-time administration) and Lady Soames (who is Churchill's daughter and the biographer of his wife Clementine). Their vivid reminiscences illuminate and conclude this volume.[3]

As such, they stand alongside the more extended memoirs and diaries of (among others) Violet Bonham Carter, Lord Moran, Sir John Colville and Harold Macmillan, which began to appear very soon after Churchill died in 1965, but forty years on, that genre is inevitably petering out.[4] Meanwhile, the official biography of Churchill was begun by Randolph Churchill and completed by Martin Gilbert in eight vast volumes between 1966 and 1988, making it the longest life of any British public figure ever written (and the publication of the companion volumes is not yet completed).[5] At the same time, the late 1960s witnessed the appearance of several instant reappraisals, some friendly, others distinctly hostile.[6] And since then, the official government records, the papers of his contemporaries and his own massive archive have all become available, the last appropriately housed at Churchill College, Cambridge, and in the process of being digitised thanks to a multi-million pound grant from the Heritage Lottery Fund. The result has been a never-ending stream of articles, monographs, biographies and multi-authored works, which taken together constitute the largest body of scholarly study devoted to one individual Briton. Today, the Churchill bibliography runs into

[3] See also *Tony Benn: Years of Hope: Diaries, Letters and Papers, 1940–1962*, ed. R. Winstone (1994); Lord Carrington, *Reflect on Things Past* (1988); M. Soames, *Clementine Churchill* (1979, rev. edn, 2002); *Speaking for Themselves: The Personal Letters of Winston and Clementine Churchill*, ed. *eadem* (1998).

[4] V. Bonham Carter, *Winston Churchill As I Knew Him* (1965); *Lantern Slides: The Diaries and Letters of Violet Bonham Carter, 1904–1914*, ed. M. Bonham Carter and M. Pottle (1996); *Champion Redoubtable: The Diaries and Letters of Violet Bonham Carter, 1914–1945*, ed. M. Pottle (1998); *Daring to Hope: The Diaries and Letters of Violet Bonham Carter, 1946–1969*, ed. *idem* (2000); Lord Moran, *Winston Churchill: The Struggle for Survival, 1940–1965* (1966); *Churchill at War, 1940–1945*, ed. [second Lord Moran] (2002); J. Colville, *The Fringes of Power: 10 Downing Street Diaries, 1939–1955* (1985); H. Macmillan, *War Diaries: Politics and War in the Mediterranean, January 1943–May 1945* (1984); *The Macmillan Diaries: The Cabinet Years, 1950–1957*, ed. P. Catterall (2003). See also *Action This Day: Working with Churchill*, ed. J. W. Wheeler-Bennett (1968); A. Montague Browne, *Long Sunset: Memoirs of Winston Churchill's Last Private Secretary* (1995).

[5] R. S. Churchill and M. Gilbert, *Winston S. Churchill* (8 vols., 1966–88); M. Gilbert, *Churchill: A Life* (1991); *idem, In Search of Churchill: An Historian's Journey* (1994); *Winston Churchill and Emery Reeves: Correspondence, 1937–1964*, ed. *idem* (1997).

[6] B. Gardiner, *Churchill in his Time: A Study in Reputation, 1939–1945* (1968); A. J. P. Taylor *et al.*, *Churchill: Four Faces and the Man* (1969); C. Thompson, *The Assassination of Winston Churchill* (1969); R. Rhodes James, *Churchill: A Study in Failure, 1900–1939* (1970).

thousands of items, it is expanding month by month and day by day, and no one can realistically hope to keep up with it all.[7]

All of which is but another way of saying that as the twentieth century has yielded to the twenty-first, so Churchill has moved from memory to history, from being a subject of personal and immediate recollection to being an object of detached and disinterested scholarly inquiry. Four outstanding and recently published books exactly exemplify this trend. Roy Jenkins's *Churchill* was written by a fellow politician-cum-biographer, who had met Churchill and (like Tony Benn) overlapped with him in the House of Commons: as such it was the heartfelt tribute of one Grand Old Man of British politics to another. Geoffrey Best's *Churchill* appeared at almost the same time, but it was a book by a professional historian with rather a different purpose. For while Churchill had been Best's boyhood hero, and while he retained an abiding admiration for him, he wrote his book to satisfy his curiosity as to how the great man would appear to future generations who had not been there in 1940.[8] Both Jenkins and Best saw Churchill in the days of his fame and glory, but a later generation of historians want to know how exactly Churchill achieved his extraordinary public renown that was both national and international. John Ramsden has explored how Churchill's reputation was projected and promoted throughout the English-speaking world, by many other people as well as himself. And David Reynolds, extending the argument he advances in this volume, has shown how Churchill wrote the *History of the Second World War* in substantial measure as an exercise in self-vindication and political re-engagement.[9]

The essays that follow move Churchill further into this post-recollection, twenty-first-century enterprise of continuing scholarly inquiry and re-assessment. Paul Addison reminds us that although Churchill believed he was a man of destiny, his career did not follow a single, upwards trajectory to the latter-day fame and glory which he had anticipated in his early novel *Savrola*. On the contrary, it crashed into ruins in 1915 in the aftermath of the Dardanelles disaster (when he may have been unduly blamed), and it only recovered in 1940 in the aftermath of the Norway fiasco (when, by an equal but opposite quirk of fate, he was lucky to survive). And these ups and downs in his career were accompanied by many apparent contradictions in

---

[7] E. L. Rasor, *Winston S. Churchill, 1874–1965: A Comprehensive Historiography and Annotated Bibliography* (2000), lists over 3,000 items.

[8] R. Jenkins, *Churchill* (2001); G. Best, *Churchill: A Study in Greatness* (2001).

[9] J. Ramsden, *Man of the Century: Winston Churchill and his Legend since 1945* (2002); D. J. Reynolds, *In Command of History: Churchill Fighting and Writing The Second World War* (2004).

his outlook and attitudes. As Roland Quinault makes plain, Churchill played a leading role in the ideological battles between democracy and dictatorship, and was a defiant defender of liberty and freedom against the Kaiser, Lenin, Hitler and Hirohito; but he was regularly abused, especially in the middle phase of his career, for being reactionary and authoritarian – a potential British Mussolini. Not surprisingly, he was often seen as the enemy of the British working class; but Chris Wrigley also shows just how respectful of trade unions Churchill was for most of his career.

So was Churchill a crusading radical or an embattled conservative? Or course, he changed his party not once but twice, and he certainly became more conservative as he got older. Stuart Ball argues convincingly that from the time he rejoined the Tories in 1923, Churchill was much closer to mainstream Conservative opinion than is generally recognised: during the 1920s *and* the 1930s, and also throughout the 1940s and early 1950s. Moreover, Ball also insists that Churchill was a much more capable party politician and effective Conservative leader than has generally admitted; and it cannot be doubted that the Tories recovered better under him after their landslide defeat of 1945 than they did under Balfour in 1906 or Hague in 1997. Not surprisingly, and as I have tried to show in my own contribution, there was also much about the conservative culture of monarchy that appealed to Churchill: as the symbol of national history, imperial greatness and a hierarchical social order. But in his radical days, Churchill had crossed swords with both King Edward VII and George V, and he was initially much disliked by King George VI and Queen Elizabeth because of his support of Edward VIII and his hostility to Neville Chamberlain and appeasement. Only after 1940 did he eventually become persona grata with the sovereign.

By the time he came to write his *History of the Second World War*, Churchill's circumstances and reputation had changed dramatically, and those six large volumes both recorded that change, and also helped to consolidate it. For as David Reynolds explains, Churchill was trying to do many things in undertaking this monumental literary enterprise. Of course, he sought to make money, to give his account of events and to place himself firmly at the centre of them. But he also genuinely wanted to know how things had happened, or failed to happen, in the way they did. This was obviously true for the first instalment, covering the 1930s, where he tried to explain why his criticisms of appeasement had been ineffectual, and why the 'unnecessary war' thus became unavoidable. But he was also, even in this first volume, arguing the case for the Anglo-American alliance – abortive (alas!) in 1938, but by the time of writing more essential than ever – the very case he had made in his 'Iron Curtain' speech at Fulton shortly before getting down to work on his memoirs in earnest. In his books on the Second World War, as in all his major works, Churchill thus combined a genuine interest in the past, a desire to give what he saw as appropriate emphasis to himself and his family, and a wish to provide historical validation for his own evolving policies and developing opinions. For most people, as E. H. Carr rightly observed, history is 'an unending dialogue between the present and the past'. But for Churchill, it was an unending dialogue between the present and the past *and the future.*[10]

One sign of this, as John Charmley points out, is that Churchill's *History of the Second World War* exaggerated the extent of Anglo-American amity, and played down the often very serious disagreements between Churchill and Roosevelt. Indeed, when pushed (as elsewhere) to its revisionist extremes, this interpretation insists that in subordinating the United Kingdom so cravenly to the United States, Churchill committed a terrible error of judgement, the full measure of which we are only now beginning to appreciate.[11] Beyond any doubt, this argument has to be considered: in the aftermath of 9/11, Britain still prefers to side with America rather than Europe, as de Gaulle always insisted (and regretted) it would. But it is also important to remember that from 1940 to 1945, Churchill's options were very limited, and he knew it. At home, his cabinet colleagues included Tory appeasers and radical socialists: neither could be fully relied upon. Abroad, his two great allies, America and Russia, both disliked the British Empire and hoped to see it fall. Under these circumstances, it can be argued that Churchill in fact did very well: he preserved the Empire against Cripps and Roosevelt and Stalin; it was largely thanks to the United States that Britain regained all its Far Eastern possessions; and in the eastern Mediterranean, Churchill had carved out a wholly new sphere of British influence. This was no mean achievement for the (by then) junior partner in the Grand Alliance.

Churchill's post-1945 career has only recently begun to receive the serious and sustained study it merits, and the later essays in this volume rightly draw attention to his role as Leader of the Opposition, to the complex agenda of his war memoirs and to his activities as an international statesman. By the time he returned to Downing Street he was, as Peter Hennessy explains, old and tired and ill; but he was determined to pull off a last triumph (and perhaps the Nobel Peace Prize?) by brokering a deal that would significantly lessen the Cold War tensions between America and Russia. Or was he? Not according to David Carlton, who argues that Churchill was always and incorrigibly

[10] E. H. Carr, *What Is History?* (1961), 24.
[11] J. Charmley, *Churchill: The End of Glory* (1993); *idem, Churchill's Grand Alliance* (1995).

hard-line anti-Communist; that he would have preferred to go to war with Stalin's Russia than make peace with it; and that his search for détente in his last administration was a desperate and cynical ploy for clinging on to office. Not so, counters John W. Young, who insists that Churchill's desire for a 'parley at the summit' was genuine, and that it was a characteristically imaginative political initiative, but that he was defeated by a combination of American un-enthusiasm, Russian equivocation, cabinet hostility and his own declining health. Clearly, Churchill's final administration remains a subject of vigorous and unresolved controversy, which these essays intensify rather than settle. On this as many other subjects, the jury is still out.

Is it, then, possible to discern the outlines of a twenty-first-century Churchill from the contributions that follow? The answer must be a tentative but encouraging 'yes'; and it consists in the serious undermining of the 'Two Churchills' model with which this prologue began. The idea that Churchill was an erratic figure, inclined to go from one extreme to the other, was a commonplace throughout his career; and in addition to Low's vivid cartoon version, it may also be appreciated by juxtaposing the famous Karsh of Ottawa wartime picture (the 'angry lion' full of fire and energy and defiance) with the Graham Sutherland eightieth-birthday portrait, subsequently destroyed (a gross, cruel and past-it monster). Yet the main conclusion to emerge from these essays is that Churchill was a more complex figure than these extreme and one-dimensional images suggest. He operated at many different levels, in his speeches, his state papers, his memoranda, his conversation, his books and his journalism. He tried out different arguments on different audiences for different purposes. His rhetoric was often defiant and belligerent, but he preferred accommodation and compromise, and all his life he believed that 'jaw-jaw was better than war-war'. 'Appeasement', he once remarked, in words that reappear more than once in these pages, 'from weakness and fear is . . . fatal. Appeasement from strength is magnanimous . . . and might be the surest way to peace.'[12]

This is scarcely the Churchill that British Prime Ministers and American Presidents repeatedly delight in invoking in support of intransigent military action against dictators and aggressors, and in unswerving support of the transatlantic alliance, come what may. This is regrettable, but not surprising. For the three-dimensional Churchill that historians have been uncovering for more than a generation has still to make his way into the popular perception or political consciousness. In the course of his astonishingly long and

---

[12] *Winston S. Churchill: His Complete Speeches, 1897–1963*, ed. R. Rhodes James (8 vols., 1974), VIII, 8143.

varied career, Churchill was indeed many things: a radical and a conservative, a class warrior and a national hero, the saviour of his country and the statesman in the age of decline.[13] Yet the Churchill the twenty-first century urgently needs is not the caricature of Low or Karsh or Sutherland, or of Thatcher or Reagan or Bush or Blair, but the Churchill who understood the transience of life, the fallibility of humankind, the capriciousness of fate and the sheer bewildering complexity of events, and who regarded the prime task of statesmanship as seeing the way forward and finding a way through. That, it is becoming increasingly plain, was the authentic historical Churchill in his time. This book is offered in the hope that he may become the authentic contemporary Churchill in our time.

---

[13] A. J. P. Taylor, *English History, 1914–1945* (Oxford, 1965), 29 n. 1; D. Cannadine, *History in our Time* (London 1998), 216–32.

CHURCHILL'S THREE CAREERS
By Paul Addison

FOR twenty years after the Second World War Winston Churchill's status as 'the greatest living Englishman' was seldom questioned. Biographers celebrated his life, contemporaries paid tribute in their memoirs, and potters designed Churchill toby jugs adorned with quotations from his speeches. As a general rule, historians had little to say about him. They regarded events since 1914 as too recent for historical enquiry: hence the leading authority on Churchill's life and times was the great man himself. His six volume history *The Second World War*, was generally accepted as a definitive interpretation.

Since Churchill's death in 1965, custody of his memory has passed gradually out of the hands of contemporaries and into the hands of historians and historically minded biographers. For many years all other work was overshadowed by the publication in eight volumes (1966–88) of the official biography, a stupendous work begun by Randolph S. Churchill and triumphantly completed by Martin Gilbert. But Churchill was a subject of growing interest and controversy and by the 1990s books and articles were pouring from the press. In his recent bibliography Professor Eugene Rasor lists and annotates some 3,099 relevant items – though, admittedly, he has cast his net widely.[1]

This expanding literature was accompanied by a diversity of interpretations which sometimes produced explosions of controversy. The spectrum of opinion ran all the way from historians who still thought of Churchill as 'the saviour of his country' in 1940 to historians like John Charmley who maintained that his war leadership was responsible for the destruction of Britain as a great power.[2] The arguments between admirers of Churchill on the one hand, and critics on the other, were many-sided. At one level there were separate if overlapping controversies about major events in which Churchill had been involved. Professor Rasor lists fifteen major areas of controversy, including the Dardanelles, allied intervention in Russia, the General Strike and the Second Front, but others, such as Tonypandy, the strategic bombing offensive, or Churchill's role in Anglo-American relations, could easily be added. The many articles and monographs which dealt with such topics were

---

[1] Eugene L. Rasor, *Winston S. Churchill 1874–1965: A Comprehensive Historiography and Annotated Bibliography* (2000).

[2] John Charmley, *Churchill: The End of Glory* (1993).

also contributions to a larger controversy about Churchill's place in history and the role of myth and reality in the making of his reputation. Here again, a number of different but related questions were involved; biographical questions about the nature of the man himself, and historical questions about the consequences of his actions.

At the beginning of the twenty-first century Churchill's reputation is in the melting-pot. In place of the national icon of the mid-twentieth century we have a multiplicity of competing images and a confusingly disconnected debate. It seems unlikely that historians will ever agree on the subject, but they may perhaps succeed in clarifying the issues. The differing premises on which assessments of Churchill are based are scattered through the pages of biographies, or half buried in the dense undergrowth of learned articles. The rest of this article is an attempt to outline, in a more explicit and systematic fashion, the contours of one view of Churchill.[3]

Churchill's active political life spanned a period of more than half a century, beginning with his election to the House of Commons in 1900, and ending with his resignation from the premiership in 1955. It was a life twice transformed by world war: the two great turning-points were 1915 and 1940. In a career of many snakes and ladders 1915, the year of Gallipoli, was the longest of the snakes on which he landed. For a time his career and reputation lay in ruins and it was only through heroic feats that he managed partially to restore them. The year of Britain's 'finest hour', 1940, turned out to be the longest of the ladders. It took him to heights of fame and glory achieved by no other British politician of the twentieth century. But the two world wars were not only turning-points in Churchill's fortunes: they were turning-points in the roles he played. Between 1905 and 1915 Churchill was one of the most prominent figures in the Liberal governments of Campbell Bannerman and Asquith. But the First World War led to the disintegration of the Liberal party and after 1918 Churchill metamorphosed into one of the most bellicose Tory politicians of the interwar years. He was always to remain a Tory and indeed became leader of the party in 1940. But after 1940 he was reincarnated as a national hero and international statesman.

In a sense, therefore, Churchill's political life consisted of three careers within a career. Since he was twenty-five when he was first

---

[3] Any concise overview is bound to resemble a ten-minute production of *Hamlet*. Quite apart from the fact that so much has to be left out, many problematical issues have to be touched on lightly, and assertions made with only brief reference to the evidence on which they are based. Nor is there space fully to acknowledge my debt to the work of other historians and biographers. I am, however, very grateful to Roland Quinault for his comments on the lecture of which this article is a revised version.

elected to parliament in 1900, forty when he fell from office in 1915, and sixty-five when he became prime minister in 1940, the three careers also corresponded approximately with youth, middle age and old age. Like most attempts to divide the past neatly into the periods, this is no doubt a simplification, but it does highlight one of the main problems in any interpretation of Churchill's life: the paradoxes and contradictions. Here was a politician who travelled all the way from the left wing of the Liberal party to the right wing of the Conservatives, to become in the end a symbol and embodiment of national unity. Here too was a politician who was frequently written off up to 1939 as the most dangerous and irresponsible of decision-makers, hailed after 1940 as the greatest strategist and statesman of the age.

How are such apparent contradictions to be explained? The thesis adopted here is that that Churchill's character and opinions, his repertoire of political roles, and his view of the world, were largely settled by 1915. Of course he continued after 1915 to grasp new problems and frame new policies. But he was to remain, as he was later to write, 'a child of the Victorian age', and a statesman attached to the social and imperial order which existed before the First World War. Within himself, therefore, Churchill changed little after 1915. His second and third careers were to a great extent repetitions of the first, but in new historical contexts which transformed the significance of his actions.

A parallel line of reasoning applies to the history of Churchill's reputation. Churchill in 1940 was the very same man he always had been. But perceptions were changed by a new historical context in which aspects of 'Winston' which had previously been regarded as flaws were transformed into precious virtues and strengths. The consequence was that a politician whose career had frequently been written off during the 1930s as a failure was now hailed as the most triumphant and victorious of statesmen.

Compulsive ambition, colossal egotism, prodigious energy, a thirst for adventure – such were the characteristics blazingly apparent in the young Winston Churchill. Like other young men in a hurry, Churchill was hungry for office and aiming for the greatest prize of all, the premiership. Far from concealing the fact, he talked noisily of his ambition to get to the top and his calculations of how to get there. But Churchill's ambitions always extended beyond the possession of office and power. He believed that he was a man of destiny. He saw himself at some future date performing great deeds on the stage of history. To Churchill therefore, office was not an end in itself, but a means to an end: the winning of great political victories, the achievement of great reforms, the saving of the nation. At a house party in January 1915 Margot Asquith heard him exclaim: 'My God! This is living history.

Everything we are doing and saying is thrilling – it will be read by a thousand generations: think of that!'[4]

Churchill's drive for power was harnessed to the workings of a brilliant mind which, at this period, may well have been at the height of its powers. It was no accident that he was the most highly paid war correspondent of the day, or generally recognised as one of the most formidable of orators. The speed with which he mastered new subjects, and the fertility of his writing, put him in the same league as his friend H.G. Wells. By 1906 he was the author of six books of which two – *The River War* and *Lord Randolph Churchill* were major works ranking with those of professional historians. In politics he schooled himself, between 1900 and 1915, in the politics of free trade and protectionism, colonial affairs, social reform, the House of Lords, Ireland, grand strategy and foreign policy. His intelligence, however, operated through a rapid process of impressionism rather than slow and methodical analysis. According to Anthony Storr, Churchill's character matched Jung's description of a psychological type, the 'extraverted intuitive', which is 'never to be found among the generally recognized reality values, but is always present where possibilities exist'.[5] His cabinet colleagues, Grey and Birrell, feared that 'the tendency in him to see first the rhetorical potentialities of any policy was growing and becoming a real intellectual and moral danger'.[6]

Churchill's dynamism was one of the reasons why he was able to embark on a political career so early in life. The other, of course, was the fact that he was born into the governing class – the son of Lord Randolph Churchill, and grandson of a duke. But if he was an aristocrat he was also an adventurer who relished the company of other adventurers, most of whom were self-made men like F. E. Smith, Beaverbrook and Lloyd George. Through his mother, meanwhile, he was half-American and the grandson of a Wall Street financier. All in all, Churchill was closer in spirit to the City of London and the world of 'gentlemanly capitalism' than he was to the vanishing world of the landed estate. Beatrice Webb, meeting him for the first time in 1903, described him as 'more the American speculator than the English aristocrat ... He looks to high finance to keep the peace ... the cosmopolitan financier being the professional peacemaker of the modern world, and to his mind the acme of civilisation.'[7]

The young Winston Churchill was also a fervent believer in the

[4] Martin Gilbert, *Churchill: A Life* (1991), 294.
[5] Anthony Storr, 'The Man' in A.J.P. Taylor *et al.*, *Churchill: Four Faces and the Man* (Harmondsworth, 1973), 231.
[6] Lucy Masterman, *C.F.G. Masterman: A Biography* (1939), 128.
[7] Norman and Jeanne MacKenzie (eds.), *The Diary of Beatrice Webb*, II: *1892–1905* (1983), 287–8, entry for 8 July 1903.

British Empire. A more humane imperialist than many of his contemporaries, he was aware of the arrogance and cruelty which sometimes disfigured British rule, and did his best to mitigate them. Nevertheless he drank deeply of the heady imperialism of the 1890s. His late Victorian vision of the hierarchy of races and the 'civilising mission' of the British, was intensified by his experience of the 'barbarism' and 'fanaticism' of the Pathans on the north-west frontier of India and the Dervishes of the Sudan. The war in South Africa, by contrast, was for Churchill a 'White man's war' in which it would be wrong to employ non-white troops against a European enemy.[8] As he explained to the House of Commons in 1906, there were five black inhabitants of South Africa for every one white. The 'black peril' was 'as grim a problem as any mind could be forced to face' and 'the one bond of union' which might lead to a reconciliation between British and Boer settlers.[9]

The fact that Churchill had been a soldier before entering politics was ever present in the minds of his contemporaries. His experience of the South African war had convinced him that civilians like himself understood the principles of warfare as well or better than the generals. It is not clear whether he believed in hereditary genius but the example of his ancestor, the first duke of Marlborough, was always before him and he felt that he possessed a special flair. As he wrote to his wife, Clementine, after attending a military field day in May 1909: 'These military men very often fail altogether to see the simple truths underlying the relationship of all armed forces ... Do you know I would greatly like to have some practice in the handling of large forces. I have much confidence in my judgment on things, when I see clearly, but on nothing do I seem to *feel* the truth more than in tactical combinations.'[10]

In party politics young Winston was initially a Tory, but inwardly unreliable. He thought of himself principally as the son and heir of Lord Randolph Churchill: in his eyes a far-sighted Tory statesman with strong radical and popular sympathies who had been ill-treated by the leaders of the party. Never a wholehearted Tory, he wrote to his mother from India in 1897: 'I am a Liberal in all but name. My views excite the pious horror of the Mess. Were it not for Home Rule – to which I will never consent – I would enter Parliament as a Liberal. As it is – Tory Democracy will have to be the standard under which I shall range myself.'[11] Churchill's ambivalence in party politics reflected a

[8] Randolph S. Churchill, *Winston S. Churchill: Companion*, 1, part 2 (Boston, 1967), 1216, Churchill to Joseph Chamberlain, 16 November 1900.

[9] Randolph S. Churchill, *Winston S. Churchill: Young Statesman 1901–1914* (1967), 164.

[10] Mary Soames (ed.), *Speaking for Themselves: The Personal Letters of Winston and Clementine Churchill* (1998), 23, Winston to Clementine, 30 May 1909.

[11] Randolph S. Churchill, *Winston S. Churchill*, 1 (1966), 318, Winston to Lady Randolph, 6 April 1897.

deeper truth. His creed was egotism – the right to express his own opinion on the merits of every issue. He was sceptical of party doctrines and resented the constraints they placed on the statesmanship of great men. As A.G. Gardiner wrote of him in 1914: 'More than any other man of his time, he approaches an issue without mental reserves or the restraints of party calculation or caution. To his imperious spirit a party is only an instrument. *Au fond* he would no more think of consulting a party than the chauffeur would think of consulting the motor car.'[12] Hence Churchill's partiality for coalitions of kindred spirits, free from the demands of the more partisan wings of the two main parties. His political ideal, he explained to Rosebery in 1902, was a 'Government of the Middle . . . free at once from the sordid selfishness and callousness of Toryism one the one hand, and the blind appetites of the Radical masses on the other.'[13]

Churchill could rightly claim that in crossing the floor of the House to join the Liberals in 1904 he was acting in defence of a cause the Conservatives were abandoning – free trade. But his change of parties cost him dear. In the eyes of the Conservatives he was a shameless opportunist, a turncoat and a cad. The Liberals, though grateful for the loan of his talents, could never forget his Tory and military origins. Most implausible of all, so it seemed, was Churchill's role as a radical and social reformer in alliance with David Lloyd George. The campaigns they waged in favour of welfare reforms, land taxes and the People's Budget seemed indistinguishable to the Tories from dema-goguery and class warfare. But whereas Lloyd George had impeccable credentials as a radical, Churchill's attacks on his own class, and his professions of concern for 'the left-out millions', exposed him to charges of hypocrisy.

He was, in fact, more consistent in his political beliefs than was generally recognised. He had entered the House of Commons as an old-fashioned radical preaching Victorian political economy. As Churchill saw it, competitive capitalism was the mainspring of economic and social progress. His commitment to free trade and rejection of protectionism followed logically on from this and gave him a legitimate pretext for joining the Liberals, even if other motives were involved. His adoption after 1906 of the 'New Liberalism' marked his conversion to policies of welfare reform intended to provide a 'safety net' or 'minimum standard' below which the poor would not be allowed to fall. But as Churchill was careful to explain, his fundamental belief in the virtues of the market was undiminished. 'The existing organisation of society', he declared, 'is driven by one mainspring – competitive

---

[12] A.G. Gardiner, *Prophets Priests and Kings* (1914), 234.
[13] Paul Addison, *Churchill on the Home Front 1900–1955* (1992), 26.

selection. It may be a very imperfect organisation of society, but it is all we have got between us and barbarism ... I do not want to see impaired the vigour of competition, but we can do much to mitigate the consequences of failure.'[14] Welfare reforms were therefore the antithesis of socialism, which he condemned in no uncertain terms. Churchill, in other words, was preaching the virtues of a Darwinian society, but one in which the winners behaved mercifully towards the losers. Nor was this a temporary posture on Churchill's part. We have only to look at the reforms Churchill introduced at the Admiralty in the conditions of the lower deck, or at the way he behaved as an officer towards his men on the western front in 1915, to see at once that he was a genuine paternalist who wished to improve the lot of the underdog.

The radical agenda of Churchill and Lloyd George included attempts to cut the army and navy estimates, and something very close to an alternative foreign policy of friendship with Germany. This too might appear out of character, but only if we picture Churchill as a perpetual militarist prophesying conflict. For much of the Edwardian period he was confident that the long European peace would continue. It was nonsense, he declared in 1908, to talk of the inevitability of war between Britain and Germany.[15]

Churchill was to remain one of the leading members of a Liberal cabinet up to 1915. He continued therefore to champion Liberal policies such as Irish Home Rule, and to belabour the Tory opposition. But from 1910 onwards there were a number of signs that he was moving to the Right. Why was this? The most plausible explanation is that changing political circumstances brought out two hitherto latent aspects of Churchill's political identity: the conservative statesman, defending the social order; and the military leader, inspired by a sense of destiny.[16]

In the first of the two general elections of 1910 the Liberals lost their overall majority and became dependent on the votes of the Labour Party and the Irish Nationalists. Later in the year Liberal and Conservative leaders entered into secret but abortive negotiations for the establishment of a coalition. Although the negotiations fell through they marked a turning-point in Churchill's political attitudes. Whereas previously Churchill and Lloyd George had been leading the radical wing of the Liberals in alliance with Labour, Churchill now hoped for some kind of reconciliation or agreement with the Conservatives. He

---

[14] Michael Freeden, *The New Liberalism: An Ideology of Social Reform* (1978), 161.

[15] Robert Rhodes James (ed.), *Winston S. Churchill: His Complete Speeches, 1897–1963* (8 vols., New York, 1974), II, 1085, speech of 14 August 1908.

[16] Arguably the most accurate term for Churchill is 'Whig' and we should think of him as Whig with both radical and conservative aspects which alternated in response to events. But this seems to me too complex a formula for the purpose of this article.

continued to speculate hopefully on the prospects for a coalition, and made strenuous but fruitless efforts to repair his own relations with the Conservatives by defusing the Irish question – which eventually blew up in his face.

Two likely explanations for this rightward shift present themselves. The year 1910 marked the beginning of the 'great industrial unrest' which preceded the First World War. Churchill, who as home secretary was the minister responsible for the maintenance of law and order, drew a sharp distinction between purely industrial disputes, in which he claimed to be neutral, and syndicalist attempts to coerce the government through 'direct action' or a general strike, which he regarded as assaults on the constitution. Whether or not syndicalism posed a serious threat, Churchill certainly believed that it did. Thoroughly alarmed by the national rail strike of August 1911, he despatched troops on his own authority to key points of the railway network. Together with his conduct of the Tonypandy affair, his actions were strongly condemned in the House of Commons by Keir Hardie and Ramsay MacDonald. Churchill was becoming anti-Labour, and Labour anti-Churchill.

The other likely explanation of Churchill's retreat from radicalism after 1910 was a growing pessimism about Anglo-German relations. At the Home Office the information he received from the intelligence services convinced him that Britain was honeycombed with German spies, a real or imagined danger that inspired some of his more illiberal measures, such as the Official Secrets Act of 1911. He became fearful of German intentions, an anxiety redoubled by the Agadir crisis of 1911. In Churchill's view, the prospect of a major war strengthened the case for the creation, out of the Liberal and Conservative parties, of a 'national party' committed both to land reform and conscription.[17] It also awoke in him the soldier and strategist. Many years later Sir Ralph Hawtrey recalled an incident which occurred in 1910 or 1911, when he was motoring down to Brighton with Churchill and Lloyd George: 'Churchill began to talk about the next war. He described how, at the climax, he himself, in command of the army, would win the decisive victory in the Middle East, and would return to England in triumph. Lloyd George quietly interposed, 'And where do I come in?'[18]

The moment war broke out in August 1914 Churchill began to intervene in the conduct of naval operations. In October he went to see Asquith, begged to be relieved of the Admiralty and given a high military command. 'His mouth waters', Asquith wrote, 'at the sight and thought of Kitchener's new armies. Are these "glittering commands" to

[17] Addison, *Churchill on the Home Front*, 159.
[18] Martin Gilbert, *In Search of Churchill* (1994), 175.

be entrusted to "dug-out trash", bred on the obsolete tactics of 25 years ago ... he was quite three parts serious and declared that a political career was nothing to him in comparison with military glory.'[19] Asquith refused and Churchill sought instead for some means by which the Royal Navy could achieve a decisive breakthrough. The consequence, of course, was Gallipoli, the moment of truth at which Churchill's sense of destiny was thwarted by political reality.

Though Churchill was only partly to blame for Gallipoli he was made into the scapegoat while Asquith and Kitchener, who were equally if not more responsible, held on to their posts. To some extent, of course, Gallipoli was only a pretext for the removal of a politician whose bumptious and aggressive style had made numerous enemies and few friends. His maverick role in party politics had thoroughly alienated the Conservatives without winning the trust of the Liberals. The Conservatives therefore insisted on his removal from the Admiralty as a precondition of their entry into a coalition government, while the Liberals made little attempt to defend him in his hour of need.

Churchill's downfall was also the result of growing doubts about his judgement. How long such doubts had existed, and how far they were shaped by malice and distortion, is very difficult to say. But they were real enough and focused on the very field in which Churchill felt that his abilities were strongest: military operations and strategy. They seem to have been crystallised for the first time by Churchill's role in the defence of Antwerp in October 1914. 'Winston', Lloyd George declared, 'is becoming a great danger ... Winston is like a torpedo. The first you hear of his doings is when you hear the swish of the torpedo dashing through the water.'[20]

Few professional politicians doubted that Churchill possessed elements of genius. Even Bonar Law, who greatly disliked and distrusted him, acknowledged his outstanding abilities. But Gallipoli confirmed a consensus among the political elite that Churchill was a genius *manqué*, and the qualification was lethal. The missing component in the otherwise wonderful mechanism of the Churchill brain was *judgement*: hence there was always a danger that he would plunge his companions into disaster. It was an assumption that might well permit Churchill to return to office in a subordinate post, but it ruled out a Churchill premiership as unthinkable.

By the time that peacetime politics returned in 1918 Churchill had

[19] Michael and Eleanor Brock (eds.), *H.H. Asquith: Letters to Venetia Stanley* (Oxford, 1982), 266, letter of 7 October 1914.
[20] John M. McEwen (ed.), *The Riddell Diaries 1908–1923* (1986), 91–2, entry for 10 October 1914.

recovered sufficiently to be included in the postwar coalition, but he was a wounded figure heavily dependent on the good will of Lloyd George. At the same time he found himself entering a new political world. At home the Liberal party was fatally divided and the Labour party emerging as the main alternative to the Conservatives. The electorate, which now included women over the age of thirty, had increased in size from seven million in 1910 to twenty-one million in 1918. There was a resurgence of industrial militancy and with it the renewed threat of a general strike. The British Empire was shaken by nationalist movements in India and Egypt, paralleled by the revolt of Sinn Fein in Ireland. The most fundamental challenge of all was the Bolshevik revolution of 1917, which threatened to spread from Russia into the heart of central Europe. From about 1921 onwards the worst of the immediate crisis was over and a period of relative stability followed, but it was also clear that the pre-1914 political order had vanished.

What was Churchill's role? There were flashes of the old radicalism especially during his period as Chancellor of the Exchequer. Although he eventually succumbed to the pressure to restore the Gold Standard at the pre-war rate of parity between the pound and the dollar, it was not without interrogating his advisers about the effects on industry and employment. He resumed with relish the role of champion of peace, retrenchment and reform. He cut naval expenditure, put the Ten-Year Rule on a revolving basis in 1928, and insisted that there was no danger whatever of a war with Japan. When the great slump occurred, he came up with the idea of an economic parliament. Churchill also developed new international themes. At the end of the First World War, and again during the world slump, he proclaimed the idea of the common heritage and destiny of Britain and the United States. In 1930 he put the case for a United States of Europe – one in which Britain would play little part.

In spite of such forward-looking moments the general character of Churchill's response to the postwar world was clear. 'Don't you make any mistake', he said to Lloyd George, 'you're not going to get your new world. The old world is a good enough place for me, & there's life in the old dog yet.'[21] Much of his political life between the wars consisted of a prolonged rearguard action, first as a coalition Liberal, and later as a Conservative, against the new political forces released by the First World War. The pattern was set at the very beginning of the period by his response to the Bolshevik revolution.

Anti-Bolshevism was the material from which Churchill fashioned a

[21] A.J.P. Taylor (ed.), *Lloyd George: A Diary by Frances Stevenson* (1971), 196–7, entry for 17 January 1920.

new political identity after 1919, and the foundation on which he built a new career. No other cause for which he stood brought so many aspects of his politics into a single, concentrated focus. In the first instance it united Churchill the military leader, conducting the British war of intervention in Russia, with Churchill the conservative statesman, engaged in an ideological crusade against a creed which represented the antithesis of everything he stood for. Since Churchill claimed that the Kremlin was fomenting nationalist revolts against British rule in Ireland, Egypt and India, it also involved the defence of the imperial order. At home the intelligence services provided Churchill with evidence of Bolshevik interference in industrial disputes and the payment of subsidies to the socialist *Daily Herald*. Churchill could therefore argue that hard-line anti-socialism in domestic affairs was the necessary counterpart of anti-Bolshevism abroad. Anti-Bolshevism therefore gave Churchill a new and powerful rationale for his favourite project of a Centre Party or permanent coalition of Liberals and Conservatives. It also supplied him with a rich if dubious source of propaganda against the Labour party. During the general election of October 1924 he declared: 'Spellbound by the lure of Moscow, wire-pulled through subterranean channels, Mr Ramsay MacDonald and his associates have attempted to make the British nation accomplices in Bolshevik crimes.'[22]

Churchill's strident anti-Bolshevik, anti-socialist line was of crucial importance in restoring him to favour with the Conservatives. He continued to pursue a strong anti-Soviet line throughout his period as Chancellor of the Exchequer in the Baldwin government, and into the 1930s. In Churchill's view fascism was the consequence of communism and the necessary antidote to it. Hence his praise for the government of Mussolini, whom he described in a speech to the Anti-Socialist Union in 1933 as 'the greatest law-giver among living men'.[23] In the opening stages of the Spanish Civil War he leaned strongly towards Franco and the Nationalist side. With unconscious irony he also declared in a debate in the House of Commons in 1937: 'I will not pretend that if I had to choose between Communism and Nazi-ism, I would choose Communism.'[24] In foreign affairs, this was exactly the choice he would make and was, perhaps, making already.

Anti-Communism was not the only front on which Churchill fought for the old world against the new. Throughout the 1920s he defended the commanding heights of free trade against the protectionist wing of the Conservative party. When the free trade cause was fatally under-

[22] Martin Gilbert, *Churchill: A Photographic Portrait* (1974), photos nos. 168–9.

[23] Martin Gilbert, *Winston S. Churchill*, v (1976), 457.

[24] David Carlton, *Churchill and the Soviet Union* (Manchester, 2000), 57. This very stimulating and original book seems to me to overstate the consistency of Churchill's hostility to the Soviet Union.

mined by the Slump, and he was compelled to abandon it, he put himself at the head of the India diehards in opposition to the policies of Baldwin, the leader of his own party.

For the first time in thirty years Churchill found himself acclaimed at gatherings of the constituency activists of the Tory party. But his relationship with the Conservatives between the wars was highly reminiscent of his relationship with the Liberals up to 1915. Churchill's views were often indistinguishable from those of the average Tory, but for all that he remained an independent grandee in a contractual relationship with the party, or whichever section of the party he was allied with at the time. There was, however, one important difference between the Liberal and the Tory phases of his career. During the Liberal phase there was always the possibility, if he could manage it, of rejoining the Conservatives. But once he had rejoined them in 1924 there was nowhere else for him to go. His fate, therefore, was entirely in the hands of the Conservative party. Over India and again over the question of rearmament Churchill demonstrated that he could attract the support of powerful bodies of Tory opinion. But as ever the support he obtained was strictly related to the issue in question. He never managed to convert it into a personal following based on trust in his judgement or faith in his political philosophy. When he came out in opposition to the Munich agreement in October 1938 his only supporters in the House of Commons were Brendan Bracken, Duncan Sandys and Robert Boothby. His isolation in the winter of 1938–9 was almost complete: this was the true period of exile in the wilderness. By January 1939, therefore, Churchill's career as a party politician was at an even lower ebb than it had been in the naval estimates crisis of January 1914, when he had almost been driven out of the Cabinet.

Churchill was still haunted by Gallipoli. Ever since 1915 he had struggled to set the record straight, defending his actions in evidence to the Dardanelles Commission and later at very great length in his book *The World Crisis*. To some extent he succeeded. Much, though not all of the blame, was lifted from his shoulders, and there was always a minority school of thought which praised Churchill as the author of a brilliant strategic conception that failed only through poor execution. No matter: 'Gallipoli' was shorthand for the charge which Baldwin, Chamberlain and their allies continued to level against him in the 1930s: lack of judgement. Churchill, of course, denied this, but there was some truth in it. Impulsive, rhetorical and visionary, he tended to confuse the desirable with the attainable. Both his war of intervention in Russia and his India campaign were quixotic affairs in which his imagination parted company with reality.

As for the Opposition, the Labour Party was as hostile to Churchill between the wars as the Conservatives had been in the Edwardian age, and ironically for the same reason: he was perceived as a dangerous enemy in the class war. In March 1933 the *Daily Herald* carried a cartoon of Churchill entitled 'Nazi movement: local version', depicting Churchill, dressed as a stormtrooper, giving the Nazi salute.[25] By the late 1930s Churchill was putting out olive branches to Labour but with little success. Three weeks after Munich Robert Fraser, a leader-writer for the *Herald*, wrote to Hugh Dalton: 'There is only one danger of Fascism ... and that will come if Chamberlain is overthrown by the Jingoes in his own party, led by Winston, who will then settle down, with his lousy and reactionary friends, to organise the nation on Fascist principles for a war to settle scores with Hitler.'[26]

Churchill's appointment as Prime Minister marked the beginning of a revolution in his reputation. In retrospect it is a revolution we tend to take very much for granted as the inevitable consequence of inspiring leadership in a time of national crisis. While that certainly is part of the explanation it is not the whole story. It scarcely diminishes Churchill to point out that in one sense he was supremely fortunate in 1940. Having been out of office for most of the 1930s he could not be held responsible for Britain's plight: this time the scapegoats were the 'men of Munich'. The circumstances of the time were such that what had previously been regarded as weaknesses or flaws in his make-up now became strengths. Few now complained that he was a warmonger or a would-be Napoleon: the zeal with which he waged war was now a precious asset. Nor was it any longer a black mark against him that he thought of himself as above party. What better recommendation could there be for the leader of a government of national unity? As for the allegation that he was an impossibilist, an impossibilist was exactly what was called for in 1940. Churchill's profound but irrational faith in victory was infectious and exhilarating and turned out to be right.

The year 1940 therefore transformed perceptions of Churchill, but this is not to say that sceptics and opponents disappeared. With the general public Churchill proved to be phenomenally, though not universally, popular. As for the political elite, most politicians and officials seem to have developed a great admiration for Churchill, but working as they did in close proximity with the great man they were always aware of his faults, and there were rows behind the scenes of which the general public knew nothing at the time. The effect of 1940, therefore, was to create something of a gulf between the war hero of the popular press, and the brilliant but fallible being who inhabited the corridors of power. Within the political elite, attitudes varied according

[25] Gilbert, *Churchill: A Photographic Portrait*, photo no. 200.
[26] Addison, *Churchill on the Home Front*, 324.

to the individual concerned and the state of the war at the time. As one defeat succeeded another during 1941, and the first half of 1942, there was much grumbling and plotting behind the scenes. In October 1941 Sir John Dill, the Chief of the Imperial General Staff, showed Sir John Reith an album of photographs of the Atlantic meeting between Churchill and Roosevelt. According to Reith's diary Dill said: ' "Our empire is worth saving. We must save it if we can from what others may do with it." "What do you mean?" I asked. There was a picture of Churchill on the page before us. He stabbed at it with his thumb. "That".' Dill was succeeded as Chief of Staff by Alan Brooke, whose love–hate relationship with Churchill was recorded in his diaries. 'God knows where we should be without him', Brooke wrote on 4 December 1941, 'but God knows where we shall go with him!'[28]

When they were eventually published, in two volumes edited by Arthur Bryant in 1957 and 1959, the diaries produced a sense of shock. They revealed for the first time the difference between the insider's view of Churchill and the wartime public image, and called into question the majestic self-portrait contained in his own *The Second World War*. The sensation would have been even greater but for the fact that some passages had been tactfully deleted. Thus in September 1944 Brooke wrote: 'He knows no details, has only got half the picture in his mind, talks absurdities, and makes my blood boil to listen to his nonsense. The wonderful thing is that three quarters of the population of the world imagine Churchill is one of the great strategists of history, a second Marlborough, and the other quarter have no conception of what a public menace he is.'[29]

The publication of the diaries marked the beginning of a more realistic assessment of Churchill's war leadership. The subsequent historiography is far too extensive to summarise here but the main tendency has been to demonstrate that after 1940, as before, Churchill's career was a very uneven mixture of success and failure. The war, however, raised Churchill's activities to a much higher plane, so it is more appropriate to employ the terms he himself used in the title of the last volume of his war history: 'Triumph and Tragedy'.

As a war leader Churchill can be assessed both as a military leader and as a statesman. On the military side his role has been analysed by historians such as Stephen Roskill, who is severely critical of his interference in naval operations, and John Keegan, who praises Churchill's overall grasp of grand strategy in Europe, while recognising that

[27] Charles Stuart (ed.), *The Reith Diaries* (1975), 281, entry for 2 October 1941.
[28] Arthur Bryant, *The Turn of the Tide 1939–1943* (1943), 299.
[29] *Daily Telegraph*, 24 January 2001.

he was badly mistaken about the Far East.[30] The sinking of the *Prince of Wales* and the *Repulse*, and the loss of Singapore, are not easily explained away. Churchill, it seems, was never quite the military genius he imagined himself to be. But the sources of triumph and tragedy have to be sought elsewhere.

Churchill's primary objective in World War Two was the defeat and destruction of the Third Reich. This was both a military and a political goal and it was Churchill's greatest strength as a war leader that he pursued it with single-minded tenacity. And whatever mistakes he made along the way, he achieved his aim. Between 1940 and 1943 it was Churchill who determined the main course of British and later Anglo-American strategy in Europe, and by May 1945 the Third Reich lay in ruins.

This was his triumph, but the price was much higher than he expected. The objective of defeating and destroying Nazi Germany led Churchill to abandon or undermine the conservative statesmanship for which he had stood between the wars. Since 1919 he had marked out clear-cut lines of resistance to the Labour party, the Soviet Union, and the enemies of imperial rule. During the Second World War he was no more in favour of socialism, communism, or the dissolution of the empire than he had been before. But he was compelled to wage war by coalition. This entailed first of all the establishment of a coalition government at home, with the Conservative party in alliance with Labour, the trade unions, and liberal reformers like Beveridge. On a global scale it involved the creation of a Grand Alliance in partnership with the United States and the Soviet Union. As a war leader, therefore, Churchill was compelled to compromise with forces whose ambitions were at odds with his own, and became the reluctant agent of policies of which he would have disapproved in peacetime. In 1942, for example, under pressure from Labour but also from Roosevelt, he was obliged to send Sir Stafford Cripps to India with an offer of self-government after the war. The Cripps mission failed, and repressive measures were adopted, but the pledge of self-government remained.

The Anglo-Soviet alliance, meanwhile, led to the virtual suppression of all public criticism of the Soviet regime. Churchill himself was silent about all those aspects of the communist system he had once denounced with such passion: nor could he admit in public to knowledge of Soviet atrocities like the massacre in the Katyn Woods. He was equally powerless to prevent the advance of the Red Army into eastern Europe, the annexation by Stalin of Polish territory, or the establishment of satellite regimes. On the home front, meanwhile, Labour and the Left

[30] Stephen Roskill, *Churchill and the Admirals* (1977); John Keegan, 'Churchill's Strategy' in Robert Blake and W.R. Louis (eds.), *Churchill* (Oxford, 1993), 327–52.

exercised much power and influence, more no doubt than Churchill realised until his defeat in the general election of 1945. The advance of socialism at home was, perhaps, the least of his problems, but in the end it reinforced all the others by depriving him of any direct role in the post-war settlement of the world.

Churchill had one great post-war aspiration of his own: the establishment of an Anglo-American world order on the basis of an ever closer union of the two great branches of the 'English-Speaking Peoples'. In 1943, when his hopes of Anglo-American harmony were at their zenith, he even proposed the establishment after the war of a common citizenship. The irony was, of course, that one of the war aims of the Roosevelt administration was the liquidation of the British Empire, and the expansion of American power and influence at the expense of Britain. By the end of 1943 it was clear to Churchill that he could no longer rely on American co-operation. As he explained to Violet Bonham Carter: 'When I was at Teheran I realized for the first time what a very *small* country this is. On the one hand the big Russian bear with its paws outstretched – on the other the great American Elephant – & between them the poor little British Donkey – who is the only one that knows the right way home.'[31]

As a war leader, therefore, Churchill tended to undermine and negate his *alter ego*, the conservative statesman. The self-cancelling process was exacerbated by his immersion in military affairs to the exclusion of almost everything else. For the most part he postponed the discussion of post-war questions, both domestic and international, until it was too late to do very much about them. The price Churchill paid for victory was partly due to the fact that for long periods the soldier in him displaced the statesman altogether.

After 1945 Churchill harboured doubts about the extent of his wartime achievement. 'Historians', he mused, 'are apt to judge war ministers less by the victories achieved under their direction than by the political results which flowed from them. Judged by that standard, I am not sure that I shall be held to have done very well.'[32] This is only one of a number of melancholy post-war reflections such as his remark to Clark Clifford on the train to Fulton in 1946: 'America has now become the hope of the world. Britain has had its day ... if I were to be born again, I'd want to be born an American.'[33] As old age

[31] Mark Pottle (ed.), *Champion Redoubtable: The Diaries and Letters of Violet Bonham Carter 1914–1945* (1999), 313.

[32] Tuvia Ben-Moshe, *Churchill: Strategy and History* (1992), 329. Ben-Moshe's own fundamental criticism of Churchill is that he lacked long-term political aims and therefore failed to integrate strategic and political objectives.

[33] Paul Addison, 'Winston Churchill's Concept of the English-Speaking Peoples' in Attila Pok (ed.), *The Fabric of Modern Europe: Studies in Social and Diplomatic History* (Nottingham, 1999), 115.

advanced and the 'Black Dog' took possession of him, Churchill began to fear that his life's work had been in vain.

There is no need to endorse this verdict. For Churchill and indeed for Britain the price of victory was high but the price of defeat would have been very much higher: the permanent establishment of a Nazi-controlled Europe of which Britain itself might eventually have become a part. In the final analysis there are two reasons why Churchill deserves to be remembered as an exceptionally great man. First of all, he was right in all essentials about the rise of Nazi Germany, and without him all might have been lost in 1940. Secondly, whether he was right or wrong over one particular question or another, he was a great man in himself, in all three of his careers. When he died the Labour politician, Michael Foot, wrote an obituary that was sharply critical of many aspects of Churchill's record. But he also wrote:

> Seen from any angle the scale of the figure on the vast canvas is stupendous. Not merely does Churchill bestride the century; not merely has he been a foremost performer in British and world politics for a longer period than almost any rival in ancient or modern times. The same giant lineaments are revealed when his particular faculties are examined. His vitality, his brainpower, his endurance, his wit, his eloquence, his industry, his application, were superabundant, superhuman. The first and last impression left by the Colosseum concerns its size. So with Churchill: the man was huge.[34]

In the summer of 1939 Churchill was invited by Julian Huxley to see the giant panda at the London Zoo. Churchill gazed at the animal for a long time, then shook his head approvingly and said: 'It has exceeded all my expectations ... and they were very high.'[35] For historians, it seems to me, Churchill is just like the giant panda. He exceeds all our expectations.

[34] Michael Foot, *Loyalists and Loners* (1986), 168.
[35] Julian Huxley, *Memories* (Harmondsworth, 1972), 237.

CHURCHILL AND DEMOCRACY
By Roland Quinault

CHURCHILL'S views on democracy – both in theory and in practice – are of interest for many reasons. He played a leading role in the ideological battles between democracy and dictatorship in the first half of the twentieth century and he was one of the principal architects of the modern democratic world order. Yet Churchill was widely regarded, particularly in the middle phase of his career, as a reactionary and anti-democratic figure. This conundrum will be examined by considering Churchill's attitude to the concept of democracy and democratic reform – both at home and abroad – over his long career. Churchill was born in 1874 when the great majority of adults in Britain were still disenfranchised and he died in 1965 the year when the Voting Rights Act ended electoral racial discrimination in the United States. Thus his life roughly spanned the period during which universal suffrage democracy became the basis of political legitimacy in the western world.

Churchill's engagement with democracy began early in his life. In his famous address to the US Congress, in 1941, he declared:

> I was brought up in my father's house to believe in democracy. 'Trust the people' that was his message ... Therefore I have been in full harmony all my life with the tides which have flowed on both sides of the Atlantic against privilege and monopoly and I have steered confidently towards the Gettysburg ideal of 'government of the people by the people for the people'.[1]

When Winston was born, however, the political outlook of his father, Lord Randolph Churchill, was still strongly conservative. In 1878, for example, Lord Randolph complained that recent Tory legislation was based 'upon principles which were purely democratic'.[2] It was not until 1884, that Gladstone's introduction of a new Parliamentary Reform Bill prompted Randolph to embrace the principle of democracy, albeit for conservative ends: 'Trust the people ... and they will trust you – and they will follow you and join you in the defence of the Constitution

---

[1] Winston S. Churchill, *The Unrelenting Struggle: War Speeches* (1942), 334: 29 December 1941.

[2] *Parliamentary Debates* (hereafter *Parl. Deb.*), 3rd series, 238, (1878), 907.

27

against every and any foe. I have no fear of democracy.'[3]

Thereafter Randolph was generally associated, in the public mind, with the concept of 'Tory democracy', which he defined, somewhat paradoxically, as both 'a democracy which supports the Tory party' and a government inspired 'by lofty and by liberal ideas'.[4] Randolph's concept of Tory democracy had a profound and lasting influence on Winston's political ideology. He considered that Tory democracy was his father's 'central idea', but conceded that it was 'necessarily a compromise ... between widely different forces and ideas'.[5]

In 1897 – two years after his father's death – Winston privately confessed that he was 'a Liberal in all but name' but went on to state that because he opposed Irish Home Rule, 'Tory Democracy will have to be the standard under which I shall range myself.' At the same time, he advocated manhood suffrage, universal education, payment of members and a progressive income tax.[6] In some contemporary notes, however, he expressed some pragmatic reservations about the extension of democracy:

> Ultimately 'one man, one vote' is logically and morally certain. The question as to the rate at which we move to so desirable a goal is one which depends on local and temporary circumstances ... I would extend the franchise to the whole people not by giving votes to the ignorant and indigent, but by raising those classes to the standard when votes may be safely given. This will take time ... The principle is one of levelling up.[7]

Churchill also expressed opposition to female suffrage on the grounds that it would increase hysterical faddism and religious intolerance and make women the dominant power in the community.[8]

When Churchill began his parliamentary career as a candidate at Oldham, in 1899, he described himself a Tory democrat and declared that the Tory democracy was 'the backbone of the party'.[9] After his election for Oldham in 1900 he continued to regard himself as a

---

[3] Winston S. Churchill, *Lord Randolph Churchill* (1907) 239: speech at Birmingham, 16 April 1884.

[4] *Ibid.*, 240: speech at Birmingham, 9 April 1888. See also: Roland Quinault, 'Lord Randolph Churchill and Tory Democracy 1880–1885', *Historical Journal*, 22 (1979), 141–65.

[5] Churchill, *Randolph Churchill*, 237–8, 821.

[6] Randolph S. Churchill, *Winston S. Churchill* (hereafter Randolph Churchill, *Churchill*): *Companion*, I, part 2 (1967), 751: Winston Churchill to Lady Randolph Churchill, 6 April 1897.

[7] *Ibid.*, 767: notes on the Annual Register.

[8] *Ibid.*, 765.

[9] Robert Rhodes James (ed.), *Winston S. Churchill: His Complete Speeches, 1897–1963* (8 vols., New York, 1974) (hereafter Churchill, *Speeches*), I, 33–5: Oldham, 24, 26 June 1899.

democratic Tory, even when mixing with aristocratic friends and relatives.[10] His cousin's wife, the duchess of Marlborough – the American heiress, Consuelo Vanderbilt – thought that Churchill 'represented the democratic spirit so foreign to my environment, and which I deeply missed'.[11]

Churchill's conversion to Liberalism, in 1904, strengthened his faith in democracy. In 1905 he introduced a motion to reduce the duration of parliaments from seven to five years in order to strengthen the authority of the legislature against the increasing power of the executive.[12] He also favoured longer general election campaigns and a second ballot to 'secure a proper majority representation'.[13] Churchill believed that tariff reform could only be defeated by 'the sledge hammer of democracy' – a massive vote for free trade at the polls.[14] This was achieved by the 1906 'Liberal landslide' and thereafter Churchill used the term 'democracy' as a synonym for mass support for Liberalism.[15]

Churchill's conversion to Liberalism was followed by a change of heart on female suffrage. In 1904 he voted in favour of extending existing franchise rights to women on an equal basis.[16] However his support for some female suffrage was undermined by the actions of the suffragettes, who disrupted his election meetings in 1906, 1908 and 1910. He responded by denouncing their tactics as undemocratic.[17] Churchill observed that 'the frenzy of a few' was no substitute for the 'earnest convictions' of millions.[18] He described the 1910 Female Suffrage Bill as 'anti-democratic' because it proposed to enfranchise propertied women rather than wage earners. He preferred to enfranchise either a proportion of women from all classes or all adults over twenty-five.[19]

When Churchill became a Liberal, he also became an outspoken critic of the House of Lords. As a young Tory, he had shewn no partiality for peers as politicians, but he had regarded the House of Lords as a bulwark of the constitution.[20] In 1904, by contrast, he complained that the Lords had become 'the merest utensil of the Carlton Club'.[21] When the peers rejected the Liberal Education Bill,

[10] *Parl. Deb.* 4th series, 89 (1901), 409.
[11] Consuelo Balsan, *The Glitter and the Gold* (1953), 103.
[12] *Parl. Deb.*, 4th series, 150 (1905), 363–6.
[13] Churchill, *Speeches*, I, 538: Manchester, 8 Jan. 1906.
[14] Churchill, *Speeches*, I, 396: Newcastle, 5 Dec. 1904.
[15] Churchill, *Speeches*, II, 1158 : Nottingham 29 Jan. 1909.
[16] *Parl. Deb.*, 4th series, 131 (1904), 1366.
[17] Churchill, *Speeches*, I, 530: Cheetham, 5 January 1906.
[18] Churchill, *Speeches*, I, 1335: Dundee, 18 Oct. 1909.
[19] *Parl. Deb.*, 5th series, 19 (1910), 224.
[20] Randolph Churchill, *Churchill: Companion*, I, part 2, 698: Winston Churchill to Lady Randolph Churchill, 4 Nov. 1896; Churchill, *Speeches*, I, 44: Shaw, 28 June 1899.
[21] *The Times*, 22 Oct. 1904.

Churchill denounced the hereditary composition, landed character and partisan politics of the Lords. He counselled the Liberals to pass 'one or two good Radical Budgets', create new peers and 'educate the country on the constitutional issues involved' before they confronted the Lords.[22] The Lords' rejection of the 1909 Budget incensed Churchill who believed that 'the whole foundation of democratic life depended on the control of the finances being wielded by the House of Commons'.[23] He claimed that the past prominence of hereditary peers merely reflected the extent to which power had been engrossed by a 'small, limited and unrepresentative class'.[24] Churchill wrote to Asquith early in 1911:

> We ought to go straight ahead with the Parliament Bill & carry it to the Lords at the earliest date compatible with full discussion. We ought as early as possible to make it clear that we are not a bit afraid of creating 5000 peers – if necessary ... our representatives would be far more capable & determined politicians than the Tory nobles.[25]

When the Parliament Bill was introduced, Churchill declared that as the nation advanced, the influence and control of the peers should be reduced.[26]

The passage of the Parliament Bill precipitated a new crisis over Irish home rule. Churchill gradually abandoned his opposition to home rule after he became a Liberal and from 1908 he supported it on broadly democratic grounds. Speaking in 1912, on the Home Rule Bill, he stated that the great majority of the Irish people had a right to a parliament of their own. He acknowledged 'the perfectly genuine apprehensions of the majority of the people of north-east Ulster', but denied that they had the right 'to resist an Act of Parliament which they dislike'.[27] He regarded the Unionists' threats to prevent home rule as a challenge to democracy:

> This will be the issue – whether civil and Parliamentary government in these realms is to be beaten down by the menace of armed force ... It is the old battle-ground of English history ... From the language which is employed it would almost seem that we are face to face with a disposition on the part of some sections of the proprietary

---

[22] Churchill, *Speeches*, I, 717: Manchester, 4 Feb. 1907.

[23] Churchill, *Speeches*, II, 1393: Bolton, 7 Dec. 1909.

[24] *The Times*, 18 Dec. 1909.

[25] Randolph Churchill, *Churchill: Companion*, II, part 2 (1969), 1031: Winston Churchill to Asquith, 3 Jan. 1911.

[26] *Parl. Deb.*, 5th series, 21 (1911), 2029.

[27] *Parl. Deb.*, 5th series, 37 (1912), 1719.

classes to subvert Parliamentary government and to challenge all the civil and constitutional foundations of society.[28]

Churchill denounced the self-styled 'party of law and order' for acting above the law and setting a bad example to the British democracy 'millions of whom are ... repeatedly urged to be patient under their misfortune until Parliament has the time to deal with their problems'.[29] Churchill's condemnation of the Unionists for undermining parliamentary goverment paralleled his contemporary criticisms of the suffragettes, syndicalists and anarchists and was a precedent for his later stance towards other groups who believed in direct, as opposed to parliamentary action.

In 1912 Churchill was moved by reports of heroic self-sacrifice during the sinking of the Titanic:

> The whole episode fascinates me. It shows that in spite of all the inequalities and artificialities of our modern life, at the bottom – tested to its foundations, our civilisation is humane, Christian, & absolutely democratic.[30]

Churchill's faith in the democratic spirit of the age was reinforced by a much greater tragedy – the outbreak of the First World War:

> It is well that the democratic nations of the world – the nations ... where the peoples own the Government and not the Government the people – should realise what is at stake. The French, English and American systems of government by popular election and Parliamentary debate ... are brought into direct conflict with the highly efficient imperialist bureacracy and military organization of Prussia. That is the issue ... no sophistry can obscure it.[31]

Germany, however, was more democratic than Russia with whom Britain and France were allied during the war. Consequently Churchill welcomed the Russian revolution of February 1917 as a victory for democracy which strengthened the Allied cause:

> All the countries whose Governments owned the people, as if they were a kind of cattle, are on one side, and the countries where the people owned the Government, which are controlled by free citizens acting through Parliamentary institutions, and based on popular

[28] Churchill, *Speeches*, III, 2230: Bradford, 14 March 1914.

[29] *Parl. Deb.*, 5th series, 61 (1914), 1577.

[30] *Speaking for Themselves: The Personal Letters of Winston and Clementine Churchill*, ed. Mary Soames (1998), 65: Winston to Clementine, 20 April 1912.

[31] Churchill, *Speeches*, III, 2236: press release, 29 August 1914.

elections, are on the other ... Governments must never again own the people in any part of the world.[32]

In 1918 Churchill hailed the Armistice as an ideological, as well as a military, victory: 'We have beaten the Germans not only out of their trenches. We have beaten them out of their political system.'[33] Britain's own democratic credentials had been strengthened by the 1918 Reform Act which nearly tripled the electorate and enfranchised women over thirty. Churchill played no part in this reform and wrote before the 1918 general election:

The only uncertain element is the great one, this enormous electorate composed of so many of the poorest people in the country. I am pretty confident, however, that we shall secure very large majorities indeed.[34]

His confidence was justified and this bolstered his faith in democracy. In 1919 he boasted to MPs: 'We are elected on the widest franchise obtaining in any country in the world.'[35]

The interwar years provide the acid test of Churchill's commitment to democracy. His strong opposition to the Russian Bolsheviks, British Socialists and nationalists in the empire, together with his return to the Conservatives, led many Left-leaning contemporaries to question his commitment to democracy. For example, David Low, the political cartoonist, wrote of Churchill in the early 1920s: 'A democrat? An upholder of democracy? Um-ah-yes ... when he was leading it. Impatient with it when he was not.'[36] This view has been implicitly endorsed by many historians like Maurice Cowling, who argued that Churchill, after the First World War, abandoned 'the rhetoric of progress for the rhetoric of resistance'.[37] In fact, Churchill's political ideology remained essentially the same as it had been before the war – what changed was the political context, both at home and abroad, in which he operated.

Churchill's hostility to the Bolsheviks was prompted mainly by his distaste for their undemocratic and violent methods. He wrote to a Dundee constituent in December 1918:

With regard to Russia, you have only to seek the truth to be assured of the awful forms of anti-democratic tyranny which prevail there

[32] Churchill, *Speeches*, III, 2562: Dundee 21 July 1917.

[33] *Ibid.*, 2643: Dundee, 26 Nov. 1918.

[34] Martin Gilbert, *Winston S. Churchill* (hereafter Gilbert, *Churchill: Companion*), IV, part 1 (1977), 429: Winston Churchill to Clementine Churchill, 27 Nov. 1918.

[35] *Parl. Deb.*, 5th series, Commons, 114 (1919), c. 1254.

[36] David Low, *Low's Autobiography* (1956), 146.

[37] Maurice Cowling, *The Impact of Labour 1920–24* (1971), 166.

... The only sure foundation for a State is a Government freely elected by millions of people, and as many millions as possible. It is fatal to swerve from that conception.[38]

In 1920 Churchill denounced Lenin and Trotsky because they had dissolved the Russian parliament and established an autocratic regime which was not 'fit company for a democratic government like ours'.[39] He declared that his hatred of the Bolsheviks was founded, not on their 'silly system of economics' or 'absurd doctrine of ... equality', but on their 'bloody and devasting terrorism'.[40]

Churchill's critique of Bolshevism had more force than many of his radical contemporaries were prepared to admit, but it led him to favour one anti-Commmunist who was hardly a democrat. On a visit to Rome, in 1927, Churchill praised Mussolini:

> Your movement has abroad rendered a service to the whole world. The greatest fear that ever tormented every Democratic or Socialist leader was that of being outbid or surpassed by some other leader more extreme than himself. It has been said that a continual movement to the Left, a kind of fatal landslide towards the abyss, has been the character of all revolutions. Italy ... provides the necessary antidote to the Russian virus.[41]

Churchill's comments were partly prompted by the need for good Anglo-Italian relations, but he clearly preferred Italy to be Fascist, rather than Communist.[42] His stance reflected the new ideological polarity in Europe, but it also echoed a personal concern which he had first voiced thirty years before. In his only novel, *Savrola*, written in 1896, Churchill traced, in his own words, 'the fortunes of a liberal leader who overthrew an arbitrary Government only to be swallowed up by a socialist revolution'.[43] His early fear that the principal threat to democracy came from the Left, not the Right, was later reinforced by the Bolshevik revolution. Nevertheless Churchill, in his Rome speech, stressed that Britain had a very different way from Mussolini of dealing with Bolshevism and when he returned home, he declared that *all* forms of tyranny – aristocratic, theocratic, plutocratic, bureaucratic, democratic – were equally odious.[44]

Churchill's postwar Irish policy was broadly consistent with his

[38] Winston S. Churchill, *The Aftermath* (1941), 48–9.
[39] Churchill, *Speeches*, III, 2937–8: Dundee, 14 Feb. 1920.
[40] *Parl. Deb.* 5th series, 131 (1920), 1728.
[41] Churchill, *Speeches*, IV, 4126: Rome, 20 January 1927.
[42] A point Churchill later acknowledged in 1944, see: *Parl. Deb.*, 5th series, 406 (1944), 938.
[43] Winston S. Churchill, *My Early Life* (1943), 169.
[44] Churchill, *Speeches*, IV, 4213: Albert Hall, 6 May 1927.

prewar democratic stance. He wrote to Lloyd George in 1918: 'I have always shared your view that home rule should be give to that part of Ireland which so earnestly desires it and cannot be forced upon that which at present distrusts it.'[45]

The IRA's subsequent campaign against the British authorities aroused Churchill's usual pugnacity and hostility to political violence. Nevertheless – as Paul Addison has pointed out – Churchill neither initiated, nor sought to prolong, British coercion in Ireland which he regarded as a prelude to a settlement, not an alternative to one.[46] He accepted the right of the Ulster Unionists to decide their own fate, but he continued to hope for the re-union of Ireland within the British Empire.[47]

In Britain, Churchill's postwar objective was to forge a progressive alliance between what he called 'the democratic forces in the Conservative party and the patriotic forces in the Liberal and Labour parties'.[48] He justified the continuance of Lloyd George's coalition government by referring to his father's call for a Tory democratic government animated by liberal ideas.[49] After the fall of the coalition, in 1923, he told Sir Robert Horne:

I am what I have always been – a Tory Democrat. Force of circumstance has compelled me to serve with another party but my views have never changed and I should be glad to give effect to them by rejoining the Conservatives.[50]

In 1924 Churchill called for Conservative co-operation with 'a Liberal wing on the lines of 1886' which would 'afford the nation the guarantee it requires against retrogression'.[51] At the 1924 general election, Churchill stood as a 'Constitutionalist' candidate for Epping. In his election address he compared his position to that of the Liberal Unionists in 1886 and also observed:

I am entirely opposed to minority rule ... the will of the majority ... is the only healthy foundation of the State ... 'Trust the people!' These words of Lord Randolph Churchill ... embody and express the fundamental principles of British national life and government.[52]

[45] Gilbert, *Churchill: Companion*, iv, part 1, 411: Churchill to Lloyd George, 9 Nov. 1918.
[46] Paul Addison, 'The Search for Peace in Ireland', in *Churchill as Peacemaker* ed. James W. Muller (Cambridge, 1997), 197–202.
[47] For a wider consideration of Churchill's Irish policy see Mary C. Bromage, *Churchill and Ireland* (Notre Dame, Indiana, 1964).
[48] Churchill, *Speeches*, iii, 2816: London, 15 July 1919.
[49] *Ibid.*, 2816–7.
[50] Martin Gilbert, *Winston S. Churchill*, v (1976), 8: Riddell's diary, 30 May 1923.
[51] *The Times*, 8 March 1924.
[52] *The Times*, 13 Oct. 1924.

After the election, Churchill joined Baldwin's new Conservative government as Chancellor of the Exchequer. In 1925 he concluded a major speech to the Primrose League, by endorsing his father's belief in 'Government of the people, for the people, by the people'.[53]

The postwar rise of Labour did not undermine Churchill's faith in democracy, partly because he had prewar experience of confronting Labour. He had personally been opposed by Labour candidates at every election since 1908 and his opposition to socialism went back even further. In 1906 he had claimed that moderate Liberalism enlisted 'hundreds of thousands upon the side of progress and popular democratic reform whom militant socialism would drive into violent Tory reaction.'[54] In 1908 he had stressed the fundamental dichotomy between Liberal and socialist principles – a view which he re-stated in 1922: 'Socialism is the negation of every principle of British Liberalism'.[55] In the same speech he observed:

> There never was a Government yet erected that would own the people as a Socialist government would. No Tsar, no Kaiser, no Oriental potentate has ever wielded powers like these. When the only employer in the country is the state, a strike becomes a rebellion. No strikes therefore can be tolerated.[56]

Nevertheless Churchill did not question the democratic right of the Labour party to seek a majority at the polls.[57] When Ramsay MacDonald formed the first Labour government in 1924, Churchill wrote to congratulate him and received an appreciative reply. Yet Churchill's antipathy to socialism remained as strong as ever and in 1926 he expressed the fear that a future Labour government would try to implement socialism and thus curtail 'our liberty'.[58]

Churchill regarded the General Strike in May 1926 as a threat to democracy because it attempted 'to compel Parliament to do something which it otherwise would not do'. He predicted that the conflict would end either 'in the overthrow of Parliamentary Government or its decisive victory'.[59] After the end of the strike, Churchill declared that 'government by talking ... is better than government by shouting and ... by shooting'. He denied that 'the age of democracy spells ruin to Parliamentary government' and claimed that parliament was 'the greatest instrument for associating an ever-widening class of citizens

[53] Churchill, *Speeches*, IV, 3592: the Albert Hall, 1 May 1925.
[54] Churchill, *Speeches*, I, 675: Glasgow, 11 Oct. 1906.
[55] *Churchill: Speeches*, I, 146–8: Dundee, 4 May 1908; IV, 3306: Dundee, 8 April 1922.
[56] Churchill, *Speeches*, IV, 3306: Dundee, 8 April 1922.
[57] Churchill, *Speeches*, III, 2943: Dundee, 14 Feb. 1920.
[58] Churchill, *Speeches*, IV, 3821: Bolton, 21 Jan. 1926.
[59] *Parl. Deb.*, 5th series, 195 (1926), 124.

with the actual life and policy of the State'.[60] Nevertheless Churchill was not keen on extending citizenship to young women. In 1927 he initially opposed the Equal Suffrage Bill because he feared it would harm the Conservative party at the polls, but he later decided to support it 'on the well known principle of making a virtue of necessity'.[61] He declared: 'we must not only trust the people ... but trust the whole people'.[62]

In his 1930 Romanes lecture, Churchill observed that parliamentary government 'seems to lose much of its authority when based upon universal suffrage' and that many European parliaments had been undermined:

> Democracy has shown itself careless about those very institutions by which its own political status has been achieved. It seems ready to yield up the tangible rights hard won in rugged centuries to party organizations, to leagues and societies, to military chiefs or to dictatorships in various forms.[63]

Churchill believed that the British parliament, by contrast, had retained both its power and prestige and provided 'the closest association yet achieved between the life of the people and the action of the State'. Nevertheless he doubted whether, even in Britain, the right economic decisions could be reached by 'institutions based on adult suffrage', since no single political party would adopt necessary, but unpopular, economic policies for fear of their electoral consequences. Consequently he recommended the creation of a subordinate 'Economic parliament' made up of businessmen and technocrats.[64]

The financial crisis of 1931 confirmed Churchill's fears about the limitations of modern democracies:

> Democracy as a guide or motive to progress has long been known to be incompetent. None of the legislative assemblies of the great modern states represent in universal suffrage even a fraction of the strength or wisdom of the community ... Democratic governments drift along the line of least resistance, taking short views, paying their way with sops and doles ... Never was there less continuity or design in their affairs, and yet towards them are coming swiftly changes which will revolutionize for good or ill not only the whole economic

[60] Churchill, *Speeches*, IV, 3968–9: Westminster, 26 May 1926.
[61] Gilbert, *Churchill: Companion*, V, part 1 (1979), 958–60: Churchill's Cabinet memorandum, 'The Question of extending Female Suffrage', 8 March 1927. *Speaking for Themselves*, 315: Winston to Clementine, 22 Oct. 1927.
[62] Churchill, *Speeches*, IV. 4333: Chingford, 24 Oct. 1927.
[63] Winston S. Churchill, 'Parliamentary Government and the Economic Problem', in *Thoughts and Adventures* (1942), 194.
[64] *Ibid.*, 196–203.

structure of the world but the social habits and moral outlook of every family.[65]

Churchill's comments reflected contemporary dissatisfaction – on the left, as well as on the right – with parliamentary party politics. This feeling encouraged Ramsay MacDonald to form, in August 1931, a coalition national government. Churchill, like his father before him, favoured the concept of a national government, but he was excluded from its ranks. Nevertheless he welcomed the national government's landslide victory at the polls, on the grounds that 'universal suffrage has sent the largest majority of Tory members to Parliament which has ever been dreamed of'.[66] By 1934, however, Churchill had concluded that the dominance of the House of Commons by one party was 'most unhealthy'. He advocated constitutional changes including a 'weighted' franchise with extra votes for heads of households and fathers of families and the creation of 'a strong and effective Second Chamber' able 'to keep the main structure of our national life beyond the danger of sudden and violent change'.[67]

Churchill's opposition, in the early 1930s, to the Government of India Bill reflected his belief that Asia was unsuited to democracy. As a young officer in India, he had observed: 'East of Suez democratic reins are impossible. India must be governed on old principles.'[68] But Churchill did not believe that India should be governed in an arbitrary or coercive way. In 1920 he endorsed the enforced retirement of General Dyer after the Amritsar Massacre and observed:

> Our reign in India or anywhere else has never stood on the basis of physical force alone and it would be fatal to the British Empire if we were to try to base ourselves only upon it.[69]

In 1931 Churchill opposed the Indian policy of MacDonald's government because it was proposed to transfer many British responsibilities to 'an electorate comparatively small and almost entirely illiterate'. He claimed that the Congress party represented the elite Brahmins who 'spout the principles of western Liberalism and democracy, but ... deny basic human rights to the 60 million untouchables'.[70] Churchill preferred the Indian government to be responsible to Westminster which he considered was 'the most democratic parliament in the world.'[71]

[65] Churchill, 'Fifty Years Hence', in *Thoughts*, 236.

[66] Churchill, *Speeches*, v, 5089: Chingford, 30 October 1931.

[67] *Ibid*, 5319–20: Broadcast, 16 Jan. 1934. *Parl. Deb.*, 5th series, 253 (1931), 102–6.

[68] Churchill, *Churchill: Companion*, I, part 2, 751: Churchill to Lady Randolph Churchill, 6 April 1897.

[69] *Parl. Deb.*, 5th series, 131 (1920), 1731.

[70] Churchill, *Speeches*, v, 5007: Albert Hall, 18 March 1931.

[71] Churchill, *Speeches*, v, 4986: Epping, 23 Feb 1931.

Churchill's doubts about democracy in India were increased by the failure of democracy in much of Europe. He claimed that the supporters of Congress had been influenced by 'all those books about democracy which Europe is now beginning increasingly to discard'.[72] In 1935 he described the proposals contained in the Government of India Bill as the 'faded flowers of Victorian Liberalism which, however admirable in themselves, have nothing to do with Asia and are being universally derided and discarded throughout the continent of Europe'.[73] Churchill's reservations were shared by some maharajahs and members of the orthodox Hindu society, Varnashrama Swarajya, who believed that western democracy was unsuited to Indian traditions.[74]

Churchill's reluctance to apply democratic principles to India contrasted with his readiness to deplore the lack of them in Nazi Germany. Soon after Hitler became chancellor, Churchill observed that German parliamentary democracy, which had been a security for Europe after the First World War, had been replaced by a dictatorship characterised by militarism and anti-semitism.[75] In 1934 he pointed out that the Nazi government was free from 'those very important restraints which a democratic Parliament and constitutional system impose upon any executive Government'.[76] He feared that the apparent success of the Nazi regime posed a threat to the continuance of democracy throughout western Europe:

We have to consider ... whether the Parliamentary Governments of Western Europe ... are going to be able to afford to their subjects the same measure of physical security, to say nothing of national satisfaction, as is being afforded to the people of Germany by the dictatorship which has been established there.[77]

Nevertheless Churchill continued to regard the Communists, as well as the Nazis, as a threat to democracy. At Paris, in 1936, he welcomed the opposition of the French, British and American democracies to both the Nazis and Communists. His speech was applauded as a 'magnificent defence of democracy'.[78] Churchill feared that in Spain, where civil war had broken out, the Communists were waiting to seize

[72] Ibid.
[73] Parl. Deb., 5th series, 302 (1935), 1921.
[74] Winston S. Churchill, Chartwell Papers, Churchill College, Cambridge (hereafter Churchill Papers), CHAR: 2/193/41–45: Stanley Bratle to Churchill, 15 April 1933; 2/123/163–7: Maharajah of Alwar to Churchill 19 July 1922; 2/189/123: cutting from The Times, 22 Nov. 1932.
[75] Parl. Deb., 5th series, 276 (1933), 2790.
[76] Parl. Deb., 5th series, 286 (1934), 2071–2.
[77] Parl. Deb., 5th series, 302 (1935), 1496.
[78] Churchill, Speeches, VI. 5788: Paris, 24 September 1936; Churchill Papers, CHAR 2/258/79: Arthur Cummings to Churchill, 24 Sept. 1936.

power as they had done in Russia in 1917. He did not, however, endorse Franco's revolt against the Republican government for he believed that 'whoever wins in Spain, freedom and free democracy must be the losers'.[79] By the end of 1938 Churchill was more favourable to the republican cause because he thought that the influence of the Communists and anarchists had waned. He feared that if Franco won he would practise 'the same kind of brutal suppressions as are practised in the Totalitarian States'.[80]

In the late 1930s it was President Roosevelt, rather than Churchill, who led the rhetorical campaign in the English-speaking world against the European dictators.[81] The president's peace initiative in 1938 inspired Churchill to issue his own call to the transatlantic democracies:

Have we not an ideology – if we must use this ugly word – of our own in freedom, in a liberal constitution, in democratic and Parliamentary government ... Ought we not to produce in defence of Right, champions as bold, missionaries as eager, and if need be, swords as sharp as are at the disposal of the leaders of totalitarian states.[82]

After the Munich agreement, Churchill claimed that the ideological antagonism between Nazidom and democracy strengthened the free world.[83] In April 1939 Churchill again echoed Roosevelt's recent defence of democracy by citing the British legacy of Magna Carta, Habeas Corpus, the Petition of Right, trial by jury, the English Common Law and parliamentary democracy.[84]

Churchill opposed Chamberlain's appeasement policy partly because he feared that it would undermine democracy in Britain:

I foresee and foretell that the policy of submission will carry with it restrictions upon the freedom of speech and debate in Parliament, on public platforms, and discussions in the Press, for it will be said ... that we cannot allow the Nazi system of dictatorship to be criticised by ordinary, common English politicians[85]

This fear had some foundation for Churchill's attack on the Munich

[79] Winston S. Churchill, *Step By Step* (1939), 51–2: 'The Spanish Tragedy, August 10, 1936'.

[80] *Ibid.*, 313: 'The Spanish Ulcer, December 30, 1938'.

[81] For a comparison between Churchill and Roosevelt's comments on democracy see: Roland Quinault 'Anglo-American Attitudes to Democracy from Lincoln to Churchill' in *Anglo-American Attitudes: From Revolution to Partnership*, ed. Fred M. Leventhal and Roland Quinault (Aldershot, 2000), 132–6.

[82] Winston S. Churchill, *Into Battle: War Speeches* (1945), 17–18: Manchester, 9 May 1938.

[83] Churchill, *Battle*, 58: broadcast to the USA, 16 Oct. 1938.

[84] Churchill, *Battle*, 100: London, 20 April 1939.

[85] *Parl. Deb.*, 5th series, 339 (1938), 371.

agreement led to calls for him to be disowned by his constituency association. But Churchill warned that parliamentary democracy would not survive if the constituencies returned subservient MPs and tried to stamp out independent judgement.[86]

When Churchill entered the Cabinet, at the outbreak of war in 1939, he called for tough measures which would convince the world that the democracies were more than a match for the dicatorships.[87] Throughout the war he remained convinced that democracy was on trial as much as dictatorship. In 1942 he told Roosevelt: 'Democracy has to prove that it can provide a granite foundation for war against tyranny.'[88] Yet Churchill's famous speeches in the summer of 1940 employed the old language of freedom, rather than the new language of democracy. Thereafter Churchill's use of specifically democratic rhetoric was constrained by contradictory pressures from Britain's two major allies. In 1941 Hitler's invasion of the Soviet Union provided Churchill with a welcome ally but undermined the democratic credentials of the anti-Nazi front. Soon afterwards, Churchill and Roosevelt signed the Atlantic Charter which, although it asserted the right of people to choose their own form of government, made no reference to democracy. This prevented embarrassment not only for the Soviet Union, but also for imperial Britain. When the US entered the war, Roosevelt privately called on Churchill to give independence to India, but he refused to consider the matter until after the war was over.[89] In 1944 Churchill even told Roosevelt that British imperialism 'has spread and is spreading democracy more widely than any other system of government since the beginning of time'.[90]

Churchill's most important wartime statement on democracy was made in opposition, not to the Nazis, but to the Communists. In December 1944 he defended British intervention in Greece and other parts of liberated Europe as action designed to ensure the rule of democracy, which he defined as free and secret voting for the candidate of one's choice. He claimed that throughout his life he had 'broadly' stood 'upon the foundation of free elections based on universal suffrage'. He accused the Communists of creating 'a swindle democracy ... which calls itself democracy because it is Left Wing':

---

[86] Churchill, *Battle*, 78: Waltham Abbey, 14 March 1939.
[87] Churchill, *Battle*, 133–4: broadcast, 1 October 1939.
[88] CHAR 20/70/79–80: Churchill to Roosevelt, 20 Feb. 1942.
[89] Lord Moran, *Winston Churchill: The Struggle for Survival 1940–65* (1966), 30–1.
[90] Warren F. Kimball (ed.), *Churchill & Roosevelt: The Complete Correspondence III. Alliance Declining February 1944–April 1945* (Princeton, 1987), 140: Churchill to Roosevelt, 21 May 1944.

Democracy ... is not based on violence or terrorism, but on reason, on fair play, on freedom, on respecting the rights of other people. Democracy is no harlot to be picked up in the street by a man with a tommy gun. I trust the people, the mass of the people, in almost every country, but I like to make sure that it is the people and not a gang of bandits ... who think that by violence they can overturn constituted authority, in some cases ancient Parliaments, Governments and States.[91]

The end of the war in Europe led Churchill to fear a renewed threat to democracy at home. The break-up of the coalition government led to a return to party politics and a general election at which Churchill re-issued a warning he had made twenty years before. He denounced socialism as a threat to liberty in Britain – 'the cradle and citadel of free democracy throughout the world' – and he even suggested that a Labour government would have to rely on some sort of gestapo.[92] Nevertheless he accepted Labour's landslide victory at the polls:

I avow my faith in Democracy, whatever course or view it may take with individuals and parties. They may make their mistakes and they may profit from their mistakes. Democracy is now on trial as it never was before, and in these islands we must uphold it, as we upheld it in the dark days of 1940 and 1941 ... While the war was on and all the Allies were fighting for victory, the word 'Democracy', like many people, had to work overtime, but now that peace has come we must search for more precise definitions.[93]

In 1946, in his famous Fulton speech, Churchill laid down the general principle that 'the people of any country have the right and should have the power by constitutional action, by free unfettered elections, with secret ballot, to choose or change the character or form of government under which they dwell'. He was mainly concerned with the lack of democracy behind the 'Iron Curtain' in Eastern Europe, but his exhortation to the British and American peoples to 'practise what we preach' implied that they should also defend democracy at home.[94] Later that year, Churchill denounced Socialist state control in Britain by an 'aristocracy of privileged officials' and in its place advocated 'a property-owning democracy'.[95] In 1947 Churchill criticised

[91] *Parl. Deb.*, 5th series, 406 (1944), 927–8.
[92] Winston S. Churchill, *Victory: War Speeches* (1946), 188–9: election broadcast, 4 June 1945.
[93] *Parl. Deb.*, 5th series, 413 (1945), 86.
[94] Winston S. Churchill, *The Sinews of Peace: Post-War Speeches* (1948), 97: Westminster College, Fulton, Missouri, 5 March 1946.
[95] *Ibid.*, 214: Conservative Party Conference, 5 Oct. 1946.

the 'we are the masters now' mentality of the Labour government:

> Democracy is not a caucus, obtaining a fixed term of office by promises, and then doing what it likes with the people. We hold that there ought to be a constant relationship between the rulers and the people. Government of the people, by the people, for the people still remains the sovereign definition of democracy. There is no correspondence between this broad conception and the outlook of His Majesty's Government.[96]

Churchill thus linked Labour with an unfavourable image of American democracy: government by caucus.

At the 1950 general election, Labour was returned to power with a narrow parliamentary majority, although it received fewer votes than the combined total for Conservatives and Liberals. This led Churchill to favour proportional representation which he had first endorsed in 1931 – when Labour had also been in office.[97] In 1950 he drew the attention of parliament to the 'constitutional injustice' whereby 2,600,000 Liberal voters had returned only nine MPs.[98] But his call for a select committee on electoral reform attracted no support from Tory backbenchers.[99] Churchill was also out of step with many Tories in his attitude to reform of the House of Lords. During the debate on the 1947 Parliament Bill, he reminded the House that he had actively supported the 1911 Parliament Act, but he attacked the new Bill because it retained the hereditary peers instead of introducing fundamental reform.[100] In 1952 Lord Salisbury noted that Churchill regarded the Lords 'as a rather disreputable collection of old gentlemen'.[101] When Churchill retired from the premiership, he refused a peerage and in 1961 he supported Anthony Wedgwood Benn's attempt to renounce his peerage and retain his seat in the Commons, which led to the 1963 Peerage Act.[102]

Churchill disliked the hereditary character of the House of Lords, but he regarded the elected House of Commons as 'the enduring guarantee of British liberties and democratic progress'. In 1953 he told MPs: 'We are not only a democracy but a Parliamentary democracy, and both aspects of our political life must be borne in mind.' He even

[96] Parl. Deb., 5th series, 444 (1947), 203.

[97] Parl. Deb., 5th series, 253 (1931), 102–6.

[98] Parl. Deb., 5th series, 472 (1950), 143–4.

[99] Stuart Ball (ed.), Parliament and Politics in the Age of Churchill and Attlee: The Headlam Diaries 1935–1951, Camden Fifth Series, vol. 14 (Cambridge, 1999), 622–3: diary entries for 7 and 9 March 1950.

[100] Parl. Deb., 5th series, 444 (1947), 202.

[101] Moran, Struggle for Survival, 376: diary entry for 22 Feb. 1952.

[102] Winston Churchill, Letter to Anthony Wedgwood Benn (Bristol, 1961). See also Tony Benn's comments in the 'Churchill Remembered' section.

claimed 'that elections exist for the sake of the House of Commons and not that the House of Commons exists for the sake of elections'.[103] He regarded himself as the servant of the House of Commons and he opposed the American system which separated the executive from the legislature.[104]

During his second premiership, Churchill was still reluctant to extend democracy to the non-white population of the British Empire, particularly in Africa. In 1954 he observed to Eisenhower:

> I am a bit sceptical about universal suffrage for the Hottentots even if refined by proportional representation. The British and American Democracies were slowly and painfully forged and even they are not perfect yet.[105]

Churchill's reference to the Hottentots echoed an 1886 speech by Lord Salisbury, who had argued that majority government could not be safely conferred on Hottentots, Indians or other non-Teutonic peoples.[106] Churchill was sceptical, not without reason, whether democracy could operate effectively in countries where there were high levels of poverty and illiteracy and no tradition of mass participation in institutional politics. Nevertheless he did not rule out democratisation in the colonies if the conditions were right. Indeed in 1953 British Guiana was given a constitution based on universal suffrage, although it was soon suspended after disturbances broke out. In the same year the possibility of giving autonomy to the Gold Coast was also considered, although Jock Colville doubted if Churchill was interested 'in the inhabitants of those parts'.[107] Churchill's preference for gradual democratisation reflected his historical perspective. His remark to Eisenhower about the slow and imperfect emergence of democracy in Britain and America was fully justified. Britain had only recently adopted a one person one value franchise and still retained an hereditary monarchy and second chamber, whilst in the USA many non-whites were still disenfranchised.

In 1914 Churchill expressed the hope that he had 'a firm grip of democratic principles'.[108] How justified was this claim with respect to his career as a whole? Churchill's commitment, in principle, to democracy in Britain never wavered, even in the interwar years. He always

[103] *Parl. Deb.*, 5th series, 520 (1953), 21–2.

[104] Winston S. Churchill, *The Unrelenting Struggle: War Speeches* (1942), 334: 29 December 1941; Sir John Colville, *Parliamentary Democracy: History and Practice* (Toronto, 1986), 7–10.

[105] Anthony Montague Browne, *Long Sunset: Memoirs of Winston Churchill's Last Private Secretary* (1996), 164.

[106] *The Times*, 17 May 1886: Salisbury's speech at St James's Hall, 15 May.

[107] Moran Diaries, 434: 14 July 1953.

[108] *Churchill: Speeches*, III, 2232 : Bradford, 14 March 1914.

believed that the fundamental source of political authority was the will of the people expressed through the medium of free and secret parliamentary elections. However Churchill's commitment, in practice, to democracy in Britain was less impressive than his rhetoric. Although he supported the principle of manhood suffrage, he did little to advance its implementation. He quickly accepted the principle of women's suffrage, but he opposed female franchise bills both before and after the First World War. Moreover Churchill was not entirely committed to an equal franchise. Montague Browne noted Churchill's interest, in the 1950s, in schemes for cumulative votes for heads of families and others with special responsibilites, but thought that he did not seriously wish to put them into practice.[109] However Churchill had also proposed such schemes in the 1930s, which suggests that he had a fairly serious interest in them.

Churchill often expressed reservations about democracy. He did so, not only in the early 1930s – when democracy was being undermined by economic and political developments – but also after the Second World War when western democracy had triumphed. In 1947 he called democracy 'the worst form of Government except all those others that have been tried'.[110] He thought that democracy was riddled with faults and dangers, and a perpetual popularity contest, though it was still better than alternative systems.[111]

It is tempting to ascribe Churchill's reservations about democracy to his ancestral Conservatism. Sir John Colville noted that Churchill was a strange mixture of radical and traditionalist and in that respect, he resembled his father, Lord Randolph, who had wished, in Winston's words, to reconcile 'the old glories ... of King and country ... with modern democracy'.[112] Winston certainly saw no contradiction between democracy and monarchy. In 1943 he approved the marriage of the exiled King of Yugoslavia on the grounds that it would give him a chance of perpetuating his dynasty and then added, incongruously, 'are we not fighting this war for liberty and democracy?'[113] Yet Churchill's belief that monarchy and democracy were compatible was based on more than just Conservatism. His hope, at the end of the Spanish Civil War, that the restoration of a constitutional monarchy would end old emnities was vindicated by events after Franco's death.[114]

Churchill's reservations about democracy stemmed not just from his

[109] Browne, *Long Sunset*, 180.
[110] *Parl. Deb.*, 5th series, 444 (1947), 207.
[111] Browne, *Long Sunset*, 180.
[112] John Colville, *The Fringes of Power*, 128; Churchill, *Thoughts and Adventures*, 42.
[113] Winston S. Churchill, *The Second World War*, v: *Closing The Ring* (1952), 571–2: Churchill to the Foreign Secretary, 11 July 1943.
[114] Churchill, *Step By Step*, 334: 'Hope in Spain, 23 February 1939'.

Conservatism, but also from his Liberalism. In 1906 he noted that the 1884 Reform Act had been followed by twenty years of Tory ascendancy:

Who could possibly have foreseen that ... enfranchised multitudes would constitute themselves the buttresses of privilege and property; that a free press would by its freedom sap the influence of debate and through its prosperity become the implement of wealth; that members and constituencies would become less independent, not more independent; that Ministers would become more powerful, not less powerful; that the march would be ordered backward along the beaten track, not forward in some new direction...[115]

Churchill was a Liberal when he wrote this comment, but he made similar remarks in the 1930s when he was a Conservative.

Churchill also feared that democracy could breed jingoism and war. In 1901 he observed: 'Democracy is more vindictive than Cabinets. The wars of peoples will be more terrible than those of kings.'[116] In 1947, in an imagined conversation with his father, he said: 'We have had nothing else but wars since democracy took charge.'[117] This was ironic because Churchill believed that peace was the only secure foundation for democracy. In 1906 he observed that 'the first indispensable condition of democratic progress must be the maintenance of European peace'.[118] This conviction underlay his support for European unity both before and after the Second World War. In 1947 he declared: 'The whole purpose of a united democratic Europe is to give decisive guarantees against aggression.'[119]

Churchill's anti-Socialism, which tarnished his reputation as a democrat in the eyes of the Left, reflected his Liberalism more than his Conservatism. His belief that socialism was an inherently illiberal political system may seem excessive in retrospect, but it was borne out, during his lifetime, in half of Europe and much of the rest of the world. Even in postwar Britain, the growth of the socialistic state alarmed not just the Right, but also moderate Labour politicians like Roy Jenkins. Today, by contrast, New Labour in Britain and the new socialists in Europe have rejected the full-blooded socialism which Churchill so strongly mistrusted.

Churchill's reputation as a democrat was also undermined by his reluctance to democratise Britian's non-white empire. But his stance

---

[115] Churchill, *Lord Randolph Churchill*, 219.

[116] *Parl. Deb.*, 4th series, 93 (1901), 1572.

[117] Winston Churchill, 'The Dream', in Martin Gilbert, *Winston S. Churchill*, VIII (1988), 369.

[118] Churchill, *Speeches*, I, 671: Glasgow, 11 Oct. 1906.

[119] Winston S. Churchill, *Europe Unite: Speeches 1947 and 1948* (1950), 83: Albert Hall, 14 May 1947.

on this issue was shared by most of his parliamentary contemporaries including many Liberals and some socialists.[120] His attitude was based mainly on pragmatic considerations of culture, wealth, class, education and stability rather than on racial prejudice, for even in Britain Churchill only favoured a gradual 'levelling up' to full democracy. Nevertheless Churchill's stalwart defence of democracy during the Second World War strengthened the post-war demand for democracy throughout the Empire.

Churchill's attitude to democracy was essentially late-Victorian in character. He favoured a democracy which was evolutionary, not revolutionary; parliamentary, not plebiscitary; monarchical, not republican, liberal not socialist. His outlook was indelibly influenced by his father's concept of Tory democracy which, in turn, drew on the Victorian Liberal tradition of Gladstone and Mill. Like them, Churchill trusted 'the people' but was not entirely committed to electoral equality and believed that legislation and administration should be in the hands of those able to lead. Churchill had great confidence in his own abilities in this respect and one of his favourite definitions of democracy was 'the association of us all through the leadership of the best'.[121] However Churchill never forgot that he was a representative of the people. On his eightieth birthday – at the height of his fame – he modestly observed that it was the British people who had the lion's heart during the war, while he merely had 'the luck to be called upon to give the roar'.[122]

[120] See the comments by Tony Benn MP and Lord Carrington in the 'Churchill Remembered' section.

[121] Winston S. Churchill, *Stemming The Tide: Speeches 1951 and 1952* (1953), 82–3: Glasgow, 18 May 1951.

[122] Winston S. Churchill, *The Unwritten Alliance: Speeches 1953 to 1959* (1961), 203: speech at Westminster Hall, 30 November 1954.

CHURCHILL AND THE TRADE UNIONS
By Chris Wrigley

WINSTON CHURCHILL combined a rhetoric of Tory democracy with a shrewd political realism in his approach to the trade unions. When class conflict was strong and law and order under threat, as in 1911–26, the rhetoric evaporated and Churchill became the champion of the anxious propertied classes. So much so that his persistent Dundee opponent, Edwin Scrymgeour, observed during the 1922 general election campaign, shortly after Mussolini took power in Italy, that it would not surprise him in the event of civil war in Britain 'if Mr Churchill were at the head of the Fascisti party'.[1] While this view ignored Churchill's deep commitment to democracy and the British constitution, it did reflect concerns about his apparent revelling in the role of Defender of Order. Yet both before and after 1911 – 26 his approach to the trade unions was emollient.

Trade unions were an important pressure group which could affect his political prospects in Oldham, where he first sought and secured a parliamentary seat. In going for Oldham he was attempting to put into practice, and to benefit from, Tory democracy. His father, Lord Randolph Churchill, had been personally encouraged by Disraeli and had taken up his mantle when proclaiming Tory democracy. As Lord Randolph put it in 1885, the Tory Party's 'great strength can be found, and must be developed, in our large towns as well as in our country districts'.[2] Winston Churchill advanced on Oldham believing he was carrying on where his father had left off.[3] 'I am a Tory Democrat', he stated early on in the 1899 by-election campaign. 'I regard the improvement of the condition of the British people as the main aim of modern government.' To this ringing declaration he added qualifications sufficiently ample to have equalled Disraeli in such matters: 'I shall therefore promote to the best of my ability all legislation which, without throwing the country into confusion and disturbing the present concord, and without impairing that tremendous energy of production on which the wealth of the nation and the good of the people depend, may yet

---

[1] Martin Gilbert, *Winston S. Churchill*, IV (1975) 879.
[2] At Cambridge University Carlton, 6 June 1885; Winston S. Churchill, *Lord Randolph Churchill*, I (1906), 295.
[3] See *inter alia*, Robert Rhodes James, *Churchill: A Study in Failure 1900–1939*, (Harmondsworth, 1973), 19–23, and Roy Foster, *Lord Randolph Churchill* (Oxford, 1981), 390–6.

raise the standard of happiness and comfort in English homes.'[4]

Winston Churchill stood in a double by-election for the two-member Oldham constituency with James Mawdsley. He was one of the first, quite possibly the first, trade unionists with whom Churchill had substantial contact. The young aristocrat running in harness with the trade unionist was very Young England. Initially, Churchill was going to run with Robert Ascroft, who was well known to Oldham's textile workers as solicitor to the Amalgamated Association of Card Blowing and Ring Room Operatives and for his part in negotiating wage agreements in 1889 and 1890 and helping to resolve the major 1892–3 cotton lock-out. With Ascroft's sudden death, the Conservatives triggered a double by-election with Mawdsley as the candidate who it was hoped would pull the textile workers' votes to the Conservatives. Churchill believed he was part of a winning combination, writing to his mother on 25 June 1899, 'Owing to the appearance of a Tory Labour candidate it is quite possible we shall win.'[5]

The candidature of Mawdsley with Churchill is a very interesting episode illustrating Churchill's attitudes towards trade unionists and trade unionism. On the one hand, Churchill and Mawdsley shared many views. On the other, one can wonder if the young Churchill grasped – or was even interested in – Mawdsley's political views. In *My Early Life* he wrote of Mawdsley as 'a Socialist' and of a partnership between 'a "scion" of the ancient British aristocracy' and a socialist, a view echoed by Randolph Churchill in the official life and by Robert Rhodes James in the *Complete Speeches*. Peter Clarke in *Lancashire and the New Liberalism* rightly noted that Mawdsley's social reform programme amounted mostly to municipal control of utilities, as he put it, his 'claims were utilitarian and they were pitched low'.[6] By 1930, when he wrote *My Early Life*, Churchill was clear enough about what then constituted socialism. Thirty years earlier, Mawdsley was only a socialist in the dubious sense of favouring state intervention and regulation of industry, of a measure of collectivism.

Mawdsley was a bigger trade union figure and more of a Conservative than most writers about Churchill have realised. He was a member of the TUC's executive body, its parliamentary committee, 1882–3, 1884–90 and 1891–7, and was the TUC's chairman in 1886. He also served on the Royal Commission on Labour, 1891–4. He was a notable anti-

---

[4] At Oldham, 26 June 1899; Robert Rhodes James (ed.), *Winston S. Churchill: His Complete Speeches, 1897–1963* (8 vols., New York, 1974) (hereafter *Complete Speeches*), 1, 35. Paul Addison, *Churchill on the Home Front* (1992).

[5] Randolph S. Churchill, *Winston S. Churchill: Companion*, 1 (1967), 1009, 1022, 1024–5 and 1028–30.

[6] Winston S. Churchill, *My Early Life*, (1930), chapter 17. Randolph S. Churchill, *Winston S. Churchill*, 1, (1966), 444–5.

socialist, resigning from the parliamentary committee in 1890 in protest at the growing influence of New Union socialists in the TUC. Then he deemed socialist ideas fit only for the 'scum of London'. In 1895 he was instrumental in forging a cotton and coal alliance which changed the TUC rules so as to undercut many of the socialists.[7] In the general election of that year he was the conduit for 'Tory gold' to reach an Independent Labour party candidate, providing the money on a no questions asked basis.[8] Churchill would have found Tom Mann or Bob Smillie very different kinds of 'socialist' from Mawdsley. Nevertheless, Mawdsley was an effective trade union leader and was one who believed he could secure more labour regulation in parliament by working through the existing parties.

The young Churchill's approach to trade unionism combined a Tory democrat desire to do something for working people, provided it did not affect the competitiveness of industry, with a concern to maintain social stability. As early as 1897 he had held forth on industrial relations at the time of the great engineering lock-out. Appropriately, his audience was a Primrose League gathering at Bath. Then he had talked vaguely of some form of profit sharing, but one which would make the workers willing to suffer income losses in bad economic times.[9] In the 1899 by-election he was explicit that Tory democracy benefited the existing social order. 'For many years the Conservative Party has guarded the interests of labour', he told an Oldham audience, 'Their efforts have not been without reward, for Tory democracy has now become the stoutest bulwark of the constitution.'[10]

Churchill's attitude towards labour all his life had this element of *noblesse oblige*, but such benevolence was tempered by an expectation of good behaviour in return. The aristocratic expectations of playing a leading role in events and for others to minister to his needs was strong in him. Charles Masterman commented of him, 'He desired in England a state of things where a benign upper class dispensed benefits to an industrious, *bien pensant*, and grateful working class.'[11] Although mostly a kind man, Churchill had been brought up to expect employees to provide service, and quickly. Even his warmest admirers on occasion shuddered at his sometimes insensitive treatment of waiters, valets,

---

[7] A. Bullen, 'The Making of Brooklands' in Alan Fowler and Terry Wyke (eds.), *The Barefoot Aristocrats* (Littleborough, 1987), 99. Alan Fowler, 'Lancashire to Westminster: A Study of Cotton Trade Union Officials and British Labour, 1910–39', *Labour History Review*, 64, 1 (1999), 1–22. H.A. Clegg, A. Fox and A.F. Thompson, *A History of British Trade Unions Since 1889*, I, (Oxford, 1964), 115, 256 and 259.

[8] Sir James Sexton, *Sir James Sexton: Agitator* (1936), 146.

[9] On 26 July, 1897 at Claverton Down, Bath; *Complete Speeches*, I, 27.

[10] On 26 June 1899; *Complete Speeches*, I, 36.

[11] Quoted in Rhodes James, *Churchill*, 45.

chauffeurs and others.[12] One recalled with dismay his ringing for service, observing that when you want a drink you should ring, and keep ringing until it appears. Such an outlook was not in harmony with trade union notions of the dignity of labour. He also had a patrician, indeed Whig, attitude towards history. His historical writings do not deal much with the common man or woman. 'War, politics, violence, these are the stuff of Churchill's history: but glorious not nasty' was one way J.H. Plumb put it. On another occasion, more in caricature, he wrote of Churchill's history as 'a saga world of killer patricians, entangled by tradition and events in a few human decencies'.[13]

As well as this aristocratic outlook and his notions of Tory democracy, a further major aspect of Churchill's attitude to the trade unions was a deep-rooted belief in market forces and individualism. Churchill spoke of the economic struggles between nations when commenting on the 1897 engineering lock-out.

> Whoever is right, masters or men – both are wrong, whoever might win, both must lose. In the great economic struggle of nations no quarter is ever shown to the vanquished. Every individual has, no doubt the right to buy the best goods in the cheapest market, and if British manufacturing cannot produce goods for export at the lowest price in the market our trade ... would simply go to the German emperor...[14]

He long remained an articulate expounder of the merits of free market forces. In October 1906, in one of his celebrated social reform speeches, he commented:

> The existing organisation of society is driven by one mainspring – competitive selection. It may be a very imperfect organisation of society, but it is all we have got between us and barbarism ... and great and numerous as are the evils of the existing condition of society in this country, the advantages and achievements of the social system are greater still. Moreover that social system is one which offers an almost indefinite capacity for improvement ... I do not want to see impaired the vigour of competition, but we can do much to mitigate the consequences of failure. We want to draw a line below which we will not allow people to live and labour, yet above which they may compete with all the strengths of their manhood.[15]

[12] Maurice Ashley, *Churchill As Historian*, (1968), 9.
[13] In a book review in *The Spectator*, 1964, partly reprinted in J.H. Plumb, *The Making of an Historian: The Collected Essays of J.H. Plumb* (Brighton, 1988), 226.
[14] At Claverton Down, Bath, 26 July 1897; *Complete Speeches*, I, 27.
[15] At Glasgow, 11 October 1906; Winston S. Churchill, *Liberalism and the Social Problem* (1909), 82.

He echoed these words in a speech to the 1947 Conservative party conference.

Like Lloyd George, Churchill was more concerned to help the underdogs of society, not labour which was organised. With the Trade Boards Act, 1909, he made what he emphasised was an exceptional modification to laws of supply and demand to ensure 'adequate minimum standards' in sweated trades, 'where ... you have no organisation, no parity of bargaining, the good employer is undercut by the bad and the bad employer is undercut by the worst; [and where] the worker, whose livelihood depends upon the industry, is undersold by the worker who only takes up the trade as a second string'. This Act initially covered 200,000 workers, of whom 140,000 were women and girls, in tailoring, box-making, lace making and chain making.[16]

But what of trade unions? He himself was a great individualist. In a speech to a well-to-do audience in November 1901, he lamented, 'In trade vast and formidable combinations of labour stand against even vaster and more formidable combinations of capital, and, whether they war with each other or co-operate, the individual in the end is always crushed under.' He declared, 'I believe in personality.'[17] Yet as a Conservative MP he favoured the reversal of the Taff Vale Judgement, 1901, being one of seventeen Conservative MPs to vote for a TUC backed bill in 1903.[18] When the Bill was moved again in 1904, he supported it observing that although 'it was difficult to find a logical reason for relieving trade unions of their responsibilities and leaving them their power', there was the practical reason that the pre-Taff Vale legal position had enabled the trade unions to function well, being 'less violent and unjust' than before, and had not damaged the economy. He commented of the 1875 legislation that it 'was the work of a Tory government; it was introduced by so good a Tory as Lord Cross, had the *impimatur* of Disraeli; and was one of the great agencies by which ... the Tory democracy had been built up in this country'.[19]

While such comments might be construed as examples of his ability to manufacture plausible arguments to meet his current political needs, more probably they reflect his views. For he was to make very similar points after the Second World War. Moreover, in the period before

---

[16] House of Commons Debates, fifth series, vol. 4, col. 388, 28 April. (The passage is rephrased in *Liberalism and the Social Problem*, 240.) Addison, *Churchill on the Home Front*, 78–9.

[17] At the Philomathic Society dinner, Liverpool, 21 November 1901; *Complete Speeches*, I, 109.

[18] F. Bealey and H. Pelling, *Labour and Politics 1900–1906* (1958), 204. Addison, *Churchill on the Home Front*, 42.

[19] In the House of Commons; *House of Commons Debates*, fourth series, vol. 133, col. 999, April 1904.

1911 it is sometimes overlooked that his contact was with the more moderate trade unionists in industries marked on the whole by less tumultuous industrial relations: the textile workers of Oldham, Manchester and Dundee. Later, in 1911–26, he was to be alarmed by militant miners, railwaymen, dockers and engineers.

In the Edwardian period he readily praised the level-headedness of trade unionists. Thus, in October 1906, he said that if any group could claim to speak for the working classes,

> it is the trade unions that more than any other organisation must be considered the responsible and deputed representatives of Labour. They are the most highly organised part of labour; they are the most responsible part; they are from day to day in contact with reality...
>
> The fortunes of the trade unions are interwoven with the industries they serve. The more highly organised trade unions are, the more clearly they recognise their responsibilities; the larger the membership, the greater their knowledge, the wider their outlook.[20]

Two years later, when he elaborated on these comments, he went so far as to reconcile the trade unions to his belief in individualism. At Dundee, when proclaiming them as 'the bulwarks of a highly competitive industrial system', he commented,

> Trade unions are not socialist. They are the antithesis of socialism. They are undoubtedly individualistic organisations, more in the character of the old Guilds, and much more in the culture of the individual, than they are in that of the smooth and bloodless uniformity of the masses.[21]

Yet in these years Churchill, as after 1945, was explicit as to the importance of the right to strike. Thus, for instance, he observed in November 1904,

> It is most important for the British working classes that they should be able if necessary to strike – although nobody likes strikes – in order to put pressure upon the employers for a greater share of the wealth of the world or for the removal of hard and onerous conditions, but in the socialist state no strike would be tolerated.[22]

On several occasions in the period before 1911, Churchill spoke on what David Metcalf has dubbed the trade unions' 'sword of justice'

---

[20] At Glasgow, 11 October 1906; *Liberalism and the Social Problem*, 72–3. For similar sentiments specifically linked to the cotton trade unions, see his speech at Oldham, 21 October 1903; *Complete Speeches*, 1, 219.

[21] At Dundee, 4 May 1908; *Complete Speeches*, 1, 1030.

[22] In a speech to working men in the Liberal Club, Coatbridge; *Complete Speeches*, 1, 384.

role. In January 1908, when speaking of the Liberal government's social reforms, Churchill observed, 'While I believe in the advantages of a competitive system under which man is pitted against man, I do not believe in allowing men to be pitted against each other ruthlessly until the last drop of energy is extracted, and there the trade unions come in as safeguards and checks.'[23] Earlier, when opposing tariff reform, he had argued that tariffs would give big profits to employers and destabilise industrial relations. He explained, 'We are told that wages were to be raised. If they are, it can only be through the pressure of the trades unions.'[24]

In his early career Churchill was willing to listen to local trade union leaders and to come to his own judgement on issues. When he was seeking election in Oldham in 1899, J.R. Clynes, then secretary of Oldham Trades Council, led a trades council delegation to press on him various labour issues. Clynes later recalled,

> I found him a man of extraordinarily independent mind, and great courage. He absolutely refused to yield to our persuasions, and said bluntly that he would rather lose votes than abandon his convictions.[25]

Yet later, in 1903, Churchill was convinced of the justice of reversing the Taff Vale Judgement after a correspondence with Clynes.

In looking at Churchill's attitudes to trade unionism it is especially important not to read back the later importance of the Labour party or TUC to the pre-1911 period. Both Churchill and Mawdsley were able to contemplate British politics with a trade union movement attaching itself to the existing parties, as in the USA. For Mawdsley, it was possible to pursue labour concerns in parliament through any party, but his preference was for the Conservative party. For Churchill in 1899, it was easy to herald Mawdsley's emergence as a parliamentary candidate as marking 'the birth of a new party which has for a very long time been in the minds of a great section of our fellow-countrymen – a Conservative Labour Party'.[26]

While favourable to trade unionism in these years, Churchill was very hostile to socialism. He proclaimed the necessity of private property and decried state employment as a recipe for low output. He frequently created caricatures of socialism to jeer at in his speeches. Of the fiery socialist Victor Grayson, he observed, 'The socialism of the Christian era was based on the idea that "all mine is yours", but the socialism of

---

[23] At Manchester, 22 January 1908; *Complete Speeches*, 1, 873.

[24] At Oldham, 21 October 1903; *Complete Speeches*, 1, 219.

[25] J.R. Clynes, *Memoirs 1869–1924* (1937), 97. Others later commented on this characteristic; for example, W.H. Thompson, *I Was Churchill's Shadow*, (1951), 169.

[26] At the Co-operative Hall, Greenacres, Oldham on 29 June 1899; *Complete Speeches*, 1, 45.

Mr Grayson is based on the idea that "all yours is mine".[27] When
Charles Masterman suggested that Keir Hardie would go to heaven
quickly, Churchill replied, 'If heaven is going to be full of people like
Hardie...well, the Almighty can have them to himself.'[28]

Like Lloyd George, Churchill was well aware of the growth of the
SPD in Germany. In a speech to a working-class audience in the
Liberal club at Coatsbridge in November 1904 he contrasted, in a
traditional Liberal manner, the quality of the British constitutional
system with that of Germany. In Britain he said they 'should try to
improve the lot of the masses of the people through the existing
structure of society rather than by the immediate demolition of that
structure and the building up of an entirely new system'. In contrast,
he asserted, 'If I were in Germany I would be a socialist myself. I
would be against militarism, conscription, the high protective tariff,
and the despotic form of government ...'[29] In this Churchill was in
tune with prevailing working-class sensitivities. In the more democratic
states, working-class politics was predominantly moderate (as in Britain,
France and the USA), whereas under the more repressive regimes it
was more revolutionary (as in Russia and Germany).

Churchill was very aware of the power of the propertied classes in
Britain, France and the USA. He might have added Germany to his
list. In such countries he felt the stability of the state rested on the 'vast
numbers of persons who are holders of interest-bearing, profit-bearing,
rent-earning property, and the whole tendency of civilisation and of
free institutions is to an ever-increasing volume of production and an
increasingly wide diffusion of profit'. He predicted that in such societies
revolution would provoke counter-revolution. He argued that Liberalism offered the alternative to class war, as through gentle reforms
it would enable British society 'to slide forward, almost painlessly ...
on to a more even and more equal foundation'. He elaborated
the historic function of the Liberal party: 'By gradual steps, by steady
effort from day to day, from year to year, Liberalism enlists hundreds of thousands upon the side of progress and popular democratic
reform whom militant socialism would drive into violent reaction.'[30]
In this Churchill unknowingly was predicting his own political trajectory in the face of militant trade unionism at home and Bolshevism
abroad.

Winston Churchill became much involved in industrial relations
while president of the board of trade (April 1908–February 1910) and

[27] At Cheetham, 22 January 1908; *Complete Speeches*, 1, 874.
[28] Lucy Masterman, *C.F.G. Masterman: A Biography* (1939), 164 (in late September or
early October 1910).
[29] At Coatsbridge, 11 November 1904; *Complete Speeches*, 1, 384.
[30] At Glasgow, 11 October 1906; *Liberalism and the Social Problem*, 77–8.

then home secretary (February 1910–October 1911). At the board of trade Churchill utilised the knowledge of several trade union leaders when he was preparing industrial reforms. In the case of safety in the mines, Churchill responded to both the recommendations of the Royal Commission on Accidents in Mines and representations from the TUC and mining trade unions.[31]

He was also, like Lloyd George before him, very willing to adopt a high profile in trying to resolve industrial disputes. Soon after taking office he set out to strengthen the board of trade's powers of intervention beyond the powers in the 1896 Conciliation Act. One proposal considered was the introduction of a version of the Canadian Lemieux Act, so that the board of trade could appoint a court of inquiry and introduce a cooling-off period while a settlement was sought.[32] While this failed to gain support from either side of industry, Churchill pressed on with the formation of a standing court of arbitration, which he saw as 'consolidating, expanding and popularising the working of the Conciliation Act'.[33] Churchill tried hard, but unsuccessfully, to achieve agreement to a new sliding scale in the cotton industry, in order to provide 'a more scientific process' for resolving differences than the persistent strikes and lock-outs.[34]

Churchill continued to express sympathy and support for trade unionism after he went to the home office. This was most notably the case with the Trade Union Bill, 1911 (which was passed in 1913 and substantially undid the Osborne Judgement, 1909, which had undercut trade union political funds). Then, in May 1911, Churchill declared,

I consider that every workman is well advised to join a trade union. I cannot conceive how any man standing undefended against the powers that be in this world could be so foolish, if he can spare the money from the maintenance of his family, not to associate himself with an organisation to protect the rights and interests of labour, and I think there could be no greater injury to trade unionism than that the unions should either be stripped of a great many strong and independent spirits ... or that they should split into rival bodies and that attempts should be made to make party trade unions – Liberal

---

[31] See, for instance, his speech to a deputation from the Parliamentary Committee of the TUC and some mining unions at the Home Office, 21 April 1910; *Complete Speeches*, II, 1556–7.

[32] Chris Wrigley, 'The Government and Industrial Relations' in Chris Wrigley (ed.), *A History of British Industrial Relations 1875–1914* (Hassocks, 1982), 145–6. E. Wigham, *Strikes and the Government 1893–1974* (1976), 22.

[33] Memorandum, 1 September 1908; Randolph S. Churchill, *Winston S. Churchill: Companion*, II, part 2 (1969), 836–8.

[34] Report of a conference at the Board of Trade, 4 March 1909; *Complete Speeches*, II, 1181–3.

and Socialist party trade unions – and so break the homogeneity and solidarity of the great trade union movement.[35]

However, by this time Churchill's sympathy with labour was beginning to diminish, and in cabinet he had opposed reversing the Osborne Judgement.

At the home office Churchill was responsible for law and order, causes dear to his heart, and as violence associated with industrial disputes escalated, so Churchill's emphasis on order put him in conflict with many trade union activists. Yet, in the earlier big disputes, Churchill still went out of his way to praise the solid trade union majority. After the riots in Tonypandy Churchill stated in the Commons that he believed that they were the work of 'rowdy youth and roughs from outside' not 'the well-educated, peaceable, intelligent and law-abiding class of men', the miners of South Wales.[36] Later in 1911 he spoke of most railwaymen being part of 'a self-respecting and respectable class' who 'have been all for peace and order throughout'.[37] In these remarks he was not only respecting the Lib-Lab voters but stating his own view.

The controversy over Churchill's role or non-role in the deaths of trade unionists in South Wales, at Llanelli not Tonypandy, has distracted attention from the part he delighted in playing in these industrial conflicts. As home secretary, as he was not slow to assert, his role was not to judge who was right or wrong but to maintain the peace. Though having made statements to that effect, he frequently promptly indicated his view. Thus, in the case of the Newport docks strike of May–June 1910 he made it clear he felt the employer was being unreasonable, whereas in the case of the 1910 South Wales coal strike he observed, 'both seemed to have behaved very unreasonably. Both sides seem to be intent on quarrelling without the slightest regard to the common interest and without paying any attention to the public welfare which is gravely compromised by their action.'[38] In practice he often annoyed both sides of industry, for his heart was with those enforcing law and order, the police and the soldiers.

J.R. Clynes, who was often a shrewd judge of people, wrote in the 1930s of Churchill, 'Churchill was, and has always remained, a soldier in mufti. He possesses inborn militaristic qualities, and is intensely proud of his descent from Marlborough.'[39] Churchill was more interested in efficient operations of the police and the soldiers, and asserting order,

[35] *House of Commons Debates*, fifth series, vol. 26, cols. 1017–8, 30 May 1911. Addison, *Churchill on the Home Front*, 145–7.

[36] *House of Commons Debates*, fifth series, vol. 21, col. 239, 7 February 1911.

[37] *House of Commons Debates*, fifth series, vol. 29, col. 2247, 18 August 1911.

[38] *House of Commons Debates*, fifth series, vol. 18, col. 73–80, 22 June 1910, and vol. 20, col. 416, 24 November 1910.

[39] Clynes, *Memoirs*, I, p. 97.

than helping businessmen *per se*. In 1911 he appears to have found the notion that the police may have used excessive force, including on women and children, hard to believe.[40] He was also a warm champion of the conduct of the soldiers. Of the troops in South Wales, he commented that soon 'they did not look upon the whole body of strikers as if they were wild beasts, as they were described in so many of the London newspapers ... In a week they were playing football matches with them...'[41]

However, if this was shades of the general strike, so was Churchill's concern to maintain transport and food supplies. At the end of unrest in London in mid 1911, Churchill informed the Commons, 'If the strike continued a regular system of convoys would have had to be organised.' He also stated that it would be 'the duty of the government in the event of the paralysis of the great railway lines upon which the life and food of the people depend, to secure to the persons engaged in working them full legal protection...'[42] With industrial unrest spreading, accompanied by more violence, Churchill became increasingly alarmist about transport strikes leading to a serious social breakdown in Britain. Four days after the national rail strike of 18–19 August 1911, in which Churchill had deployed large numbers of soldiers in London and thirty-two cities and towns, he made a notably alarmist speech in the Commons. In it he graphically recounted the disastrous effects in the Euphrates in the fifteenth century when the Nimrod Dam broke, after which thousands of people 'were wiped from the book of human life'. He then commented, 'These are the considerations which it is no exaggeration to say have to be borne in mind at the present juncture.' He referred to the recent dock and rail disputes observing of the industrial north and midlands,

> it is practically certain that a continuance of the railway strike would have produced a swift and certain degeneration of all the means, of all the structure, social and economic, on which the life of the people depends. If it had not been interrupted it would have hurled the whole of that great community into an abyss of horror which no man dare to contemplate ... I am sure the House will see that no blockade by a foreign enemy could have been anything like so effective in producing terrible pressures on these vast populations as the effective closing of those great ports coupled with the paralysis of the railway service.[43]

[40] For instance, in response to George Lansbury's questions, 10 August 1911; *House of Commons Debates*, fifth series, vol. 29, cols. 1360–1.

[41] *House of Commons Debates*, fifth series, vol. 21, col. 236, 7 Feb 1911.

[42] *House of Commons Debates*, fifth series, vol. 29, cols. 1987 and 1991, 16 August 1911.

[43] *House of Commons Debates*, fifth series, vol. 29, cols. 2323–34, 22 August 1911.

Churchill was very taken aback by the pre-First World War strikes in key sectors of the economy. At the board of trade in 1909 he had been disconcerted at the response to a threat to pass emergency legislation to refer a mining dispute to compulsory arbitration. Sir George Askwith, the board of trade's conciliator, recalled, 'As he was leaving the room, Mabon, the famous Welsh leader, turned on him with the remark, in a strong Welsh accent, "Mr Churchill, you cannot put 600,000 men into prison." '[44] At the time of the 1911 national rail strike, he was dejected when the men rejected Lloyd George's proposed settlement, commenting, 'The men have beaten us ... We cannot keep the trains running. There is nothing we can do. We are done!' But when Lloyd George secured a settlement Churchill telephoned him regretting it, commenting, 'I'm very sorry to hear it. It would have been better to have gone on and given these men a good thrashing.'[45]

By July 1911 Churchill was anxious about industrial relations generally. According to Asquith's cabinet report to the king on 21 July he raised the issue with his colleagues, referring to 'the almost daily outbreak of strikes, direct and sympathetic, accompanied by a growing readiness to resort to violence, and imposing heavy labour responsibilities both on the police and military'. He called for a public inquiry, perhaps chaired by the prime minister, 'into the causes and remedies for these menacing developments'.[46] His colleagues agreed with his concern, but did not set up a public inquiry.

Churchill's concern was to do with more than a wave of strikes. He was alarmed by rioting crowds, in South Wales, London and Liverpool in particular. In the case of Liverpool he was not alone among ministers, Herbert Samuel writing to his wife in August 1911, commented 'Liverpool is verging on a state of revolution.'[47] The king took the same view. Churchill noted that in Liverpool and elsewhere poor people often joined in the unrest. In the House of Commons he read out the chief constable's report which stated that in Liverpool, the riot began with a fringe of the crowd at the great demonstration of the National Transport Workers' Federation, 'the fringe at this corner consisted no doubt of the roughs from the adjoining Irish district, always ready for an opportunity to attack the police'.[48] Churchill, like his former leader Lord Salisbury, had forebodings about social disintegration. He often had an aristocratic concern about Robespierre and the French Revo-

[44] Lord Askwith, *Industrial Problems and Disputes* (1920), 131.
[45] Masterman, *Masterman*, 207-8.
[46] Asquith's report to the King, 21 July 1911; Asquith Papers, 6, f. 58. The king shared Churchill's anxieties as revealed in Asquith's Cabinet Paper on Industrial Unrest, 8 September 1911; PRO, CAB 37/107/107.
[47] Samuel to his wife, 17 August 1911; Samuel Papers, A157, f. 615.
[48] *House of Commons Debates*, fifth series, vol. 29, col. 1989, 16 August 1911.

lution, if not about Napoleon whom he greatly admired. He was easily teased by Lloyd George and Masterman. At the time of the 1909 People's Budget, Lucy Masterman recorded,

... they began talking wildly, absolutely in fun, of the revolutionary measures they were proposing next: the guillotine in Trafalgar Square; and nominating for the first tumbril. Winston, whose sense of humour is not very quick, became more and more indignant and alarmed...[49]

As Paul Addison has commented, Churchill in the summer of 1911 'fatally compromised' his standing as a radical reformer as he adopted 'a belligerent posture' and a determination that 'the spirit of insubordination must be broken'.[50] Churchill remained on the side of those wanting a tough stance, not a settlement through legislation, during the big 1912 coal dispute.[51] However, by this time he was at the admiralty and so in charge of one of the armed forces.

Churchill dealt again with labour as minister of munitions during the First World War. As in the Second World War, he was readily willing to make concessions to the trade unions if these would secure greater effort for the needs of the war. In August 1917 he responded to pressure from the skilled engineering unions to drop proposals to extend dilution of labour to private work. Instead he pushed quickly through parliament an emollient Munitions of War Amendment Bill, which included the abolition of the much-hated leaving certificate (needed from employers before workers could leave for other employment) and gave the minister of munitions powers to increase skilled workers' hourly rates of pay in order to remove financial inducements for skilled men to transfer to more highly paid less skilled work (mostly on piece rates).[52]

Churchill made use of these powers again in the autumn of 1917 to try to remedy the widespread and ominously growing grievances over pay. In so doing he displayed a lack of awareness of the sensitivity of altering some groups of workers' pay. He unleashed a series of strikes as workers not included in the initial 12.5 per cent pay rises strove to restore their differentials (their relative position with regard to pay). In November the matter was deemed so urgent by Lord Milner, Churchill

[49] Masterman, *Masterman*, 139.
[50] Addison, *Churchill on the Home Front*, 150.
[51] Asquith's Cabinet report to the king, 16 March 1911; Asquith Papers, 6, f. 119.
[52] Chris Wrigley, *David Lloyd George and the Labour Movement* (Hassocks, 1976), 203. Chris Wrigley, 'The Ministry of Munitions: An Innovatory Department' in Kathleen Burk (ed.), *War and the State* (1982), 32–56.

and others that the war cabinet was summoned half an hour earlier to deal with it.[53]

In the succeeding months the government was forced to concede further pay rises to other groups, with Churchill and the civil servants trying to protect the public purse. On one occasion a Belfast engineer spoke of Dr Macnamara and Churchill at the admiralty with regard to dockyard labour, 'whenever he [or Macnamara] went as Secretary for a shilling for the "bottom dog" he was always received in the finest manner; Mr Churchill was always in favour of giving a shilling to the "bottom dog" '. To this, the civil servant Sir Thomas Munro responded, 'Mr Churchill's generous instincts have to be a little curbed by those of us here.'[54] Churchill, having unleashed the initial pay awards, himself pressed on iron and steel trade union officials that in wartime, with employers able to pass costs on, the old check on pay rises had gone and the state had to be firm. When he learned in January 1918 that a general extension of 7.5 per cent in pay was about to be authorised, he wrote to Lloyd George stating this was 'too foolish' and that such a concession should not be given 'on the eve of a tussle with labour which may lead to strikes instead of keeping it as a counter for bargaining a peace with'.[55] However, in such moves Churchill was trying to bolt the stable door after the horse had galloped out and run away. The 12.5 per cent pay rise episode did nothing to enhance Churchill's reputation for dealing with labour.

Churchill's time at the ministry of munitions was also marked by him being impressed by the effectiveness of the Ministry's interventionist role in industry. At a dinner to mark his departure from the Ministry, Churchill commented,

> I have not been quite convinced by my experience of the Ministry of Munitions that socialism is possible, but I have been very nearly convinced. I am like one of those people who are trembling on the border-line between individual enterprise proceeding in fierce competition in all industries, and a vast organised machinery of production supported and equipped by all that is best in the nation and proceeding on calculation and design to multiply enormously the prosperity of the whole people. I am bound to say, I consider, on the whole, the achievements of the Ministry of Munitions con-

[53] Maurice Hankey to Lloyd George, 17 November 1917; Lloyd George Papers F/23/1/28. Wrigley, *David Lloyd George*, 219–22.

[54] Conference with the Belfast engineers, 22 November 1917; PRO MUNS-82–342/23. Munro had been one of the three commissioners who enforced dilution on the Clyde in 1916.

[55] Conference with the iron, steel and bricklayers unions, 3 January 1918, PRO MITNS79–341/12. Churchill to Lloyd George, 21 January 1918; Lloyd George Papers, F/8/2/4.

stitute the greatest argument for state socialism that has ever been produced. Nothing like it has ever been attempted in any part of the world.[56]

This was a long way from his pre-war anti-state stereotyping, as expressed in November 1904 when he stated, 'Whenever we have men working on assured and fixed salaries drawn from the state we can be quite certain that while they do their duty they will not over-exert themselves.'[57]

After the end of the First World War Churchill took similar political postures towards industrial unrest to those he had adopted during the serious industrial unrest of 1911. While again he showed some caution in deploying troops in industrial disputes, he was emphatic that where strikes threatened food supplies or utilities he was willing to take strong measures. In February 1920 when the cabinet was in alarmist mood about major strikes leading to serious unrest, Churchill was a vigorous supporter of the emergency transport system, observing 'It is not strike-breaking, it is feeding the people.' He also stated that while the Territorial Army could not be used in a strike or local riot 'but if there was a grave national emergency then there could be a Royal Proclamation and the Territorial Force would be embodied and available'.[58]

Nevertheless, he continued to see trade unionism as a bulwark against revolution. When supporting recognition of the Railway Clerks Association in February 1919, he commented,

> the trade union organisation was very imperfect, and the more moderate its officials were the less representative it was, but it was the only organisation with which the government could deal. The curse of trade unionism was that there was not enough of it, and it was not highly enough developed to make its branch secretaries fall into line with head office. With a powerful union either peace or war could be made.

However, at that time of acute industrial unrest even Bonar Law, the Conservative leader, observed that 'the trade union organisation was the only thing between us and anarchy, and if the trade union organisation was against us the position would be hopeless'.[59]

---

[56] At a dinner given by the higher staff of the Ministry of Munitions, 22 January 1919; PRO MUNS-12–200/53.

[57] At Coatsbridge, 11 November 1904; *Complete Speeches*, II, 383. Even allowing for the different audiences, this displays a notably different view.

[58] Notes of a cabinet meeting, 2 February 1920; K. Middlemas (ed.), *Thomas Jones: Whitehall Diary*, II (Oxford, 1969), 99–103. See also P. Dennis, 'The Territorial Army in Aid of the Civil Power in Britain', *Journal of Contemporary History*, 16 (1981), 705–24.

[59] Chris Wrigley, *Lloyd George and the Challenge of Labour* (Brighton, 1990), 117.

Churchill's deeper fears of mob rule and revolution were accentuated by developments in Russia from October 1917 and in Central Europe in 1918–19. Such fears seem to have prompted alarmist talk and action on his part, all the more worrying to those who did not share his concerns as he held the office of secretary of state for war. As Paul Addison has aptly put it, 'Churchill's Marlborough complex was coupled with a primal hatred of the Bolshevik revolution.'[60]

While Churchill was very much a *bona fide* anti-Bolshevik and anti-socialist, like Lloyd George he was very willing to play up anti-Labour fears to encourage middle-class voters to continue to feel a need for the coalition government. At Loughborough on 4 March 1922, he warned, 'A socialist will coax and wheedle you and argue you into ruin, and the Communist will ram ruin down your throat with a bayonet on the Russian plan.'[61] Also, given the massive swings to Labour in London county council and then borough elections in 1919 and 1920, Churchill had additional political reasons for promoting Conservative–Liberal coalition politics at the local level as well as 'fusion' nationally. Moreover, there was a consistency in both his tough line in favour of 'order' and his continuing support for social reform, including housing and unemployment measures as well as supporting special taxes on war wealth.

This pattern was repeated in his period as chancellor of the exchequer in Baldwin's 1924–9 government. He remained vehemently anti-Communist, be it the Third International or the Communist party of Great Britain, and anti-socialist. Hence, in January 1927, his praise for Mussolini's 'triumphant struggle against the bestial appetites and passions of Leninism'.[62] He continued to pretend publicly that Ramsay MacDonald and the other Labour party leaders were wolves in sheep's clothing, whereas most were sheep in sheep's clothing, with the odd sheep in wolf's clothing. He also hoped to push forward with some social reforms, notably in the areas of housing and pensions, such as he had pressed for in the past as part of his Tory democracy or pre-war Radicalism.[63] By 1924 he had written off the trade unions as Labour supporters, and consistent with his view in cabinet on the Osborne Judgement in 1911, he favoured making trade unionists contract-in to the unions' political levy. Yet he maintained his view (to use Gladstone's phrase) that working people should be 'within the pale of the constitution' and that state funding would enable them to exercise 'to the full their constitutional rights and to be continuously assimilated into the British parliamentary system'.[64]

[60] Addison, *Churchill on the Home Front*, 211.
[61] Martin Gilbert, *Winston S. Churchill*, IV, 772.
[62] Addison, *Churchill on the Home Front*, 274.
[63] Diary entry, 28 November 1924; Jones, *Whitehall Diary*, I, 307.

With the general strike Churchill identified the mass action as a constitutional outrage while he deemed the coal strike a legitimate industrial action. As in 1911 he revelled in the law and order operational side of the dispute, again urging heavy troop presence, even with tanks and machine-guns, where there was anticipated to be serious unrest. Four years later, in *My Early Life*, he claimed his behaviour was consistent with earlier crises. He wrote,

I have always urged fighting wars and other contentions with might and main till overwhelming victory, and then offering the hand of friendship to the vanquished. Thus, I have always been against the pacifists during the quarrel and against the Jingoes at the close ... I thought we ought to have conquered the Irish and then given them Home Rule; that we ought to have starved the Germans and revictualled their country; and that after smashing the General Strike, we should have met the grievances of the miners.[65]

Certainly, after the general strike Churchill tried to find compromises acceptable to both sides of the coal industry. However, as Paul Addison has emphasised, having failed he proposed forcing a settlement on the miners, with 'all relief to their families to cease within one week' for men who refused to return to work.[66]

Churchill's tough line with strikers in disputes which he deemed to threaten the fabric of society made many leaders of the British Labour movement deeply suspicious of him. This was not assuaged for many by his anti-Nazi and anti-appeasement policies before the Second World War. Churchill, however, built on his First World War experiences at the ministry of munitions when he sought extra labour for admiralty war work. In January 1940, after referring to his experience in the First World War, he said, 'Millions of new workers will be needed, and more than a million women must come boldly forward into our war industry' and emphasised, 'Here we must specially count for aid and guidance upon our Labour colleagues and trade union leaders.'[67] As prime minister when speaking of the trade unions' co-operation in suspending restrictive practices 'which have taken generations to win', he specifically referred back to his own blunders of 1917, saying that he 'survived many of its political vicissitudes,

[64] Addison, *Churchill on the Home Front*, 269.

[65] Churchill, *My Early Life*, quoted in Robert Rhodes James, 'Introduction', *Complete Speeches*, 1, 18–19.

[66] Addison, *Churchill on the Home Front*, 268.

[67] Speech at Free Trade Hall, Manchester, 27 January 1940; Martin Gilbert, *The Churchill War Papers*, 1 (1993), 695. On bringing trade union and employer representation to the Admiralty to help ensure large numbers of extra merchant ships, see *House of Commons Debates*, fifth series, vol. 369, cols. 1923–36; 27 February 1940.

including the $12\frac{1}{2}$ per cent, which, at any rate, you will admit was well meant'.[68]

Churchill, like Lloyd George in December 1916, needed Labour's support to fight the war. George Isaacs, a trade unionist and Labour MP who was to be Attlee's minister of labour, 1945–51, later commented of Churchill accession to the premiership in 1940,

> It must be stressed that the readiness of the trade unions to support the government and to set aside their old quarrels with Churchill was due in large measure to the fact that in Bevin they had a personality who could meet the Prime Minister on level terms. Bevin, as Minister of Labour, was a necessary condition for the partnership...[69]

For Churchill, Bevin soon became a rock he could rely on. As Alan Bullock has observed, 'Bevin was a new discovery in whom he recognised at once a toughness of mind, a self-confidence and strength of will which matched his own.'[70] Within five months of Bevin entering the government Churchill raised him to the war cabinet and kept him there, very much as a man who could take on much power in a crisis. While Churchill was not uncritical, he admired Bevin and his ability to ensure increased industrial output. Churchill observed frankly in July 1941, that 'he is producing ... though perhaps on rather expensive terms, a vast and steady volume of faithful effort, the like of which has not been seen before'.[71] Churchill certainly warmed to the trade union support for the war, paying warm tribute to their role in 1940 and afterwards.[72] He was especially pleased to note the far fewer strikes than in the First World War. After one of his speeches before leading trade unionists, his principal private secretary observed that he thought Churchill got on better with them than with the Tories. According to Eric Seal, Churchill replied, 'yes, they have a certain native virility – although he found himself in sympathy with the Tories on theoretical matters like free enterprise and the rights of property'. When Seal commented that the trade unionists 'were essentially conservative and not much of the pale intellectual about them', Churchill agreed.[73]

[68] Speech to employers and members of the TUC gathered in honour of US ambassador Gilbert Winant; 27 March 1941; Martin Gilbert, *The Churchill War Papers*, III (2000), 409–10.

[69] George Isaacs, 'Churchill and the Trade Unions' in Charles Eade (ed.), *Churchill by his Contemporaries* (1953), 383.

[70] Alan Bullock, *The Life and Times of Ernest Bevin*, II (1967), 4.

[71] *House of Commons Debates*, fifth series, vol. 373, cols. 1278–9, 29 July 1941. Bullock, *Bevin*, II, 67.

[72] Churchill to Luke Fawcett, 4 September 1941; Gilbert, *The Churchill War Papers*, III, 1158.

[73] Martin Gilbert, *Winston S. Churchill*, VI, 1044.

Churchill generally disliked socialists, especially middle-class ones, but admired pragmatic trade union leaders.

After the victorious end of the war but the Conservative defeat in the general election, Churchill continued to take a positive view of the trade unions. To the respect for their role in the war was added Churchill's need to woo working-class voters if a Conservative return to office was to be achieved. In the post-war years Churchill reverted to his old language of Tory democracy. Thus at the 1947 Conservative party conference, after referring to Disraeli and his legislation, Churchill declared,

> The trade unions are a long-established and essential part of our national life ... we take our stand by these pillars of our British Society as it has gradually developed and evolved itself, of the right of individual labouring men to adjust their wages and conditions by collective bargaining, including the right to strike ...

At the 1950 Conservative party conference he returned to this theme.

> The salient feature of this conference has been the growing association of Tory democracy with the trade unions. After all it was Lord Beaconsfield and the Tory Party who gave British trade unionism its charter, and collective bargaining coupled with the right to strike. I have urged that every Tory craftsman or wage-earner should of his own free-will be a trade unionist, but I also think he should attend the meetings of his trade union and stand up for his ideas instead of letting only socialists and communists get control of what is after all an essentially British institution.[74]

He also defined Conservative economic and social policy in phraseology very similar to that he used in the Edwardian period.

With his return to office in 1951, with fewer votes than the Labour party but a majority of seats, Churchill did not want to resurrect his own or the Conservative party's anti-trade union image. Nor did he wish for strikes which could disrupt the recovery of the British economy. He took up the suggestion from a Conservative party central office official that Sir Walter Monckton would be an ideal, emollient minister of labour.[75] Churchill briefed Monckton not to bring about confrontations with public-sector trade unionists, least of all the miners. Churchill himself pressed Monckton to avoid railway strikes on two

---

[74] Printed in Chris Wrigley, *British Trade Unions 1945–1995* (Manchester, 1997), 44.

[75] According to his private secretary, when Tom O'Brien, a trade union Labour MP, congratulated Churchill on Monckton's appointment, 'That was a suggestion straight from the Holy Ghost, Prime Minister', Churchill grinned and replied, 'From an even higher source than that'. It turned out the initial suggestion came from George Christ of Central office. Anthony Montague Browne, *Long Sunset* (1995), 131.

occasions, the latter in December 1954 being an occasion when Monckton otherwise intended not to give way.[76] Churchill also personally
cultivated senior trade union figures, including Vincent Tewson, the
general secretary of the TUC; this included invitations to social events
at Downing Street. His government also outdid Attlee's in the number
of trade unionists appointed to various consultative committees.[77] This
policy secured industrial peace, even if commentators at the time and
several historians subsequently have questioned its wisdom given the
rising inflation and declining relative competitiveness of British industry
in these years.

Perhaps the most notable feature of Churchill's attitude to the trade
unions was the sheer longevity of many of his attitudes. 'Tory democracy' or 'One nation' views were recurring themes, though if – as
was notably the case at times in 1911–26 – he felt industrial unrest was
threatening the social fabric of society, he was very willing to smash
'the enemy within'. George Isaacs in 1953 rightly observed, 'Sir Winston
is an individualist in an aristocratic tradition' but 'he cannot be regarded
as a "typical" capitalist or even a "typical" aristocrat.'[78] Churchill's
background, including the martial tradition of his illustrious ancestor,
the first duke of Marlborough, is very important. As well as his father,
another figure whom he much admired at the turn of the century and
who influenced his outlook was Lord Rosebery; a Whig peer who was
an Imperialist abroad, a social reformer at home and who, incidentally,
successfully offered conciliation and succeeded in settling the massive
1893 coal lock-out.

Churchill's ideas about trade unions and a free market economy
were not novel. Notions of resolving industrial clashes through joint
consultation were widespread in his period, and were shared by many
trade unionists such as Arthur Henderson, Ben Turner, J.R. Clynes,
David Shackleton and Ernest Bevin. He was notable for being a
president of the board of trade who was pro-active, who stretched the
voluntarist provisions of the 1896 Conciliation Act as far as they would
go and made some attempts to extend such powers by additional
legislation. In this he was presenting himself centre stage much as his
successful predecessor, David Lloyd George, had done. Churchill, faced
with what he deemed serious unrest, was more belligerent than Lloyd
George. With the national rail and coal disputes of 1912 Churchill
busied himself with securing law and order while Lloyd George was
skilful in negotiating deals which unlocked the disputes. Churchill was

[76] Addison, *Churchill on the Home Front*, 427–9.
[77] Anthony Seldon, *Churchill's Indian Summer* (1981), 29, 199 and 568–9. V.L. Allen, *Trade Unions and Government* (1960), 34 and 304.
[78] Isaacs, 'Churchill and the Trade Unions', 389.

less well tuned-in to the delicacies of industrial relations than Lloyd George, as was dramatically illustrated with the way he blundered in out of his depth over the 12.5 per cent pay increases in 1917. Yet, when he felt industrial disputes were not menacing the fabric of society and he was not full of anti-red sentiments, Churchill worked towards Tory democrat aspirations of industrial peace and harmony.[79]

[79] I am grateful to Stefan Berger, Chris Williams, Neil Wynne and their colleagues for their comments on an early version of this essay, given at the Department of History, University of Glamorgan, Research Seminar, 13 December 2000.

CHURCHILL AND THE CONSERVATIVE PARTY
By Stuart Ball

THE words 'Churchill' and 'party' lie in uneasy company. Winston Churchill is regarded as the least orthodox and party-minded of all those who stood in the front rank of British politics during the twentieth century, always navigating by his own compass. This view is shaped by Churchill's remarkable egotism and the well-known incidents of his career: the two changes of party allegiance, the coalitionism of 1917–22, the rebellious 'wilderness' years of the 1930s, and the premiership almost above party in 1940–5. It has been reinforced by the preponderance of biography in the writing about Churchill, and especially by those which regard him as a 'great man'. Churchill tends to be removed from his political context and separated from his peers, and there is a reluctance to see him in any conventional light. As a result, by far the most neglected aspect of Churchill's life has been his party political role, and in particular his relationship with the Conservative party.[1]

There are several reasons for this. It is the antithesis of those aspects which most attract admirers and authors – this is the Churchill of the 'Gestapo' speech, not of 'blood, toil, tears and sweat'.[2] Seeing him as a party politician is in conflict with the picture of the lone hero, the

[1] The only discussions are Lord Blake, 'Churchill and the Conservative Party', in Crosby Kemper (ed.), *Winston Churchill: Resolution, Defiance, Magnanimity* (Columbia, Mo., 1995), 141–56, a brief narrative treatment which does not go beyond 1940, and the more specific study by John Ramsden, 'Winston Churchill and the Leadership of the Conservative Party 1940–51', *Contemporary Record*, 9, no. 1 (1995), 99–119; the latter's volume in the Longman History of the Conservative Party series, *The Age of Churchill and Eden 1940–57* (1995), provides further analysis and is the most valuable exploration of this theme after 1940. Paul Addison, *Churchill on the Home Front 1900–55* (1992), is unusual in concentrating on domestic politics and makes many important points, but still leaves Churchill's relationship with the party in the background; it excludes discussion of the India revolt and thus has a comparatively short examination of 1929–39, and like most works gives less weight to the 1945–55 period. A recent substantial study by Graham Stewart, *Burying Caesar: Churchill, Chamberlain and the Battle for the Tory Party* (1999), focuses on Churchill's career during the 1930s.

[2] None of the twenty-nine essays in the last major collection, Robert Blake and W.R. Louis (eds.), *Churchill* (Oxford, 1993), discussed Churchill's relations with the Conservative party. There is a similar pattern in the various biographies, whether it is the orthodox narrative of the massive volumes of the official life, summarised by Martin Gilbert in *Churchill: A Life* (1991), or the revisionism of John Charmley, *Churchill: The End of Glory* (1993). The most recent brief synthesis, Ian Wood, *Churchill* (Basingstoke, 2000), does not even have an entry for Conservative party in the index.

unique and iconoclastic. At the same time, Churchill does not stand for any particular brand of Conservatism, and his name does not figure within the party in the same way as Disraeli, Baldwin, Macmillan, Thatcher and even (in more intellectual circles) Salisbury. Since 1945 Conservatives have certainly been glad to hail him as their own, but they raid his past for little other than the summer of 1940. Churchill is seen as a great man *of* the party, rather than a great figure *in* it, and his legacy is unclear. It is easy to say that Churchill was not an 'orthodox' Conservative, as if Conservatism was reducible to some formulaic recipe. In fact, there were three strands in Churchill's outlook which he shared with most Conservatives of his era. First was the Empire and Britain's world role; for this Churchill had an instinctively positive outlook and a sense of mission. Second was the independent spirit of the British people; the 'Tory democracy' of Disraeli and Lord Randolph, resting upon practical measures but never to be stifled or circumscribed. The third theme was a guarantor of this: a balance between the classes, without the dominance of one over the others – as needful in the taming of the unchecked House of Lords as it was in the danger of socialism.

The aim of this paper is to examine the most important themes and issues in Churchill's relationship with the Conservative party, concentrating on the period between his return to the fold in 1924 and the second premiership of 1951–5. It seeks to ask questions which are rarely raised, and to offer some different perspectives.[3] His position cannot be assessed if it is treated too much in isolation – for example, was Churchill any more 'in the wilderness' in the 1930s than Amery or the fourth marquess of Salisbury, or was he less constructive as opposition leader in 1945–51 than Balfour had been after the previous landslide defeat in 1906–11? Churchill was far from flawless as a party politician, but his abilities have been undervalued. A successful political career needs not just oratorical and executive talent, but also an awareness of relationships and the ability to work with others. Churchill is not known for the latter, but the problem is that because in his case

---

[3] The monographs on party and political history are more helpful than any biographies. In addition to Ramsden, *Age of Churchill and Eden*, and Stewart, *Burying Caesar*, see Stuart Ball, *Baldwin and the Conservative Party: The Crisis of 1929–31* (London and New Haven, 1988); Gillian Peele, 'Revolt over India', in *The Politics of Reappraisal 1918–39*, eds. G. Peele and C. Cook (1975), 114–45; Carl Bridge, *Holding India to the Empire: The British Conservative Party and the 1935 Constitution* (New Delhi, 1986); Maurice Cowling, *The Impact of Hitler: British Politics and British Policy 1933–40* (Cambridge, 1975); Neville Thompson, *The Anti-Appeasers: Conservative Opposition to Appeasement in the 1930s* (Oxford, 1971); N.J. Crowson, *Facing Fascism: The Conservative Party and the European Dictators 1935–40* (1998); Paul Addison, *The Road to 1945: British Politics and the Second World War* (1975); Kevin Jefferys, *The Churchill Coalition and Wartime Politics 1940–45* (Manchester, 1991); and Anthony Seldon, *Churchill's Indian Summer: The Conservative Government 1951–55* (1981).

the ability and egotism were more strikingly evident, he is treated as if he was of an entirely different breed.

An assumption which colours many views of Churchill is that he did not appreciate party political realities. This is untenable: Churchill was a constituency MP for several decades, and showed that he was well aware of the limits of party tolerance in the 1930s. He sat through many local functions, delivered speeches around the country, attended as many conferences as most ministers in this era, and was present at party meetings. He was aware of how the parliamentary Conservative party worked, and of the backbench groups and committees. Churchill had a better understanding of the role of party than was displayed by Lloyd George, Austen Chamberlain, Mosley, Beaverbrook and Stafford Cripps between 1918 and 1939, and his awareness of its importance was shown by his desire to underpin the Lloyd George coalition by the fusion of its followers into a single party. He also had a better feel for what the Conservative party and the public would accept than was demonstrated by Austen Chamberlain in 1922, Hoare in 1935, and Balfour and F.E. Smith more generally; the latter burned his boats more irretrievably than Churchill without leaving the party. However, in the interwar period Churchill tended to underestimate the resilience and adaptability of parties. He thought that a major crisis was likely to lead to the parties breaking up and realigning; in other words, that party in general was a constant part of the landscape, but the particular parties in their present forms were not. Up to 1939 he seemed often to be looking for a repeat of the upheaval of the 1880s which had been so crucial in his father's career. In December 1929 he thought 'that all three parties would go into the melting pot within the next two years and come out in an entirely different grouping', but when this happened in August 1931 he was not in a position to take advantage of it.[4]

There is some basis for the traditional view, especially during the Second World War. There is no doubt that Churchill wanted most of all to succeed as a war leader, and that all else was secondary. This was partly due to his patriotism and the peril which the nation faced; with invasion a real danger, party matters naturally had little call on his time. Anything which disrupted national unity or took attention away from the war effort was disliked – particularly party frictions, and later plans for postwar reconstruction. It is also true that Churchill was comfortable with coalition, and not only in wartime. He always wished to broaden the base of the government and form a ministry of all the talents. However, his desire to continue the coalition into peacetime was based upon the assumption that Labour would still be the junior

[4] Jones to Bickersteth, 23 Dec. 1929, *Thomas Jones: Whitehall Diary, Vol. 2: 1926–30*, ed. K. Middlemas (Oxford, 1969), 229.

partner, whilst the end of the war would allow more Conservative involvement on the home front. This expectation was not unreasonable in 1944–5, given Lloyd George's victory in 1918 and Labour's limited advance in the 1930s. Churchill did not spurn party as the working means of British political life, or the nature of the Conservative party as such – but he sought to broaden it, to hold the centre and contain Labour. He favoured a coalition arrangement when the elements were more equally balanced, as in 1918–22, and fusion and absorption when not, as in the Woolton-Teviot agreement with the Liberal Nationals and the offer of a cabinet post to Clement Davies, the Liberal leader, in 1951. In seeking to widen the Conservative base, and to appeal to former Liberals on the basis of moderate reformism, Churchill was following the same course as Baldwin had before him.

Churchill's tactics were often more cautious than his oratorical style might suggest. Its memorable vigour obscures the fact that his moves were generally as carefully rehearsed as his major speeches – where hours of work lay behind any apparent spontaneity. However, whilst there is no doubt that Churchill had a gift for words and an original turn of phrase, no one has ever suggested that he was a skilled tactician. If anything, the view is quite the opposite – that his decisions were poor and his judgement flawed, and that this was his area of greatest weakness. This derives mainly from three events – the failure of the Gallipoli campaign in 1915, the rejection of his charges against Hoare and Derby by the committee of privileges in 1934, and the shouting down of his speech in the abdication crisis in 1936. Yet, in the first two of these at least, it could be said that his case was sound enough and need not have led to such a setback. The abdication speech was a failure to understand the mood of the hour, but even so too much should not be construed from one blunder. In any long parliamentary career there are speeches which fall flat or have unintended results, and Churchill had no more stumbles than most. Baldwin is often considered to have been a master of the moods of the House and the currents of public opinion, but in reality his touch was as erratic as Churchill's. Churchill's approach was based upon an almost mid-Victorian concept of the importance of opinion in the House of Commons and the degree of independence of the backbench MP. Before he became leader himself, he hoped for a definition of party loyalty which was based broadly upon principles and sentiments rather than narrowly upon the present leaders. Although he was generally disappointed, throughout the century similar expectations have been held by figures from different generations, backgrounds and parties, including Mosley, Bevan, Powell, Jenkins and Heseltine.

Churchill's main forum was parliament, and only secondarily did he go beyond that to address a wider party audience. Given that in the

Conservative party policies were made by the leaders and that the strongest influence upon them was exerted by or through the parliamentary party, this was a sensible strategy. However, few excluded figures have had more than a handful of regular followers, even if they have been able to muster greater support during a crisis. Rebellions tend to occur on issues rather than in support of a personality, however respected or popular; the rebel vote of 1922 was not *for* Bonar Law any more than that of 1975 was *for* Thatcher or that of 1990 *for* Heseltine – although in each case a credible alternative leader was needed, as Meyer's failure in 1989 demonstrates. So it is not surprising that the India rebels or the anti-appeasers did not wish to be thought of as Churchill followers even when they applauded his speeches. The point of note about Churchill's two campaigns in the 1930s is not that they did not involve more Conservative MPs, but rather that they gathered so many. This was particularly the case with India, perhaps the largest sustained internal rebellion the Conservative party has ever seen – but it is also true of the smaller and less consistent band of anti-appeasers, for they were still larger than the Suez group of the 1950s, the Profumo rebels or Powellites of the 1960s, the resisters of the poll tax in the 1980s, or the Maastricht rebels in the early 1990s.

The most significant period of Churchill's relationship with the Conservative party begins with his return to the fold in 1924. Churchill's predominant theme since 1918 had been anti-Socialism, and the changes in the political landscape left him with no other natural home. His return was encouraged by the new party leader, Stanley Baldwin, and in the 1924 general election he was returned as Conservative MP for Epping, a safe seat near London.[5] Conservative doubts about Churchill in the 1920s were not due to his prewar years as a Liberal or his crossing of the floor in 1904. Much of prewar politics seemed remote by 1924, and the only leading figure of that era who was still active, Balfour, was one of the strongest proponents of Churchill's return. Indeed, it is this connection which links to the real concern about Churchill in the 1920s – his leading role in the Lloyd George coalition, and the suspicion that he would intrigue for its revival. The fear of a returned coalition was a constant theme in Conservative politics from 1922 to 1935, with plots and conspiracies being frequently suspected – and not just by such paranoid minds as J.C.C. Davidson.[6]

Any reservations were certainly not because Churchill was not

[5] Churchill contested the election as a 'Constutionalist', but he was the offically sanctioned candidate of the Epping Conservative Association and was regarded as such by Central Office (which had helped him secure the candidacy).

[6] *Memoirs of a Conservative: J.C.C. Davidson's Memoirs and Papers 1910–37*, ed. R.R. James (1969), 213, 215, 309–10; *Parliament and Politics in the Age of Baldwin and MacDonald: the Headlam Diaries 1923–35*, ed. Stuart Ball (1992), 68, 140, 150–1, 189.

Conservative enough in his views.[7] As the hammer of the Reds at home and abroad since 1918, he was if anything too much to the right. Given the tone which Baldwin wished to set in 1924, putting Churchill in any cabinet post was an ambivalent step. The danger that Churchill might give the government too belligerent a face may also help to explain Baldwin's decision to offer him the exchequer. Although prominent, it was less politically sensitive than other departments, as it was less in direct contact with Labour and the trades unions and had no immediate role in executing foreign or imperial policy. The treasury was less of a danger than a return to the home office would have been (if Joynson-Hicks caused problems with the ARCOS raid, consider the fireworks that Churchill might have set off), or ministries such as labour, health or even education; the board of trade was critical on tariff and safeguarding issues, whilst giving Churchill a military department would have been more unacceptable to party opinion and given him not enough to do – considerations which also applied to the imperial and non-departmental posts respectively.

The strategy worked well: the treasury kept Churchill occupied and returned his attention to his best regarded field of domestic reform, where he worked as effectively with Neville Chamberlain as any two such powerful colleagues and partial rivals have in any other ministry. The appointment as chancellor did not go to Churchill's head; he had plenty of ideas, but put the greatest emphasis upon loyalty to Baldwin and being a reliable member of the cabinet team. He delivered good, but not too showy or individualistic, debating performances.[8] He cultivated Conservative MPs, and was aided in this by the large influx of new members in 1924. In 1925 the clash with Bridgeman over the naval budget aroused a few fears of coalitionist plots, but the admiralty's case was not conclusive whilst the need for economy was strong. The Economy Bill which Churchill delivered in March 1926 was a response to backbench and constituency pressure, although the savings identified fell well short of the sweeping reductions for which – however unrealistically – the party clamoured.

Churchill was happy with the course of the 1924–9 government on social reform and conciliation.[9] His stance on the general strike was the same as Baldwin's: that this was a challenge to the constitution and must be defeated. If there was a difference, it was only in the vigour

[7] For example, his anti-Socialist views were set out in a long letter to *The Times*, 18 Jan. 1924, at the formation of the first Labour government.

[8] See Neville Chamberlain's rather patronising assessment at the end of the first session, Chamberlain to Baldwin, 30 Aug. 1925, Martin Gilbert, *Winston S. Churchill: Companion* (hereafter Gilbert, *Churchill: Companion*), v, part 1 (1979), 533–4.

[9] See his response to Baldwin's speech on the trade union levy bill, Churchill to Clementine Churchill, 8 Mar. 1925, *Companion Documents, Volume V (Part 1)*, 424.

of the tactics and language used, and throughout the strike Churchill accepted and discharged the tasks which he was given. Although he supported Baldwin's decision not to legislate in 1925, Churchill was more in tune than his leader with Conservative opinion on the trade union levy, another key theme of the mid 1920s. He was in favour of the change to 'contracting in' even before the general strike, and had no disagreement with the terms of the 1927 Trade Disputes Act. Another matter on which the rank and file felt strongly was strengthening the House of Lords as a bulwark against an overriding Socialist majority, and here again Churchill was of the same mind as the centre and right of the party. The de-rating scheme which he developed with Neville Chamberlain in 1927–8 was the centrepiece of the government's unemployment strategy. Although the reform failed to generate public enthusiasm, it had something to offer both urban and rural Conservatives and was well attuned to mainstream party opinion.[10] By the election of May 1929, Churchill had established a fairly secure position in both the party and the cabinet; if the Conservatives had won, he would have been seen as a positive member of the team which had secured victory. Whilst Baldwin was considering a reshuffle which would have moved him from the Treasury, there was no intention or pressure to leave him out of the next cabinet.[11] A change of post was not a snub or unwelcome; there were more creative opportunities elsewhere, and now that Churchill had worked his passage the party would be willing to give him greater latitude.

The Conservative defeat in 1929 left the Liberals holding the parliamentary balance, and Churchill was willing to seek an arrangement with them to block Labour or remove them from office after a few months. He was not the only Conservative to consider this, but few others were willing to deal directly with Lloyd George, or thought that Lloyd George would set a feasible price. Nevertheless, the revival of coalitionism, or even the rumour of it, damaged Churchill's position. Although Churchill was fairly effective in replying to Snowden in set-piece debates such as the 1930 budget, in general he did not shine on the opposition front bench; Baldwin was not alone in thinking that he had 'made one blunder after another'.[12] However, he was not the only former minister who found adapting to opposition difficult, and Austen Chamberlain and Baldwin were even more indifferent performers. The

[10] Amery diary, 24 Apr. 1928, *The Leo Amery Diaries, Volume 1: 1899–1929*, eds. J. Barnes & D. Nicholson (1980), 547.

[11] Neville Chamberlain diary, 11 Mar. 1929, Neville Chamberlain MSS, Birmigham University Library; Churchill's own recollections, Amery to Baldwin, 11 Mar. 1929, Gilbert, *Churchill: Companion*, v, part 1, 1431, 1444–45.

[12] Amery diary, 26 May 1930, *The Empire at Bay – The Leo Amery Diaries, Volume 2: 1929–45*, eds. J. Barnes and D. Nicholson (1988), 72.

revival of protectionist feeling in the Conservative party in 1929–30 was not as difficult for Churchill as might have been expected. Now back in the party mainstream, he was ready to take a more flexible view. The problems of the slump undermined the certainties of many defenders of free trade, and whilst he was still reluctant to put duties on food imports, he was not prepared to quit the front bench over this.[13] He was sensitive to the move of party opinion towards tariffs and imperial preference in the winter of 1929–30 and developed his own position alongside it, closing rather than widening the gap.[14] It is significant that when Beaverbrook was identifying the barriers to be overcome in the spring and summer of 1930, Churchill had faded into the background; Salisbury and even Percy offered more resistance, until the attack moved on to Davidson and ultimately Baldwin.

Churchill's eclipse in 1929–31 was not mainly due to the renewal of the tariff issue, or even his opposition to Baldwin's line on India. There was a third factor which affected a considerable number of the 1924–9 cabinet: the feeling against the 'old gang', and the desire to refresh the Conservative front-bench. Fanned by Beaverbrook as part of his efforts to remove obstacles to his protectionist Empire Crusade, this became a forceful pressure during 1930.[15] Inclusion in the 'old gang' was not so much a matter of age alone, but rather of style, outlook, and length of career. It affected most those who seemed to have late Victorian roots or mentalities, and so included Austen Chamberlain, Joynson-Hicks, Churchill, Salisbury and Percy, but not Neville Chamberlain, Hoare and Cunliffe-Lister. Churchill was thus only one amongst several who were washed into a backwater by this tide of party feeling. As this pressure mounted at the end of 1930, his attention turned to the India question. It was not a deliberate search for a weapon to use, but rather that the dwindling chances of his inclusion in the next cabinet removed the counterbalance to his strong convictions on this issue. In November 1929 Churchill had been deeply unhappy when Baldwin supported the Irwin Declaration of eventual dominion status, but he remained a loyal member of the front-bench team until his resignation in January 1931.[16] His departure was not a leadership bid; like Eden in 1938, Thorneycroft in 1958 and Heseltine in 1986, it was the only reaction left when an

[13] Addison, *Churchill on the Home Front*, 294, 296–9; Churchill to Baldwin, 14 [not sent] & 16 Oct. 1930, Gilbert, *Churchill: Companion*, v, part 2 (1981), 191–4.

[14] Nicolson diary, 23 Jan. 1930, *Harold Nicolson: Diaries and Letters 1930–64*, ed. Stanley Olson (1980), 14–15. He was happy to accept the referendum policy announced by Baldwin on 4 Mar. 1930 and the advance to the 'free hand' in September and October 1930, and in the budget debates of April 1931 gave public support to introducing tariffs for revenue and negotiating purposes.

[15] Ball, *Baldwin and the Conservative Party*, 115, 116, 159–61.

[16] *Ibid.*, 114–117; Hoare to Irwin, 13 Nov. 1929, Gilbert, *Churchill: Companion*, v, part 2, 111.

existing tension was stretched to breaking point. He remained loyal on other issues in 1931, and sought to help in the party's attacks on Labour.[17]

At the height of the tariff crisis in September 1930, Churchill had warned Baldwin that he cared about India 'more than anything else in public life'.[18] He was unwilling to go beyond the Simon Commission's proposals for limited regional devolution, and was appalled when the first Round Table conference ended in January 1931 with a commitment to a federal constitution including areas of native control of the central government. A few days later, on 26 January, Baldwin gave firm support to this in an ill-judged speech which dismayed Conservative MPs. He had barely consulted his front-bench colleagues, and several were angry and upset. Churchill resigned the next day, and during the following weeks sought to draw back the party's position.[19] This had some effect: despite scoring some debating points at Churchill's expense, Baldwin sounded a more careful note in his next speeches in March 1931. Between 1931 and 1935 Churchill was not using India to overthrow Baldwin and seize the leadership – not because he did not want it, but because he knew that it was not likely to be obtained in that way. Although there were a few moments when the tide of party feeling swung towards Churchill's views on India, he would not have been Baldwin's replacement. Any successor would need the support of most of the front bench and have to be able to command wider and deeper confidence amongst MPs and the constituencies than Churchill did. As the crisis of March 1931 showed, the most likely new leader would have been Neville Chamberlain.[20]

Churchill had been aware since 1929 that Chamberlain might be Baldwin's eventual successor, blocking his own chances and providing a less congenial style of leadership.[21] He had considered retirement and concentrating on making his family's financial situation more secure, even before the depression hit his investments in late 1929. In fact, he largely followed through with this, adopting a kind of semi-retirement. During the 1930s Churchill followed his own course first and foremost, and took remarkably little account of the views of others. This could be ascribed to egotism and lack of judgement, but makes more sense

[17] Churchill to Boothby, 21 Feb. 1931, *Companion Documents, Volume V (Part 2)*, 275. He delivered a powerful attack on MacDonald in the debate on the Trades Disputes Bill just after his resignation, although this could also be seen as a bid to win over Conservative MPs.

[18] Churchill to Baldwin, 24 Sep. 1930, Gilbert, *Churchill: Companion*, v, part 2, 186.

[19] Ball, *Baldwin and the Conservative Party*, 121–2, 134; Churchill had a favourable reception at the N[ational] U[nion] Central Council, 24 Feb. 1931.

[20] Ball, *Baldwin and the Conservative Party*, 135–6 201.

[21] Churchill to Clementine Churchill, 27 Aug. 1929, Gilbert, *Churchill: Companion*, v, part 2, 61–62.

as the conduct of someone who feels above the fray of the day-to-day struggle. Churchill's course was closest to that of the 'elder statesman', combining experience which should be deferred to with some detachment from the government, though not hostility.[22] This gave him the licence to concentrate on issues of particular interest, and explains the nature of his interventions. His attendance at the House was intermittent, and the habit of delivering a prepared speech and then departing was not calculated to draw in the many new members who hardly knew him. He expected to offer advice and be heard at the highest level, and to be given privileged access to information in certain areas; he played a part behind the scenes, and over air defence was certainly not 'in the wilderness'. At the same time, Churchill was giving much more of his time and energy to activities outside politics. Some of these were to make money, but others were leisure; the involvement in Chartwell, and the painting – which unlike his writing was never intended to produce income. His absence from the fray at the crucial party conference of 1934, cruising in the Mediterranean and painting, was not a tactical move but a reflection of other priorities.

It is wrong to regard Churchill as being isolated or excluded after 1931, although this is the romantic myth of the 'wilderness years'. This implies that his omission from the national government in 1931 was a consideration in its making, rather than the natural consequence of his resignation from the front bench and the limited number of ministerial places available for Conservatives in a coalition. This false perspective results from viewing events as if the political world revolved around Churchill, and assuming that such a giant could only have been marginalised by the deliberate efforts of the 'pygmies' who ruled the national government. The truth is more ordinary; he was one of a number of Conservative ex-ministers whose position and influence had declined, and who were peripheral to the events of August to November 1931. Several who were still members of the business committee found no place, such as Steel-Maitland, Peel and Amery, whilst Austen Chamberlain and Hailsham were marginalised. Nor was Churchill unusually detached from his party, being no further removed than Heseltine in 1986–90 and less so than Bevan in the early 1950s, Cripps in 1939, Austen Chamberlain in 1922–3, or Powell after 1968. Another perspective on Churchill's position in the 1930s is offered by a comparison with the two most recent Conservative chancellors of the exchequer. He was more in touch with the party mainstream on India

[22] He was described in these terms by Harold Nicolson as early as January 1930: Nicolson diary, 23 Jan. 1930. This does not mean that 'elder statesmen' do not harbour hopes of a recall to the cabinet; Austen Chamberlain's position – which was more similar to Churchill's in 1929–35 than is ususually recognised – is an example of this.

than Kenneth Clarke has been on Europe since 1997, and more respected and listened to than Norman Lamont after 1993, despite the latter's Euroscepticism. The closest parallels to Churchill's position were Balfour after 1911 and Gladstone after 1874 – for certainly he did not rule out the chance of a recall to high office, although he expected not the leadership but a cabinet post related to defence.

Churchill's conduct during the 1930s makes little sense if he really was aiming to seize the party leadership or bring down the national government. In 1931 Amery noted: 'I imagine that his game is to be a lonely and formidable figure available as a possible Prime Minister in a confused situation later on.'[23] This would have been a remote and wildly speculative strategy, but Churchill's independent course was open to misinterpretation, and the suspicion that he was seeking to overthrow the leadership was a handy weapon to use against him. However, if this was his purpose, then his judgement was deeply flawed and his tactics foolish beyond belief. His campaign over India was conducted separately from the other heavyweight former ministers who might have been allies, such as Austen Chamberlain and Salisbury. Churchill's onslaught drove them towards an ineffective middle ground, and consolidated party moderates behind Baldwin and Hoare. Mainstream opinion regarded Churchill's intemperate language and forecasts of doom as exaggerated, and their excess made the official policy more credible. Up to 1933 Churchill made little effort to appeal directly to the Conservative grass roots, and by then the firmer regime of Willingdon as viceroy provided a less worrying state of affairs in India than had been the case in 1929–31. Nor was there any real attempt to canvass Conservative MPs in general, and the rebels acted according to their own personal agendas. As the 'diehards' did not view Churchill as their leader and were often ineffective in debate, they were hardly a suitable basis for a leadership bid.

Churchill was far from being opposed to the national government in principle, for it was precisely the sort of cross-party anti-Socialist pact that he had been looking for in the 1920s. His opposition to the India policy and urging of rearmament can obscure the fact that he was in agreement on the broad range of domestic policy.[24] India would not, in any case, have been the issue on which to divide the national government. Agreement since the Irwin Declaration in 1929 had enabled Baldwin and MacDonald to feel that they could work together

[23] Amery diary, 30 Jan. 1931, *Empire at Bay*, 146.
[24] For example, his support and praise for Chamberlain's budget in 1936: Addison, *Churchill on the Home Front*, 320. This contrasted with the manifesto of the five Conservative MPs who resigned the whip over India in 1935: Atholl, Todd, Astbury, Nall and Thorp to Baldwin, 1 and 21 May 1935, Baldwin MSS 107/82–7 and 91–4, Cambridge University Library.

in August 1931, and India was one of the main factors in the latter's decision to remain in office. The round table policy was subscribed to by Labour and Liberal figures in the government, and was further reinforced when Irwin joined the cabinet in June 1932. There was no significant cave amongst the Conservative ministers on India, or fault line between them and the other parties; if this was an attempt to weaken the national government, then it was misguided in attacking one of its most cohesive fronts. Although Conservative activists in the constituencies were disturbed, especially where they had economic or personal links with India, public opinion generally was little moved. Nor was this an issue upon which to make alliance with Lloyd George or appeal to the middle ground, and some combination of mavericks from all sides was never likely.

Churchill's campaign over India was focused almost obsessively upon that single issue, and he was determined to fight to the bitter end.[25] Although he was defeated, his strategy was not unsound. At the outset he made such effective use of the Conservative party's official backbench India Committee in March 1931 that Baldwin was nearly toppled from the leadership.[26] After the national government's landslide majority in 1931, it became clear that success was not likely to be achieved through parliamentary dissent alone. From the summer of 1932 the focus was widened to the constituencies; rejection of the policy by the National Union would not bind the leadership, but it would be a difficult barrier to surmount.[27] Churchill's link with Rothermere was not foolish: contrary to myth, the party crisis of 1929–31 had showed how much impact a campaign conducted by the likes of the *Daily Mail* could have on the Conservative grass roots, especially in the safer seats of middle-class south and middle England. The official line was opposed by large minorities at the central council and annual conference meetings in 1933 and 1934, and seventy-nine Conservative MPs voted against the second reading of the India Bill in February 1935, even though on all these occasions the issue was made one of confidence in the leadership. In April 1934 Hoare admitted that 'not thirty' Conservative MPs were strong supporters of the Bill, whilst 'the great mass is very lukewarm'.[28]

Churchill's decision in 1933 to refuse a place on the joint select committee considering the white paper was not a mistake, as it would have muzzled him during the key months of the struggle, but there were other tactical errors.[29] In March 1933 his speech in the debate on

[25] Churchill to Croft, and to Carson, 31 Mar. 1933, Gilbert, *Churchill: Companion*, v, part 2, 558–9; Cazalet diary, 19 Apr. 1933, in Robert Rhodes James, *Victor Cazalet* (1976), 154.

[26] Ball, *Baldwin and the Conservative Party*, 144–5.

[27] Stewart, *Burying Ceasar*, 153.

[28] Hoare to Willingdon, 20 Apr. 1934, Gilbert, *Churchill: Companion*, v, part 2, 769–770.

[29] On the Select Committee, see the discussion in Stewart, *Burying Ceasar*, 157.

the white paper was wrecked by an unproven allegation that the government was manipulating and coercing the Indian civil service. More serious damage resulted from his accusation in April 1934 that Derby and Hoare had interfered with evidence submitted to the select committee. This was not a mistake in itself and could easily have led to Hoare's downfall; only packing the investigating committee and other dubious tactics saved him and possibly the government.[30] However, the rejection of Churchill's case when the committee of privileges reported in June reinforced views of his unfitness for office and made him almost a pariah. On this and other occasions, he was vulnerable to claims that he was seeking the destruction of the national government.[31] Nevertheless, Churchill was not alone in making mistakes. It was Page Croft – who had been campaigning within the Conservative party since Edwardian days, and should have known better – who breached unwritten conventions in sending propaganda directly to constituency delegates before the 1933 conference.[32] Although he was damned by the involvement of his son, Randolph, Churchill was very doubtful about using the by-election tactic which backfired at Wavertree and Norwood by letting Labour in.

The proper test is not whether a revolt reverses a policy or brings down a government, for it is exceptionally rare for resistances in the Conservative party to have such results. The fall of the coalition in 1922 was the product of an unusual combination of issues and groups on a wide front. More limited effects are the norm, and it is these with which the India campaign should be compared. Churchill's campaign affected government policy in several ways – in its timing, in its presentation, and to some extent in its content. It certainly put down a marker beyond which concessions could not be made, placing the emphasis upon safeguards, limited powers and the counterbalancing role of the princely states. The India campaign achieved more than the protectionist pressure to apply tariffs to iron and steel in the late 1920s, or the Suez group in the 1950s, or the opponents of the common market in 1970–1, or the critics of the poll tax in the late 1980s. The closest parallel is with the opponents of the Maastricht treaty in the Major period, and if the 'Eurosceptics' achieved more this was mainly due to Major's vulnerable majority after the 1992 election. The India campaign was fought under the largest-ever government majority; whilst this might give some MPs more latitude to express dissent, it ensured that there were many more who could be counted on for loyal

---

[30] C. Bridge, 'Churchill, Hoare, Derby, and the Committee of Priveleges: April to June 1934', *Historical Journal*, 22 (1979), 215–27.
[31] Hoare to Willingdon, 17 & 31 Mar. 1933, Gilbert, *Churchill: Companion*, v, part 2, 549–50, 557–8.
[32] Lord Croft, *My Life of Strife* (1949), 232–4.

support. Even so, the leadership had to take care, and there were several alarming moments between February 1931 and March 1935.

Churchill's developing concern about air defence in 1934–36 was shared by many within the Conservative party who feared that disarmament had gone too far. He was not the only senior figure inside or outside the government to urge swifter rearmament, although he was the most persistent and public in expressing his views. Once again there were doubts about his intentions and judgement, but the charge of scaremongering was largely deflated by German statements about the size of their air force. Churchill had seemed wild and emotional about India, but more sober and informed over rearmament and later appeasement. His tactics were less confrontational and he was building support in 1935–6, especially on the need for a ministry of supply to manage the rearmament effort. He dearly hoped to get this post, and from October 1935 to March 1936 moderated his public statements to facilitate this. However, Baldwin was concerned that he would be unwilling to accept the necessary compromises and become a disruptive force in the government. Churchill's public criticisms of the Nazis meant that his return would send a signal which conflicted with the government's efforts to negotiate peaceful resolutions of disputes. For these reasons, Baldwin and later Chamberlain decided against bringing Churchill back into the cabinet in peacetime. However, many of those who did not consider Churchill to be the best man for the job still agreed with him over the need for greater vigour in defence preparations.

The abdication crisis at the end of 1936 was a setback for Churchill, reviving the criticisms of his lack of judgement and the suspicions that he was intriguing to bring down Baldwin and the National Government. Churchill was dismayed to be shouted down in the Commons on 7 December 1936, but the storm was as brief as it was intense. Some fences were mended with more judicious words on 10 December, and two days later Churchill delivered one of his most effective speeches on defence.[33] The impact of the crisis should not be exaggerated, for his diminished impact and support in 1937 owed more to the better international atmosphere.[34] Even so, the choice of Churchill to second Neville Chamberlain's formal election as party leader in May 1937 was not just a symbol of unity, but also a sign that Churchill counted for something in Conservative politics. Chamberlain's accession to the premiership was welcomed as a positive step, and most Conservatives were persuaded that his purposeful drive for appeasement offered the

---

[33] Winterton diary, 12 Dec. 1936, in Earl Winterton, *Orders of the Day* (1953), 223; Amery diary, 10 Dec. 1936, *Empire at Bay*, 433.

[34] Addison, *Churchill on the Home Front*, 323.

best prospect of avoiding war. Rearmament still mattered, but visible progress was being made and the government was more readily accorded the benefit of the doubt. The eclipse of Churchill by the end of 1937 was a product of Chamberlain's success, for they could not both be right in their prescriptions. Churchill's message had now become predictable and its negativity was unwelcome. Conservative opinion in parliament and the constituencies rejected the anti-appeasement case because it seemed likely to lead to war rather than prevent it. Churchill's real period of isolation was the eighteen months from the autumn of 1937 to March 1939. He was discounted by the majority of Conservative opinion, and kept at a distance by the mainly younger and left-wing group of anti-appeasers who looked to Eden. Churchill was reduced to a small group of supporters who were little liked or respected: principally Bracken, Sandys and Boothby, with Spears and Macmillan in the outer circle. It is this which gives rise to descriptions of Churchill as a 'lonely figure', although dissident former ministers rarely have more than a couple of brave souls closely linked to them in parliament.[35]

Even so, during this period he was still listened to, and it was only in the months between the Munich settlement and the occupation of Prague in March 1939 that the atmosphere became bitter. An open breach and resignation of the whip seemed possible after his speech in the Munich debate and his vote with Labour on the ministry of supply issue on 17 November 1938. It was also in this period that he encountered serious opposition within his constituency association, threatening his position as a Conservative candidate. Whether or not central office had a finger in the pie, the local unrest was genuine.[36] Dissent was strongest in some of the branches, but Churchill retained the crucial support of his chairman and the central executive. He followed a prudent strategy, and was not in as much danger as other less prominent anti-appeasers such as Vyvyan Adams, Paul Emrys-Evans and the duchess of Atholl. Doubts about the Munich settlement and especially the wisdom of further appeasement were more widespread than appeared on the surface; although only Duff Cooper resigned from the cabinet, several others wavered. There were threats of resignation from junior ministers such as Crookshank, and a feeling that this had been far from 'peace with honour'.[37] After the occupation of Prague in March 1939, German conduct provided the vindication of experience and the anti-appeasers became the realists. In the summer months of 1939 the Conservative

[35] Blake, 'Churchill and the Conservative Party', 153.
[36] Colin Thornton-Kemsley, *Through Winds and Tides* (Montrose, 1974), 93–7; David Thomas, *Churchill: The Member for Woodford* (Ilford, 1995), 91–111.
[37] Crookshank diary, 30 Sep.–6 Oct. 1938, Crookshank MSS, Bodleian Library.

newspapers pressing for Churchill's return to the cabinet were led by the Baldwinite loyalist Lord Camrose's *Daily Telegraph*.

His conduct at the admiralty after the outbreak of war damped fears about his motives and judgement, and he was careful to give unmistakable public loyalty to Chamberlain. This was carried through to Churchill's speech in the Norway debate itself, and was an essential foundation for his acceptance by the party as prime minister in May 1940. Kingsley Wood's support of Churchill may show that ambition resides in every breast, but it also demonstrated his acceptability to party centrists of a different background and outlook. There was still much fear and bile from those most closely linked to Chamberlain, as shown by Butler's comments to Colville on 10 May.[38] However, Churchill's purge of the old guard and elevation of the excluded was far from sweeping, and driven more by the need for efficiency and the pressure of the moment. The dropped or sidelined were mainly those who had not shone in wartime posts or become a liability, such as Hoare, Simon, Stanley and Elliot, and a few younger figures who had not made a strong mark one way or another, such as Wallace. There was no exclusion which seemed unjust or aroused resentment, and most of the inclusions were not provocative.

The events of May to October 1940 focused attention upon Churchill at his best, and when Neville Chamberlain's health unexpectedly collapsed in the early autumn, no other successor as party leader would have been credible. The myths of the prewar decade had already begun to be woven around Churchill: when he became leader in October 1940, *The Times* pointed to the improbability of this outcome because his 'unorthodoxy has so often brought him into conflict with his party'.[39] But how true was this view, influenced as it was by the immediate past? Churchill's conflict as a young backbencher had been through holding to an old orthodoxy in the face of a new, of being a recusant Tory. As a Coalitionist after 1917 he had worked in harmony with the orthodox strain of Conservatism which was dominant up to 1922. In the 1920s he was soundly in the Conservative mainstream; along with the majority of the cabinet and most MPs he resisted the pressure of the minority to extend safeguarding to iron and steel before 1929, and then was careful to move with the protectionist tide in 1930–1. His India campaign was solidly Tory – indeed for many too hidebound in outlook – and his doubts were privately shared by many who voted for the official line. The pressure for swifter rearmament did not conflict with Conservative feeling generally in 1934–8; this was why it embarrassed the leadership,

[38] Colville diary, 10 May 1940, *The Fringes of Power: Downing Street Diaries 1939–55*, ed. J. Colville (1985), 122.

[39] *The Times*, 10 Oct. 1940; Ramsden, 'Churchill and the Leadership', 99.

who felt constrained by the broader public mood of disarmament. On appeasement Churchill was in conflict with the party leader, Chamberlain, and the major figures around him, and in unfriendly tension with central office. Over the abdication crisis and during the Munich settlement he was for a few days or weeks seriously out of step with a powerful mood in Conservative parliamentary and constituency opinion. However, as with India, the case which he put forward was closer to Conservative instincts and self-image than Chamberlain's pursuit of Gladstonian arbitration in search of an elusive concert of Europe. Many Conservatives were uneasy about appeasement, and felt that Britain was being disregarded and humiliated – a mood which spread as the sheer relief at avoiding war over Czechoslovakia wore off. As leader after 1940, Churchill was orthodoxly Conservative – the usual line of criticism is that he was not forward-looking enough.

There were two areas of tension between Churchill and the parliamentary party between 1940 and 1945. Significantly, the first and most important was a national rather than a party concern: the strategic direction of the war. Doubts emerged as military setbacks and problems in war production continued during 1941, and this became more acute during the most difficult period from late 1941 to the end of 1942. Conservative MPs were unhappy about the influence of Churchill's personal circle, in particular Beaverbrook and Bracken, and the lack of orthodox Conservatives in the cabinet.[40] The 1922 Committee provided a forum for concern, but would not support any direct attack on Churchill. This was demonstrated at the lowest point after the fall of Tobruk in June 1942, when the lack of Conservative support for the vote of censure in the Commons led its proposer, Wardlaw-Milne, to offer to withdraw it before the debate.[41] Conservative MPs did not want a different leader, but a more responsive and effective government. The feeling that Churchill paid too little attention to Conservative opinion was also balanced by consensus about the priority of the war. Thus an audience of 150 Conservative MPs at a lunch for Churchill organised by the 1922 Committee in 1941 cheered his declaration that no party would sacrifice more in the interests of victory. The turn of the tide in the war at the end of 1942 removed the pressure on Churchill, and his continuance in office was never again in doubt. That the concern had been for nation and not faction was shown by the fact

[40] 1922 Ctte., 23 July 1941. See also the comments of Hacking and Dugdale, the retiring and incoming Party Chairmen, in March 1942, Collin Brooks diary, 12 Mar. 1942, Addison, *Churchill on the Home Front*, 361; Butler's comments to Chuter Ede, Ede diary 25 Feb. 1942, *Labour and the Wartime Coalition: From the Diary of James Chuter Ede 1941–45*, ed. K. Jefferys (1987), 57; Amery diary, 27 Feb. 1944, *Empire at Bay*, 969.

[41] Headlam diary, 30 June 1942, *Parliament and Politics in the Age of Churchill and Attlee: the Headlam Diaries 1935–51*, ed. Stuart Ball (Camden 5th series, 14, 1999), 322.

that the critics of the previous months were the most pleased and reassured by the news of victory.[42]

The second area of tension concerned domestic policy; this became more important from 1942 onwards, but never threatened Churchill's position. In 1942 and 1943 Conservatives were restive over some extensions of state direction on the home front, especially when promoted by Labour ministers; there was particular hostility to the coal rationing scheme and a revolt against Bevin's Catering Wages Bill led by the former party chairman, Douglas Hacking. After the Beveridge Report, and especially in the later stages of the war, it was measures of postwar reconstruction which were most controversial. Finally, there was the concern about the lack of any distinctive Conservative policies, especially as the prospect of an election drew nearer. Churchill was not unsympathetic to Conservative resistance to creeping Socialism, and party pressure led to some compromises.[43] However, his reaction to Conservative dissent on agreed matters or awkward aspects of the war, such as the equal pay vote in March 1944 or the problems of Poland and Greece in the winter and spring of 1944–5, was much more impatient. His continued priority was to avoid any controversies which distracted from the war effort or threatened wartime unity. Thus he was hostile to R.A. Butler's efforts to reform education as well as unhappy over the need to set out postwar plans. Part of the problem was certainly Churchill's understandable wish to retain his unique stature as a prime minister almost above party. He felt ambivalent about his role as party leader, and attracted to continuing the wartime coalition. Uncertainty over this continued up to May 1945; as long as the possibility remained open, Churchill was opposed to anything which tended to emphasise separateness – such as distinctively party statements or a more forceful approach to by-elections after Conservative losses in 1944.[44] Together with his exhaustion in 1944–5, this inaction left the Conservatives committed to the coalition's reconstruction proposals without gaining any credit for them. Although a party conference was held in March 1945, it had little impact. When the election eventually was held on party lines, the manifesto had to be improvised hastily and was presented without the word 'Conservative' appearing: it was 'Mr Churchill's declaration of policy', and electors were asked to 'Vote National'. Lacking other ammunition, Churchill turned to the par-

---

[42] Report of Churchill's Parliamentary Private Secretary, Harvie-Watt, 13 Nov. 1942, Ramsden, *Age of Churchill and Eden*, 32.

[43] Churchill minuted 'good' on his PPS's report of Conservative opposition to the coal scheme: Ramsden, *Age of Churchill and Eden*, 33. He also shared Conservative dislike of left-wing broadcasts on the BBC, and of current affairs discussion in the army: Addison, *Churchill on the Home Front*, 346.

[44] 'Party Truce', Whips' files, in Ramsden, 'Churchill and the Leadership', 102.

tisanship of the misjudged 'Gestapo' broadcast and the Laski affair – more red herring than red peril. However, although the vocal young radicals of the Tory reform committee had been swept by enthusiasm for planning, Churchill was in tune with most Conservative candidates on economic and social policy.

The most common charge against Churchill is that he neglected his responsibilities as party leader in wartime, but both Asquith and Lloyd George had had little time to spare for Liberal organisation during the First World War. There were clear limits to the advisability of party activities in wartime, and it was Chamberlain and Hacking who mothballed central office and set the tone for the interpretation of the party truce in 1939–40, despite being apparently more partisan Conservatives. A recurring theme from Churchill's address to the party's central council in March 1941 to the annual conference four years later was the need to sacrifice party interests in wartime.[45] In any case, there was little Churchill could have done to prevent the tide of feeling against the 'guilty men' of Munich which swept the country in 1940–2, and the election verdict was even more a punishment of Baldwin and Chamberlain than a rejection of Churchill. There is no suggestion that Churchill was the primary cause of defeat even if some of his actions or inactions, such as the 'Gestapo' speech or being unwilling to hold party conferences, may have contributed to its extent. More could have been done by way of propaganda and election preparations, including a swifter return for local party agents from war service and a less cautious and sober manifesto. However, it strains credulity to argue that the defeat would have been avoided if Churchill had apportioned his attention differently between 1940 and 1945.

Churchill's standing as the wartime saviour protected him from criticism within the Conservative party after the election defeat. The rank and file did not wish to lose his leadership, whilst MPs and the shadow cabinet recognised that he could not be forced out. It was thought that he might decide to fold his tent after the defeat, and that age and health meant that he might not be able to stay for long. In fact, ambition to reverse the defeat soon restored Churchill's vigour, whilst his constitution held up until the major stroke of 1953. He remained leader until 1955 – a longer tenure than Baldwin, and only just surpassed by Thatcher. Yet he is never thought of as a 'party' leader in the same sense, even though the years from 1940 to 1955 were the most productive phase of his career. The period as leader of the opposition has been especially neglected; this is partly due to the general theory that it is governments which fail rather than oppositions succeed,

---

[45] Speeches at NU Central Council, 27 Mar. 1941; NU annual conference, 15 Mar. 1945.

but still more to the belief that Churchill had little to do with the recovery – indeed, that it was achieved almost despite him.[46] The picture which emerges from the memoirs of the shadow cabinet is that he was absentee, reactionary in outlook, difficult to deal with, and imprudent in his parliamentary onslaughts. The image of Churchill in 1945–51 is that of the self-indulgent rambles at the fortnightly shadow cabinet lunches at the Savoy: a poor manager of meetings and men, out of touch with modern realities, lacking a coherent strategy and disliking detail. Yet Churchill was actually a vital part of the equation in 1945–51 – not least because his role and contributions did not duplicate the style and activities of his colleagues. His known reluctance to move too far to the left was reassurance to the party mainstream, which was always dubious about the novel panaceas offered by bright young men. At the same time Churchill wanted to win, and was willing to make the compromises necessary to do so.

Churchill made an effective start in the new House on 16 August 1945 and at his meeting with Conservative MPs on 21 August, but his strategy was little more than criticising the government and waiting for them to make mistakes. His absences in the winter of 1945–6 and the confusion of command which followed produced a critical reaction in the 1922 Committee, but matters improved in 1946 with Eden discharging the role of deputy leader. From the spring of 1946 Churchill began to attack the government over shortages, ration cuts and mismanagement, linking these hardships with Socialist nationalisation, but he left it to Eden and others to present the party line in debates on social and welfare measures in 1945–7. However, it is likely that it was criticism of austerity rather than reassurance on welfare which brought voters – and especially women – back to the Conservatives in 1950, and so Churchill's priorities were not misguided. In 1946 he gave way to rank-and-file pressure for a fresh and authoritative definition of policy, which led to the *Industrial Charter* of 1947. Churchill wanted to avoid giving hostages to fortune in specific pledges, but the content was principles rather than promises; whilst he remained doubtful and out of sympathy with it, he did nothing to block it. The November 1947 local elections showed large Conservative gains, and they held a consistent lead in the opinion polls through 1948. When Labour appeared to be recovering ground in early 1949, and especially after the failure to win the Hammersmith South by-election in March, party anxieties recurred but were swiftly steadied. Churchill listened to the criticisms of the 1922 Committee once again, and the shadow cabinet agreed on 1 April to draw up a full policy statement. This time, with the election on the horizon, Churchill took a close interest in the

---

[46] This is the concluding analysis of Ramsden, 'Churchill and the Leadership', 117.

drafting, though the substance was a reworking of the various charters. Not long after, further gains in the May 1949 local elections and the economic difficulties which led to devaluation in September restored Conservative morale. His leadership during the election campaigns of 1950 and 1951, and of the opposition during the eighteen months between, has not attracted criticism. When the Conservatives returned to office in 1951 with the cautionary but workable majority of seventeen, it was Churchill's victory as much as anyone's. The policy pamphlets and committee minutes which lie in the archives are easily overvalued, whilst growing membership and larger staffs are the result of improving party fortunes rather than the cause. It may be that opposition is as much about waiting carefully for the government to run into difficulty, and that Churchill's wish to keep his powder dry was not unwise. Certainly, when the party was next in opposition in 1964–70 an extensive policy review did not result in confidence during the 1970 election campaign or a successful government afterwards.

In Paul Addison's view, between 1949 and 1953 Churchill 'led the Conservative Party with great vigour and flair towards the middle ground of politics'.[47] He was more successful at navigating the way back from defeat in 1945 than Balfour was after 1906, and hit fewer shoals than Hague has done since 1997, although admittedly the economic fortunes of the Attlee and Blair governments are poles apart. In comparison to the equivalent defeats of 1906 and 1997, after 1945 there was greater cohesion and sense of purpose. It is too easy to account for this by saying that the tariff issue for Balfour or Europe for Hague were more divisive and difficult to deal with – this may be so, but they were also not handled as well. There were tensions too after 1945, not least between the rump of Chamberlainite backbenchers who felt slighted after 1940 and the anti-appeasers who had risen above them, and between the young upstarts of the Tory reform committee and the staid provincial businessmen. Whilst mistakes and troubles are easy to detect and apportion the blame for, their absence is close to invisible, and the credit likely to be taken by whoever is the busiest bee around – in this case Butler and Woolton, and perhaps Macmillan as well. Churchill's strategy was to give the lead on the major occasions, such as votes of censure, the party conference and mass rallies like that at Blenheim in August 1947, and to delegate the detail. However, his intermittent attendance at the House remained an issue: in March 1949 a senior backbencher considered that Churchill 'is not really a party man – all he wants is to get back to power – people are beginning to realize this'.[48]

[47] Addison, *Churchill on the Home Front*, 387.
[48] Headlam diary, 7 Mar. 1949.

Whilst his interest in policy and his parliamentary performances can be criticised, Churchill was more successful in the appointments which he made as party leader. Taken as a whole, his record in this area is at least as good as other leaders, and perhaps better than any except Bonar Law. Even if he sometimes favoured candidates from his own circle, it is significant that he could be persuaded to choose someone from the mainstream who would enjoy wider confidence.[49] The role of R.A. Butler in the wartime policy exercise and in being given charge of the Conservative research department after 1945, is only the most visible example of this. For the party chairmanship, Churchill first appointed Dugdale, a former Baldwin protégé who was widely liked, and then when he fell ill chose Assheton; both were at least equal in capacity to the other Chairmen appointed since the post was created in 1911.[50] Woolton may not have been Churchill's first thought to succeed Assheton after the 1945 defeat, but still he appointed and supported him. If his appointment had been a flop Churchill would surely have been criticised, and so on the same principle he deserves his share of credit for Woolton's successes. Churchill's choices of chief whips combined orthodoxy with effectiveness: Stuart managed the delicate task of the wartime coalition period well, whilst the out-numbered opposition performed reasonably well from 1945 to 1950. In 1950–1 Labour's narrow majority was worn down, whilst in 1951–5 a fairly small Conservative majority was never seriously troubled. This cannot be put down entirely to Labour's Bevanite problems, and perhaps Buchan-Hepburn is the unsung success of Tory chief whips. Whilst failure in 1945 has obscured the fact that Churchill made sound party appointments, so in a different way did recovery in 1950 and 1951. The problem here is not criticism of his team, but the fact that they take all the credit – especially Butler and perhaps Macmillan on policy, and Woolton and perhaps Maxwell-Fyfe on organisation.

Churchill was also a good constructor of cabinets, given that all prime ministers have limited material to work with. The 1940 ministry had to be a compromise between the old guard and fresh faces, with room made for Labour. It worked competently enough through 1940, and was progressively adjusted thereafter. The 'caretaker' government of 1945 is sometimes unfairly dismissed, but it was a sound and capable team. Most of all, the quality of the 1951 cabinet – most purely Churchill's own – was unusually high, and stands well in comparison with the Conservative teams which returned to office in 1915 or 1979.

[49] Ramsden, 'Churchill and the Leadership', 111.

[50] With the exception of the special and temporary status of Neville Chamberlain as Chairman in 1930–31; see Stuart Ball, 'The National and Regional Party Structure', in A. Seldon and Stuart Ball (eds.), *Conservative Century: the Conservative Party since 1900* (Oxford, 1994), 174–5.

As well as a few prestigious outside figures such as Earl Alexander of Tunis, there was a mixture of old and new talent. The great offices were in strong hands: for Butler at the treasury and Eden at the foreign office, 1951–5 was to be the high point of their careers, and Maxwell-Fyfe at the home office was suitable and effective. As the government continued a new generation of ministers gained their spurs, including Thorneycroft, Macleod, Lennox-Boyd, Heathcoat Amory, Eccles, and Peake.

Two principal themes run through this paper. The first is that Churchill was much closer to mainstream Conservative opinion than is generally recognised. This is particularly the case for 1923–9, but it is also largely true for 1930–9 when he was in line with the national government on many areas of domestic policy. On the particular issues where he differed, his instincts and reservations were shared by many, even if they did not trust him personally or express open dissent. Hardly any Conservatives were keen on the India policy; where Churchill failed it was through the lack of a convincing alternative, which left the majority of the party uneasily trusting the 'men on the spot' in Westminster and India. Most Conservatives wanted faster rearmament as the foundation for a firmer stance which would end the humiliations swallowed from Abyssinnia and the Rhineland to the Tientsin crisis of June 1939. By 1939 Churchill was seen to stand for this, and reservations about him lessened considerably between March 1939 and May 1940. During the war Churchill provided the kind of patriotic and unifying leadership which the Conservative party admires, and his relegation of partisanship was fully in tune with party sentiment. Conservatives did not feel that they should be operating during the party truce in the way in which Labour was, but that Labour should be acting as they did. Between 1945 and 1955 Churchill led the Conservatives from the mainstream. He did not lean too far in the direction of planning and interventionism, or sound reactionary notes which would deter middle opinion. This pragmatic approach was continued after 1951, and there is little doubt that the uncontroversial course which the Churchill government followed was satisfactory and reassuring to the party as a whole.

The second theme is that Churchill was a more capable party politician and effective Conservative leader than has previously been acknowledged. This should not be regarded as tarnishing his reputation or diminishing his stature, even if it means that he is set less apart from others. Churchill should be seen as a man who spent a lifetime in politics in an age when they were dominated and defined by parties. His wartime approach to the party leadership was not necessarily unsound, and the party appointments made then and later were above the average in capacity and effectiveness. The criticism of his opposition leadership has some parallels with Neville Chamberlain's impatience with Baldwin, for it is the same difference of outlook between the grasp of detail and the appreciation of atmosphere and timing. If the leader bears the ultimate responsibility for the party's fortunes, then Churchill is due the credit for his part in the postwar recovery. Alone amongst Conservative leaders – except perhaps Bonar Law in 1922 – Churchill tends not to be given much credit for the election victory gained under his command. Yet the margin in 1950 was close and the victory in 1951 a narrow one, and it may well be that another leader – which would almost certainly have been Eden – might not have kept his nerve or had the stature to succeed. His contribution to his peacetime ministry of 1951–5 also tends to be overshadowed, partly due to the stroke which affected its second half. Churchill's course between 1946 and 1955 was consistent and coherent, revolving around the defence of freedom against an enchroaching state. This was the common link between his strong line on the Cold War and warnings of the danger of Communism abroad, and his support for the liberty of the individual and free markets at home against Socialist planning and bureaucracy. He was able to maintain a clear and distinctive Conservative identity, without either echoing the discredited past of the 1930s or losing touch with moderate opinion. It was under Churchill that the identification of the Conservatives with normality, stability, prosperity and opportunity was strongly established in the postwar era. This was the foundation not just for three consecutive terms in government from 1951 to 1964, but for the predominant role of the Conservative party in British politics in the decades to follow.

CHURCHILL AND THE BRITISH MONARCHY[1]

By David Cannadine

In early April 1955, on the eve of his retirement as prime minister, Sir Winston Churchill gave a farewell dinner at 10 Downing Street, at which the principal guests were Queen Elizabeth II and the duke of Edinburgh. At the end of the evening, as he escorted his sovereign to her car, the cameras caught the leave-taking scene: Churchill, full of years and honour, wearing the Order of the Garter which she had given him, and the Order of Merit which her father had bestowed, bowing to the queen, whom he had earlier saluted as 'the young, gleaming champion' of the nation's 'wise and kindly way of life'.[2] This sunset tableau, combining regal youth and statesmanly age, was reminiscent of Winterhalter's picture, painted one hundred years before, which had depicted the venerable duke of Wellington doing homage to the young Victoria, to Prince Albert, and to their son, Prince Arthur of Connaught, on the first of May 1851.[3] For Churchill, like the Iron Duke before him, was not only her majesty's greatest subject: he was also an ardent admirer of the institution of monarchy, and of the person and the character of the last British sovereign he himself would live to serve. Indeed, according to his wife, Clementine, he was 'Monarchical No 1'.[4]

This was scarcely surprising. For Churchill was born and grew up in what he later recalled as 'the days of Queen Victoria and a settled world order', when politics, society and government were still largely dominated by the monarchy, aristocracy and gentry, and by the pageantry and spectacle that were associated with them. This was Churchill's world where, as C.F.G. Masterman noted, 'a benign upper class dispensed benefits to an industrious, *bien pensant* and grateful

---

[1] This is, despite the overwhelming mass of pertinent material, a strangely neglected subject, with the honourable exception of P. Ziegler, 'Churchill and Monarchy', in R. Blake and W.R. Louis (eds.), *Churchill* (Oxford, 1994), 187–98, to whose pioneeringly perceptive essay this account is much indebted.

[2] Robert Rhodes James (ed.), *Winston S. Churchill: His Complete Speeches, 1897–1963* (8 vols., 1974) (hereafter *Speeches*, I–VIII), VIII, 8645–6.

[3] N. Frankland, *Witness of a Century: The Life and Times of Prince Arthur, Duke of Connaught, 1850–1942* (1993), 1–2.

[4] Randolph S. Churchill and Martin Gilbert, *Winston S. Churchill* (8 vols., 1966–82) (hereafter *Churchill*, I–VIII), VIII, 570; J.R. Colville, *The Fringes of Power: Downing Street Diaries, 1939–1955* (1985), 128.

working class'.[5] Thus understood, Britain was a 'complex society', which 'descended through every class of citizen' from the monarchy at its apex to the workers, in their 'cottage homes', at the bottom, and it was because he saw it in this way that Churchill 'accepted class distinctions without thought'.[6] Yet for all his deeply rooted belief in 'a natural, social, almost a metaphysical order, a sacred hierarchy which it was neither possible nor desirable to upset', Churchill's relations with the British royal family were more complex and controversial than that serene sunset encounter with his sovereign suggests.[7] The to-ings and fro-ings of his party-political allegiancies, combined with his decade of unrelieved opposition during the 1930s, meant there were times when he and the British crown were placed on contrary sides on the great issues of the day. And despite his devotion to the institution of monarchy, Churchill sometimes found individual sovereigns difficult to deal with, and expressed disparaging opinions which they, reciprocally, were also inclined to entertain of him.

As a politician and statesman, Churchill's relations with British sovereigns were also much influenced by his historical sense of how the monarchy had evolved, and by his constitutional sense of what the monarchy ought to be and ought to do. During the first phase of his political career, until his fall in the aftermath of the Dardanelles disaster, he tended to see Edward VII and George V as obstructing his Liberal, reforming zeal. In the interwar years, the collapse of the great continental ruling houses, combined with his own growing conservatism, meant Churchill became more appreciative of the stabilising virtues of the British crown, and it was this very appreciation which clouded his judgement at the time of the abdication. But this divisive episode meant that in 1940, there were many fences to mend between the unexpected monarch and the unexpected prime minister, and it was only when this had been accomplished during the Second World War that the final and mutually admiring phase of crown–Churchill relations was established. 'King and country, in that order', noted Lord Moran, 'that's about all the religion Winston has.'[8] But it was not always in that order; and Churchill's opinions sometimes seemed more heretical than orthodox.

[5] *Churchill*, VIII, 371; D. Cannadine, *Aspects of Aristocracy: Grandeur and Decline in Modern Britain* (1994), 156.

[6] V. Bonham Carter, *Winston Churchill as I Knew Him* (1965), 161; Lord Butler, *The Art of the Possible* (1971), 156; P. Addison, *Churchill on the Home Front, 1900–1955* (1992), 47, 52–3, 211, 311–15, 439; W.S. Churchill, *Marlborough: His Life and Times* (2 vol. edn, 1947) (hereafter *Marlborough*, I–II), I, 915–16.

[7] I. Berlin, *Mr Churchill in 1940* (nd), 12, 17, 36–7. The origins of the kingly and hierarchical social order were sketched out in W.S. Churchill, *A History of the English-Speaking Peoples* (4 vols., 1956–8) (hereafter *ESP*), I–IV, I, 53, 122, 136–38.

[8] Lord Moran, *Winston Churchill: The Struggle for Survival 1940–1965* (1966), 192.

I

Churchill's view of the British monarchy was grounded in the classic Victorian histories by Macaulay, Froude, Gardiner and Carlyle that he had initially encountered as a Harrow schoolboy and later read as a self-educating subaltern in Bangalore; and they were set out, virtually unchanged, in his *History of the English-Speaking Peoples*, which was largely written during the late 1930s, although it was not published until he was in retirement.[9] Notwithstanding the title, which implied that attention would be given to ordinary men and women, it was essentially a brightly lit cavalcade of the great public figures who had made up the nation's story, and it was headed and dominated by kings and queens. They formed a varied and diverse collection, and Churchill judged them confidently, crisply and critically. There were outstanding leaders in war and forceful adminstrators in peace, such as Alfred the Great, William the Conqueror, Henry II, Richard I, Edward I, Henry V, Henry VII, Elizabeth and William III.[10] But many monarchs were personally inept and politically disastrous, among them Stephen, John, Richard II, Richard III, Mary Tudor, James II, George III and George IV. As Robert Rhodes James rightly notes, 'Churchill's histories are populated with the Good and the Bad' – and of none was this more true than his history of the English-speaking monarchy.[11]

Yet amidst this constantly shifting kaleidescope of royal dynasties, national alliances and sovereign individuals, two general themes did stand out. One was that, despite the delinquencies of many individual monarchs, the English crown was a sacred, mystical, almost meta-physical institution, which connected the past, the present and the future, and which proclaimed the unity and identity of the nation. As Lord Moran recalled, 'the history of England, its romance and changing fortunes, is for Winston embodied in the royal house'.[12] A second was that, while European nations preferred (or suffered) kings and queens who were generally despotic and absolute, the English evolved a more admirable form of 'constitutional and limited monarchy'. Thanks to parliament, which represented the nation as a whole, and the later advent of the two party system, the sovereign's power was progressively eroded in a succession of episodes which were milestones in the advancing story of English liberties, extending from Magna Carta to

---

[9] J.H. Plumb, 'Churchill: The Historian', in *idem, The Collected Essays of J.H. Plumb*, I, *The Making of an Historian* (1988), 240–3.

[10] *ESP*, I, XIII–XIV, 92–6, 131–40, 157–69, 178–89, 224–43, 315–24; II, 13–21, 82–95, 106–115; III, 3–22.

[11] *ESP* I, 152–3, 190–202, 289–307, 378–95; II, 76–81, 304–13; III, 131–2, 135–43, 193; IV, 12–15, 32–3; Robert Rhodes James, *Churchill: A Study in Failure, 1900–1939* (1970), 312.

[12] Moran, *Struggle for Survival*, 399.

the Glorious Revolution of 1688 and beyond. The result was a happy compromise, a 'permanent parliament and a docile monarchy', whereby the sovereign reigned above the battle of party, while the Lords and Commons legislated and the politicians governed.[13]

This, then, was the British crown, as it had evolved and developed by the end of Victoria's reign, when young Winston was first learning about it. He had no doubt that she had been a great queen, who 'in spite of her occasional leanings', was 'a constitutional sovereign', who 'represented staunchness and continuity in British traditions', and who 'set a new standard for the conduct of monarchy which has ever since been honourably observed'.[14] In institutional (and Tory) terms, her crown embodied the nation's history, continuity and identity in its symbolic functions and ceremonial activities; and in practical (and Whig) terms, it was a convenient constitutional device, which left the people free to elect their representatives through whom they governed themselves. But during her reign, the monarchy also acquired two important new functions. Thanks to the happy home life of Victoria and Albert, it provided a moral example to the nation, of decent and dutiful domesticity, in a way that had not been true for much of the Stuart and Hanoverian dynasties. And Victoria was not only the head of the British nation but also became the 'great presiding personage' of the British Empire. Largely on account of Disraeli's initiative and imagination, hers had become an imperial monarchy, the focus and cynosure of a diverse and far-flung British community, extended across the seas and around the world, which was united in fealty to the queen empress.[15]

This monarchy – by turns Tory and Whig, mystical and functional, symbolic and constitutional, individual and familial, national and imperial – was in the full flower of its late-Victorian confidence and ostentation as Churchill was growing up. It seemed an apt expression of the British genius for organic constitutional evolution and working political compromise, it was widely envied around the globe, and in this particular settlement and configuration, it lasted the whole of his long life.[16] For Churchill, and notwithstanding the occasional difficulties of incompetent individuals or malevolent monarchs, it was beyond doubt the best of all possible worlds. 'Our ancient monarchy', he observed on the birth of Prince Charles in 1948, 'renders inestimable services to

[13] Plumb, 'Churchill', 227–9; *ESP*, ii, 166, 178, 190, 219, 261–3, 271, 293–303, 314–24; *ESP*, iii, viii.

[14] *ESP*, iv, 45, 225.

[15] *ESP*, vi, 43–5, 224–5, 230–1, 298–9.

[16] D. Cannadine, 'The Context, Preformance and Meaning of Ritual: The British Monarchy and the "Invention of Tradition", c. 1820–1977', in E.J. Hobsbawm and T.O. Ranger (eds.), *The Invention of Tradition* (Cambridge, 1983), 120–60.

our country and to all the British Empire and Commonwealth of Nations.' And it did so because it was 'above the ebb and flow of party strife, the rise and fall of ministries and individuals, the changes of public opinion and fortune'. Domestically, it presided, 'ancient, calm and supreme within its functions, over all the treasures that have been saved from the past, and all the glories we write in the annals of our country'. And internationally, it provided 'the mysterious . . . the magic link which unites our loosely bound but strongly interwoven Commonwealth of nations, states and races'.[17]

But Churchill never forgot that while the mystical, unifying, moral and imperial functions of the monarch were important, the whole thrust of English history had been to bring about a state of affairs where the king's government was carried on by minsters, who were primarily answerable to parliament, rather than to the crown. 'The royal prerogative', he insisted to his wife in 1909, 'is always exercised on the advice of ministers, and ministers and not the crown are responsible, and criticism of all debateable acts of policy should be directed to ministers, not to the crown.' He made the same point about parliament's pre-eminence thirty years later, when he bluntly informed the exiled duke of Windsor that 'when our kings are in conflict with our constitution, we change our kings', as had happened in 1688 – and as had happened again in 1936.[18] And in 1947, in *The Dream*, his imaginary conversation with his father, Churchill explained that the monarchy had survived because 'they took the advice of ministers who had majorities in the House of Commons'. This was the British monarchy as limited, constitutional, parliamentary monarchy. It put the crown in its place, and in political (though not social) terms, that was a subordinate place. Honouring the sovereign was right and good; but being governed by the sovereign had long since been given up.[19]

II

Such were Churchill's history and theory of the British monarchy: how, then, did his relations with successive British monarchs work out in practice? During his early years, young Winston enjoyed the sort of friendship which in those days was commonplace between the scion of a great ducal house and the royal family, characterised by a paradoxical combination of closeness and distance, approval and disapproval – and with eyes firmly to the main chance. His parents pulled strings with the duke of Cambridge, the queen's cousin and commander in chief of

[17] *Speeches*, VII, 7743; VIII, 8337.
[18] *Churchill*, II, 327; V, 1037.
[19] *Churchill*, VIII, 366; *ESP*, II, 267.

the British army, to get their son his commission, initially intended to
be in the infantry, but subsequently in the cavalry. Such shameless
lobbying was customary in high social circles at that time; but these
were also the years of Victoria's imperial apotheosis, by which the
young Churchill was deeply and lastingly affected. In Diamond Jubilee
year, he was serving in India, and as he read accounts of how the
queen had been made an empress, his romantic ardour was roused: 'I
must', he told his mother, 'array myself with those who "love high
sounding titles", since no title that is not high-sounding is worth
having.'[20]

But as someone with a career to establish and a reputation to make,
young Winston generally saw British royalty in terms of professional
contacts and social connection. In 1898, he sent the prince of Wales a
copy of his first book, *The Story of the Malakand Field Force*, and he
professed himself 'Tory enough' to be delighted at the recipient's
favourable response. Soon after, the prince wrote again, advising him
(rather shrewdly, as things turned out) that the 'parliamentary and
literary life' would suit him better than 'the monotony of military life',
and they continued to correspond while Churchill was in South Africa
during the Boer War.[21] When he took up his 'parliamentary and literary
life' in earnest, by becoming an MP for Oldham, he was soon invited
to Balmoral. 'I have been very kindly treated here by the king', he
reported to his mother, 'who has gone out of his way to be nice to
me.' As Churchill began to make a reputation as colonial under
secretary, Edward expressed delight that he was becoming 'a *reliable*
minister and above all serious politician, *which can only be obtained by
putting country before party*'. And when he became engaged, the king sent
him a congratulatory telegram, and gave him a gold headed malacca
cane as a wedding present.[22]

But Churchill's drive, brashness, ambition, opportunism, self-absorp-
tion and egotism soon grated on his sovereign, and as he moved from
being a junior Conservative backbencher to a junior Liberal minister,
Edward reluctantly concluded that he was 'almost more of a cad in
office than he was in opposition'.[23] In 1909, when president of the
board of trade, Churchill made common cause with the chancellor of
the exchequer, Lloyd George, to reduce the amount spent on the army

[20] *Churchill*, I, 75, 147–50, 205, 227, 242–3, 336.
[21] *Speeches*, VI, 6552; *Churchill*, IRI, 381–2, 420–1; Randolph S. Churchill and Martin
Gilbert, *Winston S. Churchill: Companion Volumes* (5 vols., 1966–82) (hereafter *CV*, I–V), *CV*,
I, part 2, 763, 1231–2; P. Magnus, *King Edward the Seventh* (Harmondsworth, 1967), 330–1.
[22] *Churchill*, II, 52, 158–9, 160–1, 211, 271, 274; Magnus, *Edward the Seventh*, 432.
[23] J. Vincent (ed.), *The Crawford Papers: The Journals of David Lindsay, Twenty-Seventh Earl
of Crawford and Tenth Earl of Balcarres, 1871–1940, During the Years 1892 to 1940* (Manchester,
1984), 83; K. Rose, *King George V* (1983), 112; Magnus, *Edward the Seventh*, 432.

in favour of old age pensions. The king responded by suggesting to the prince of Wales that Churchill's initials, WC, 'are well named'. When he made a speech in September 1909, attacking dukes as 'unfortunate individuals' and 'ornamental creatures' who were part of a 'miserable minority of titled persons who represent nobody', the king's private secretary, Lord Knollys, took the extraordinary step of writing to *The Times* to protest. Churchill was unrepentant. 'He and the king must really have gone mad', he retorted. 'This looks to me like a rather remarkable royal intervention, and shows the bitterness which is felt in those circles. I shall take no notice of it.' But Knollys was no less unforgiving. 'The very idea', he wrote, of Churchill's acting 'from conviction or principle ... is enough to make anyone laugh.'[24]

The same contrasts in attitude and behaviour were apparent during the early years of the reign of George V. As home secretary, Churchill successfully oversaw the trial for criminal libel of Edward Mylius, who claimed that George V had secretly married in Malta in 1890; and the king found his nightly reports of Commons proceedings 'always instructive and interesting'.[25] But while George V recognised Churchill's zeal and energy, he shared his father's view that he was 'irresponsible and unreliable'. In 1908, he had told Churchill that he did not consider Asquith to be a gentleman. As he later admitted to Lord Esher, he should never have said such a thing, 'but Winston repeated it to Asquith, which was a monstrous thing to do, and made great mischief'.[26] There were also difficulties arising from the reports of the Commons proceedings, as when Churchill observed that 'there are idlers and wastrels at both ends of the social scale'. George V opined that such views were 'very socialistic'; but Churchill stood by the offending phrase and objected to receiving 'a formal notification of the king's displeasure'. Peace was eventually restored; but the sovereign's private secretary saw this as further evidence that Churchill was 'a bull in china shop', while *he* continued to think the royal reproof unjust and a sign that the king lacked political impartiality.[27]

When Churchill moved to the admiralty, matters did not improve. The new first lord was a party politician and a zealous reformer; the king was a former naval person, head of the armed services, and a staunch believer in tradition and precedent. Churchill wanted to name a ship 'HMS Oliver Cromwell': not surprisingly, George V took violent exception to thus commemorating the regicide. Churchill then proposed 'HMS Pitt': but the king wouldn't have that, either. In both cases,

[24] Magnus, *Edward the Seventh*, 473, 506; *Churchill*, II, 326–7, 338–9.
[25] H. Nicolson, *King George V: His Life and Reign* (1967), 71; Rose, *George V*, 83–4; *Churchill*, II, 373–5, 382–3, 418–23, 426, 436.
[26] *Churchill*, II, 670–1; *Churchill*, III, 87; Nicolson, *George V*, 138; Rose, *George V*, 71.
[27] *Churchill*, II, 433–9; Rose, *George V*, 76, 111–12.

Churchill grudgingly gave way. 'I have always endeavoured to profit from any guidance His Majesty has been gracious and pleased to give me', he wrote rather stiffly and unconvincingly after this second royal rebuff.[28] Thereafter, their relations remained tense, as Churchill made no secret of his view that George V was a dim reactionary, and the king made it plain that Churchill was rude and inconsiderate. When he objected to the first lord's proposal to withdraw battleships from the Mediterranean to safeguard British waters, in May 1912, Churchill exploded to his wife: 'The king talked more stupidly about the navy than I have ever heard him before. Really it is disheartening to hear this cheap and silly drivel with which he lets himself be filled up.'[29]

These two monarchs disliked Churchill because they thought he was insufficiently respectful of their person and their prerogative, while Churchill objected to inappropriate royal interference in matters which were wholly within the realm of parliament and government. As a result, the crown and court were firmly against him by the time war broke out in 1914, and thereafter, relations deteriorated still further. When Churchill rashly assumed command at Antwerp, Lord Stamfordham opined that he must be 'quite off his head!' And when he urged the reappointment of Lord Fisher as first sea lord, George V objected on the (not unreasonable) grounds that he was seventy-three and lacked the confidence of the navy; but Churchill insisted and the king had to give way.[30] All of which meant that his downfall over the Dardanelles disaster in 1915 was greeted at Buckingham Palace with scarcely concealed relief. 'It is', Queen Alexandra informed her son, 'all that stupid, young foolhardly Winston C's fault.' And the king agreed. Churchill had become 'impossible', a 'real danger', and he was 'delighted' and 'relieved' that he had gone. So was his son, the prince of Wales and future Edward VIII: 'It is a great relief to know Winston is leaving the admiralty', he wrote to his father.[31] Thus ended the first phase of Churchill's involvement with the British crown, which scarcely presaged the mutual admiration that would characterise their relations by the last two decades of his life.

III

It was during the 1920s and 1930s that Churchill's attitudes towards the British monarchy became generally more appreciative and admiring. Like many pre-1914 Liberals, the First World War left him saddened

[28] *Churchill*, II, 646–54; *CV*, II, part 3, 1764; Rose, *George V,* 160–1.
[29] *Churchill*, III, 87–8; Rose, *George V,* 160.
[30] *Churchill*, III, 86–7, 120, 150–1, 383–4.
[31] *Churchill*, III, 454, 473; *CV*, III, part 2, 939; Rose, *George V,* 189; P. Ziegler, *King Edward VIII: The Official Biography* (1990), 78.

and uncertain, and looking out on a social, political and international landscape so brutally transformed that it bore little resemblance to the Edwardian *belle époque*, with its settled values, historic institutions, venerable titles and great estates. 'Injuries', he later wrote, 'were wrought to the structure of human society which a century will not efface, and which may conceivably prove fatal to the present civilisation.'[32] The ruling houses of Germany, Russia and Austria-Hungary had been fixed points around which much of Europe's history had revolved. Now they were gone, and the Spanish monarchy followed in 1931. Deprived of these symbols of order, tradition and continuity, 'woven over centuries of renown into the texture of Europe', the continent lapsed into anarchy, civil war, revolution and dictatorship (whether fascist or communist). Even Britain was not entirely free of this contagion: great aristocratic families were no longer as secure or prominent as they had been before 1914, and universal democracy threatened to get out of hand.[33]

These changes, in continental circumstances and in Churchillian perceptions, help explain the substantial transformation in his relations with King George V. For he no longer regarded the British sovereign as the ignorant, blimpish reactionary of his Liberal days, but as the embodiment of decency, duty and tradition, in a world of strife, anarchy and revolution; and for his part, the king now warmed to Churchill both as an old friend and fellow Conservative. The solution of the Irish problem seems to have had a great deal to do with this. Churchill greatly admired the 'unswerving sense of devotion' the king displayed in visiting Belfast in June 1921 when he urged Irishmen to 'forgive and forget', and the king applauded Churchill's 'skill, patience and tact' in seeing the Irish Treaty through in the following year. Thereafter, while Churchill was chancellor of the exchequer, their relations remained friendly, and when he visited Balmoral in 1927, Churchill 'enjoyed myself very much' and had 'a very good talk about all sorts of things'. And when holidaying at Deauville, he observed the Shah of Persia at the gaming tables, dissolutely 'parting with his subjects' cash'. 'Really', he observed to Clementine, 'we are well out of it with our own gracious monarch!'[34]

Churchill developed these views more fully in an obituary notice of

---

[32] Cannadine, *Aspects of Aristocracy*, 156–7; M. Cowling, *Religion and Public Doctrine in Modern England* (Cambridge, 1980), 320–8; *Churchill*, IV, 914–15; W.S. Churchill, *The World Crisis: 1915*, (1923), 17; *idem, The World Crisis: The Eastern Front* (1931), 82; *Speeches*, V, 5291.

[33] W.S. Churchill, *The World Crisis: The Aftermath* (1929), 18, 31; *idem, The Eastern Front*, 17.

[34] Rose, *George V*, 337; Rhodes James, *Study in Failure*, 120; *Churchill*, IV, 790–1; *Churchill*, V, 244, 303, 700–1.

George V, which he reprinted in *Great Contemporaries*.[35] In the course of the reign, great changes had destabilised the world: empires and monarchies had fallen; dictatorship and anarchy had flourished; democracy had become incontinent and unfettered. Yet, 'at the heart of the British Empire', there was 'one institution, among the most ancient and venerable, which, so far from falling into disuetude or decay, has breasted the torrent of events, and even derived new vigour from the stresses'. 'Unshaken by the earthquakes, unweakened by the dissolvent tides, though all be drifting', the 'royal and imperial monarchy stands firm.' This was 'an achievement so remarkable, a fact so ... contrary to the whole tendency of the age', that it could not be 'separated from the personality of the good, wise and truly noble king whose work is ended'. He was 'uplifted above class-strife and party-faction'; he never feared British democracy; he reconciled labour and socialism to the constitution and the crown; he 'revivified the national spirit, popularized hereditary kingship'; and in so doing won the affection of his subjects and the admiration of mankind. 'In a world of ruin and chaos', Churchill concluded, 'King George V brought about the resplendent rebirth of the great office which fell to his lot.'[36]

But then the crown passed to King Edward VIII, whom Churchill had known (and admired) for a long time. As home secretary, he had participated at the 'beautiful and moving ceremony' at Carnarvon Castle in 1911 when Edward was invested as prince of Wales, and he had met him soon after at Balmoral. Edward's delight and relief at Churchill's fall in 1915 was soon abandond, and he reverted to his earlier belief that Churchill was 'a wonderful man with great powers of work'.[37] During the 1920s, Churchill helped the prince with speech writing and speech making, he sent him copies of *The World Crisis* as the volumes appeared, they corresponded about public affairs and played polo together, and in 1932, the prince contributed to the cost of the Daimler that Churchill was bought by his friends on his return from America. Four years later, Edward was king, and Churchill wrote him a gracious and grandiloquent letter, offering 'my faithful service and my heartfelt wishes that a reign which has been so nobly begun may be blessed with peace and true glory' and that 'in the long swing of events, Your Majesty's name will shine in history as the bravest and best beloved of the sovereigns who have worn the island crown'.[38]

[35] W.S. Churchill, *Great Contemporaries*, (1942 edn), 245–56.

[36] This was not the first time Churchill had written appreciatively about the king, having earlier produced a film script for Alexander Korda to commemorate George V's Silver Jubilee: *CV*, v, part 2, 962–4, 989–1031.

[37] *CV*, ii, part 2, 1099; part 3, 1781; Ziegler, *Edward VIII*, 46.

[38] *Churchill*, iv, 525, 682–3; *Churchill*, v, 7, 809; *CV*, v, part. 1, 42–3, 1065–6; *CV*, v, part 3, 34–5; *Speeches*, v, 5291.

These hopes were sincere and heartfelt, and rested on an exaggerated sense of the king's virtues, with a blind eye turned to his faults (especially his support of appeasement); but they were nullified by the abdication. In taking the king's side against the government, and allying himself with the legendarily mischievous Lord Beaverbrook, Churchill may have been seeking to embarrass Baldwin and the national government. This was certainly the view of his critics, but his motives were more deeply grounded and disinterested than that.[39] He was a loyal friend, especially when the going got rough, and he sympathised with the king's wish for a happy home life to accompany the glitter and pomp of his lonely public position. Moreover, England had been through its constitutional revolution in 1688, and in the uncertain 1930s, neither the country nor the monarchy needed any repetition of that disruption and disturbance. And he was sure that, given time, the king would repent of his passion for Mrs Simpson, and thus retain (and adorn) his throne. On the basis of this analysis, Churchill's course was clear. With Baldwin's knowledge and consent, he rallied to the king, seeking to boost his morale, and urging him to be discreet in his relationship with Mrs Simpson. And he tried to play for time, out of fear that undue pressure or excessive haste might lead the king to make the wrong decision (abdication and marriage), and in the hope that given time and chance, he might do the right thing, and renounce her.[40]

In championing the king, Churchill did his own reputation untold harm, with the public, the politicians, and the court. In a period of mounting tension and anxiety, his plea for extra time was patently unrealistic; he failed to appreciate that Edward had already decided to give up the throne; and he seriously misjudged the character of the sovereign and the mood of the country, which was turning decisively against the king. On 7 November 1936, he rose in the Commons to plead that 'no irrevocable step be taken'. The House turned angrily on him; the speaker ruled him out of order; he shouted at Baldwin that 'you won't be satisfied until you've broken him'; and he stormed out of the chamber. Within three days, the king had abdicated, but Churchill, though shocked and disappointed, stood by him. Following Baldwin's announcement in the Commons, he praised Edward's 'qualities of courage, of simplicity, of sympathy and, above all, of sincerity rare and precious' which, he felt sure, 'might have made his reign glorious in the annals of this ancient monarchy'.[41] He helped to compose the ex-king's abdication broadcast, he was convinced his policy had

[39] *Churchill*, v, 809–31; Rhodes James, *Study in Failure*, 269–77; Vincent, *Crawford Papers*, 573–7, 580.

[40] *Churchill*, v, 810–11; *CV*, v, part 3, 450–4; Vincent, *Crawford Papers*, 577; Colville, *Fringes of Power*, 716; Ziegler, *Edward VIII*, 302–27.

[41] Colville, *Fringes of Power*, 196; *Speeches*, vi, 5820–2.

been the right one, and he remained deeply unhappy at what had occured. 'I believe', he wrote to Lloyd George at Christmas, when it was all over, 'the Abdication to have been altogether premature and probably quite unnecessary. However, the vast majority is on the other side.'[42]

But while Churchill remained personally loyal to the duke of Windsor (as Edward VIII became), he recognised that the monarchy had to be carried on, and the throne had to be supported. In the aftermath of the abdication, he served on the Commons select committee charged with arranging the civil list for King George VI and Queen Elizabeth. The government expected him to cause further trouble over making financial provisions for the duke; but on learning of his substantial private fortune, Churchill agreed that the matter should be dealt with privately, so as to avoid the public embarrassment of parliamentary discussion. When the Committee's proposals were presented to the Commons, in March 1937, Churchill made a stirring speech in support of 'the honour and dignity of the crown'.[43] He believed the crown should be well provided for because 'the glitter and splendour of ceremonial pageant' was popular and exciting, and helped associate the mass of the people with the state. But he also insisted that 'the ancient constitutional monarchy of this country' was 'the most effective barrier against one man power or dictatorship, arising whether from the right or from the left'. Embodying tradition and custom, and sustained by parliament, it brought decency and security to national life, and provided 'that element of unity, of the present with the past', which was 'the greatest hope of our freedom in the future'.[44]

IV

By the end of 1936, Churchill respected and revered the British throne as a powerful institution providing a beneficient antidote to contemporary chaos: and after seeing King George VI and Queen Elizabeth crowned at Westminster Abbey, he admitted to Clementine, 'You were right. I see now the "other one" wouldn't have done.' He published an effusive article on the new monarch in the *Strand Magazine* in May 1937, and in a speech in the following year opined that 'the king and his family play a part in our modern life more helpful and more fortifying to the state than in any former age'.[45] But this realistic recognition of royal realities did not mean he abandoned the duke.

[42] *Churchill*, v, 828, 831; *CV*, v, part 3, 489, 493–4.
[43] R. Rhodes James (ed.), *'Chips': The Diaries of Sir Henry Channon* (1967), 128.
[44] *Speeches*, vi, 5847–9.
[45] Ziegler, 'Churchill and the Monarchy', 194; *CV*, v, part 3, 519, 651–3, 1530; *Speeches*, vi, 6017.

Indeed, Henry Channon believed that Churchill was 'pro-Windsor to the end'. They exchanged letters regularly in the months after the abdication; Randolph Churchill was one of the few English friends who attended the wedding of the duke and duchess; and early in 1939, Churchill himself visited the Windsors in the south of France. When war broke out, and Churchill was recalled to the government as first lord of the admiralty, the duke wrote to him, 'not as a minister of the crown, but more as a father'. And on one occasion, they met in the basement secret room of the admiralty, where the disposition of the British navy was recorded. Lord Crawford – the embodiment of responsible respectability – was not at all amused.[46]

So, in the aftermath of the abdication, Churchill was scarcely *persona grata* with the new king, the new queen, or the new court. George VI and Elizabeth had heartily loathed Wallis, and regarded any supporters of hers as enemies of theirs; and so, with equal vehemence, did Queen Mary. Indeed, they viewed the social circle centring around Emerald Cunard, Henry Channon and Winston Churchill as embodying all that was worst of the vulgar, morally suspect, American forces that seemed to be corrupting British society.[47] And these pro-Edward-and-Wallis delinquencies were further compounded by the fact that Churchill was implacably anti-Chamberlain and anti-appeasement. The new king and queen, by contrast, were devoted supporters of the prime minister. They shared his strong sense of decent moral values, and he appeared with them on the balcony of Buckingham Palace after he returned bearing 'peace with honour' from Munich. When Chamberlain resigned on 10 May 1940, George VI told him he had been 'grossly unfairly treated' and 'greatly regretted' his going, while Queen Elizabeth wrote saying 'how deeply I regretted your ceasing to be prime minister. I can never tell you in words how much we owe you'.[48]

Chamberlain's departure was bad enough for the king and queen: the prospect that he might be followed by Churchill seemed even worse. His devotion to the institution of monarchy was not in question; but although he signed himself, as first lord of the admiralty, 'Your Majesty's faithful and devoted servant and subject', it was precisely that faith and that devotion to George VI which seemed so conspicuously lacking. Along with most of the British establishment, the king preferred

[46] *Churchill*, v, 853, 855–6, 1035, 1037; *CV*, v, part 3, 634–5; *Churchill*, vi, 12–13, 154; M. Gilbert, *The Churchill War Papers* (2 vols., 1993–4) (hereafter *WP*, i–ii), i, 369–70, 376–7, 776, 1070; Vincent, *Crawford Papers*, 604; Rhodes James, '*Chips*', 122.

[47] *CV*, v, part 3, 673–4; W.S. Churchill, *The Second World War* (6 vols., 1948–54) (hereafter *SWW*, i–vi), i, 172; Rhodes James, '*Chips*', 60–1, 80–3, 90–1.

[48] *Churchill*, vi, 313; J.W. Wheeler-Bennett, *King George VI: His Life and Reign* (1965), 443–4; S. Bradford, *The Reluctant King: The Life & Reign of George VI, 1895–1962* (New York, 1989), 274–9; A. Roberts, *Eminent Churchillians* (1994), 10–40.

Halifax as Chamberlain's successor. He was decent, religious, landed, a fox hunter and a family friend. Churchill, by contrast, was widely regarded as 'a cad', 'a 'half breed', a 'dictator', a 'rogue elephant', 'the greatest adventurer in modern political history'.[49] Jock Colville, the scion of a courtly family, and private secretary to Neville Chamberlain, was singularly unimpressed by Churchill's 'record of untrustworthiness and instability'. And his mother, Lady Cynthia Colville, who was a lady-in-waiting, received a letter from Queen Mary saying she hoped her son would remain with Chamberlain and not go to the new prime minister. Had these people known that the duke of Windsor had sent Churchill a letter of congratulation, thanking him for his 'great measure of practical and sympathetic support in the past', and clearly expecting more of the same in the future, they would have been even more alarmed.[50]

Such was the extent of courtly opposition when Churchill took office in May 1940, an appointment to which George VI was himself initially 'bitterly opposed'. The fact that Churchill immediately insisted – despite firmly expressed royal misgivings – in making the dreaded Lord Beaverbrook minister of aircraft production, and the no-less unrespectable Brendan Bracken a privy councillor, only seemed to confirm the establishment's worst fears, namely that the 'gangsters' and the 'crooks' were now in charge.[51] The new prime minister was not always scrupulous in keeping the king informed, and he was often infuriatingly unpunctual for royal audiences or luncheons. 'He says he will come at six, puts it off until 6.30 by telephone, then comes at seven', noted Colville. Chamberlain had been considerate and deferential, and the king and queen felt 'a little ruffled by the offhand way' in which Churchill treated them.[52] Moreover, he soon established himself as the personification of Britain's unity and resolve, and as the nation's supreme warlord and grand strategist, which meant he inevitably upstaged the king. For he was eloquent, charismatic and heroic, which George VI was not. 'The King and Queen feel Winston puts them in the shade', recorded Mrs Ronald Greville. 'He is always sending messages for the Nation which the King ought to send.'[53]

Nevertheless, their relations gradually improved. 'As the war pro-

[49] Cannadine, *Aspects of Aristocracy*, 161, and references cited there.

[50] Colville, *Fringes of Power*, 29, 121–3, 130.

[51] Roberts, *Eminent Churchillians*, 14–15, 38–41; Colville, *Fringes of Power*, 145; Ziegler, 'Churchill and the Monarchy', 194; R. Blake, 'How Churchill Became Prime Minister', in Blake and Louis (eds.), *Churchill*, 273; *Churchill*, VI, 316, 453–4; Bradford, *Reluctant King*, 312–14.

[52] Ziegler, 'Churchill and the Monarchy', 195; Colville, *Fringes of Power*, 160, 211; *Churchill*, VI, 560, 716; *Churchill*, VII, 655.

[53] Rhodes James, *'Chips'*, 272; Colville, *Fringes of Power*, 211, 467; Bradford, *Reluctant King*, 340.

ceeded', Jock Colville recalled, 'the King and Queen became as devoted to Winston as he consistently was to them.' George VI soon came to recognise the vigour and brilliance and sheer indispensability of his wartime leadership: 'I must confess', he wrote when giving permission in July 1941 for Churchill to leave the country to meet Roosevelt off Newfoundland, 'that I shall breathe a great sigh of relief when you are safely back home again.' And, although titanically busy, Churchill regularly lunched with the king at Buckingham Palace, and sent the royal family presents on their birthdays and at Christmas.[54] In 1941, the king publicly expressed his confidence in his prime minister by making him lord warden of the Cinque Ports, and Churchill was 'much attracted by the historic splendour of the appointment', which had been held by the younger Pitt, Wellington and Palmerston. So close did their friendship become that when Churchill wrote his wartime memoirs, he noted with pride that was as much familial as personal, that 'as a convinced upholder of constitutional monarchy I valued as a signal honour the gracious intimacy with which I, as first minister, was treated, for which I suppose there has been no precedent since the days of Queen Anne and Marlborough during his years of power'.[55]

One indication of this is that throughout the war, his letters to his sovereign displayed what Ben Pimlott has rightly described as 'extravagant courtesy', and 'exaggerated shows of deference'.[56] Here is one example. Early in 1941, George VI sent his best wishes for the new year, adding that he had 'so much admired all you have done during the last seven months as my prime minister'. Churchill replied that the sovereign's support had been 'a constant source of strength and encouragement'; that he had served the king's father and grandfather as a minister; that his own father and grandfather had served Queen Victoria; but that the king's 'treatment of me has been intimate and generous to a degree that I had never deemed possible'. The war, he concluded, putting things in a broader and more optimistic perspective, had 'drawn the throne and the people more closely together than was ever before recorded', and George VI and Queen Elizabeth were 'more beloved by all classes and conditions than any of the princes of the past'.[57] Such letters, almost Disraelian in their flattering eloquence, were warmly received at Buckingham Palace; and George VI did his best to reciprocate the same elevated sentiments, even though he could not match the same high style.

[54] Colville, *Fringes of Power*, 211, 323; *Churchill*, VI, 961, 1148; Wheeler-Bennett, *George VI*, 446–7 525–6.
[55] *SWW*, II, 335; Colville, *Fringes of Power*, 439–40.
[56] B. Pimlott, *The Queen: A Biography of Queen Elizabeth II* (1996), 81, 173.
[57] *SWW*, II, 554–5; Wheeler-Bennett, *George VI*, 467. For another, similar letter from Churchill to the king in 1943, see Wheeler-Bennett, *George VI*, 564–5.

But while Churchill's faith and devotion were as sincerely felt as they were eloquently expressed, he had not obtained supreme power with any intention of sharing it with his sovereign. He kept the king fully supplied with the appropriate papers, and was impressed by his thorough mastery of them; but they were for information only.[58] From the outset, Churchill paid great attention to parliamentary opinion, he regularly (if reluctantly) deferred to his chiefs of staff, and in the later stages of the war, he found it increasingly difficult to get his way with Roosevelt and Stalin. But as his intransigence about Beaverbrook and Bracken had signalled early on, he never seems to have changed his mind on a major matter of wartime policy or personnel at the behest of his sovereign. Only in smaller matters did the king occasionally insist, and the prime minister reluctantly give way. This was memorably demonstrated at the time of the D-Day landings, which Churchill was determined to watch at first hand from a nearby cruiser squadron. The king thought this was too great a risk, and in the end he prevailed. But even then, Churchill insisted that this in no sense overturned the general principle that as prime minister he alone could decide which theatres of war he should visit.[59]

Two other members of the British royal family took up Churchill's time during the war years, one of whom was the duke of Windsor, who was hoping for better times now he had a friend at 10 Downing Street.[60] But while Churchill remained personally sympathetic, this was another of those rare instances where he also had to take note, in what was a difficult and delicate family matter, and at a time when he himself was barely established in power, of the wishes of the king and queen. In July 1940, the duke and duchess were in Lisbon, having fled from France before the advancing German army. It was rumoured they were the object of Nazi plots and schemes, which made it imperative to get them out of the country. The duke wanted to return home, and to an important job. But the king, Queen Elizabeth and Queen Mary, were determined 'to keep him at all costs out of England'. Caught in the middle of this royal row, Churchill offered the duke the Governorship of the Bahamas, and urged him to go there directly. It was a deft solution to a difficult problem. 'He'll find it a great relief', observed Lord Beaverbrook of the duke. 'Not half as much as his brother will', replied Churchill. 'I have done my best', the prime minister told the duke, who recognised that he had. But in keeping him out of the country, Churchill also mended his own damaged fences with the king and queen.[61]

[58] Bradford, *Reluctant King*, 305.
[59] *SWW*, v, 546–51; Wheeler-Bennett, *George VI*, 600–6.
[60] P. Dixon, *Double Diploma* (1968), 115.
[61] Colville, *Fringes of Power*, 183–4, 211; Bradford, *Reluctant King*, 434–9.

The very different challenges presented by the career considerations of the king's cousin, Lord Louis Mountbatten, were a great deal easier for Churchill to deal with. For here his task was not reluctantly to relegate a tainted royal to the margins of events, but enthusiastically to propel a glittering royal towards the centre of affairs. As well as being the great-grandson of Queen Victoria, Mountbatten was young, brave, gallant, confident and dashing – an ambitious, well-connected officer after Churchill's own heart. Moreover, he was the son of Prince Louis of Battenberg, who had been obliged to resign as first sea lord in October 1914 when Churchill had been first lord of the admiralty on the wholly groundless accusations that because of his German 'birth and parentage', he was unpatriotic in his sympathies.[62] So Churchill had many reasons for wishing Lord Louis well, and he did just that, making him successively chief of combined operations in 1941, and supreme allied commander in South East Asia two years later, positions of exceptional seniority to be given to an impetuous (and foolhardy?) sailor who was only in his early forties. And with the end of the war in the Far East approaching, Churchill clearly anticipated giving Mountbatten further preferment and promotion. 'We will talk about your future', he told him, 'as I have great plans in store.'[63]

It was a sign of Churchill's transformed relations with the British monarchy, no less than of his triumphs as war leader, that on 8 May 1945, he appeared on the balcony of Buckingham Palace with King George VI and Queen Elizabeth. 'We have', he observed, in moving a loyal address to the king in the Commons, 'the oldest, the most famous, the most honoured, the most secure and the most servicable monarchy in the world.' It was, he insisted, 'an ancient and glorious institution', and 'the symbol which gathers together and expresses those deep emotions and stirrings of the human heart which make men travel far to fight and die together.'[64] But then Churchill was turned out at the general election, and the king was as dismayed to lose his prime minister as he had been reluctant to appoint him five years before. 'I was shocked at the result, and I thought it most ungrateful to you personally after all your hard work for the people', he wrote, with a fine indifference to the conventions of constitutional impartiality. 'I shall miss your counsel to me more than I can say.' He duly offered Churchill the Order of the Garter (which he refused) and later the Order of Merit (which he accepted).[65]

[62] *Churchill*, II, 551–2, 631–2; *Churchill*, III, 147–53; Nicolson, *George V*, 333.

[63] P. Ziegler, *Mountbatten: The Official Biography* (1985), 49, 132–3, 165–57, 168–9, 176–8, 216–24, 299; Colville, *Fringes of Power*, 127; *Churchill*, VIII, 100.

[64] *Churchill*, VIII, 174; *Speeches*, VII, 7164–5.

[65] *Churchill*, VIII, 109, 114–15, 177–8; Wheeler-Bennett, *George VI*, 635–7, 645, 650; Bradford, *Reluctant King*, 377–8.

V

Unlike the great duke of Marlborough, Churchill had been dismissed by the electorate rather than by his sovereign, and thereafter he remained a firm favourite with the British royal family, by many of whom he was now regarded more 'as a friend' than as an ex prime minister. The king continued to consult him about speeches and letters, Churchill sent copies of his history of the Second World War as successive volumes appeared, and he spoke effusively in parliament on the occasion of their majesties' silver wedding.[66] He was delighted when Princess Elizabeth became engaged to Lieutenant Philip Mountbatten; in seconding the Commons address of congratulation, he noted that the monarchy and the royal family, 'play a vital part in the tradition, dignity and romance of our island life'; and when he arrived (late) for their wedding in Westminster Abbey, 'everyone stood up, all the kings and queens'.[67] Churchill also remained a foul-weather friend to the duke of Windsor: he unavailingly supported his search for an honorary post at the British Embassy in Washington; and Winston and Clementine celebrated their fortieth wedding anniversary with the duke and the duchess in the south of France in 1948.[68]

On Churchill's return to power in October 1951, the king was as pleased to see him back as he had been dismayed in 1940. 'In Winston's approach to the throne', Lord Moran reported, 'his sense of history invested the monarch with a certain mystique, so that he always spoke of the royal house with touching reverence.'[69] The death of George VI in January 1952 moved him deeply, and his broadcast and parliamentary eulogies were vibrant with emotion: 'during these last months, the king walked with death, as if death were a companion, an acquaintance, whom he recognized and did not fear'. And he saluted him for being 'so faithful in his study and discharge of state affairs, so strong in his devotion to the enduring honour of our country, so self-restrained in his judgement of men and affairs, so uplifted above the clash of party politics'. In short, his conduct on the throne was 'a model and a guide to constitutional sovereigns throughout the world today, and also in future generations'. But what Churchill meant by that was revealing: George VI 'mastered the immense daily flow of state papers', and this made 'a deep mark' on the prime minister's mind; but he never suggested the king made any serious impact on government policy.[70]

[66] *Marlborough*, II, 912–13; Moran, *Struggle for Survival*, 312; *Churchill*, VIII, 390–1, 446–7, 491, 760–1; *Speeches*, VII, 7632–3.

[67] *Speeches*, VI, 7541; *Churchill*, VIII, 340–41; Rhodes James, *'Chips'*, 418.

[68] Ziegler, *Edward VIII*, 505; *Churchill*, VIII, 174, 207, 232–5, 267–8, 409–10, 431, 450; *Marlborough*, I, 906–11.

[69] Pimlott, *The Queen*, 173; Moran, *Struggle for Survival*, 414, 421.

[70] Moran, *Struggle for Survival*, 341, 372–4; Colville, *Fringes of Power*, 640; *Churchill*, VIII, 696–701; *Speeches*, VIII 8336–7.

The prime minister's feelings towards the king were genuinely warm; and with his successor, all was even more sweetness and light. Churchill had first met Princess Elizabeth at Balmoral in 1928, when she was two. She was, he told Clementine, 'a character', with 'an air of authority and reflectiveness astonishing in an infant'. Now she was queen, and the ageing prime minister saw himself playing Melbourne to her Victoria. He was the experienced world statesman, with an authority matchless and unrivalled; she, by contrast, was the young sovereign, new to her great responsibilities. The prime minister wore a frock coat and top hat for their (increasingly lengthy) weekly audiences, they talked about polo, horses, and his early life as a subaltern in India, and he returned 'overflowing with her praises'.[71] The queen, for her part, was 'very fond' of her first prime minister; she enjoyed his company at the races and at Balmoral; she gave him the Order of the Garter, which he had previously declined from her father; and she commissioned a portrait bust by Oscar Nemon to be placed in Windsor Castle. Mutual admiration could scarcely go further, and was one of the reasons why Churchill determined to stay on to be the high priest of the secular-cum-sacred splendours of her coronation.[72]

Among the greatest pleasures of Churchill's second premiership were the opportunities to give public expression to his romantic feelings for the institution of monarchy, and for the person of the new monarch. When saluting Elizabeth's accession, he hoped her reign would witness 'a golden age of art and letters', and a 'brightening salvation of the human scene'. On the evening of her coronation, he described the queen as 'a lady whom we respect because she is our queen, and whom we love because she is herself'. And when she returned from her six-month Commonwealth tour in May 1954, Churchill was even more expansive. The 'gleaming episode' of this 'royal pilgimage' had, he averred, cast a 'clear, calm, gay and benignant' light 'upon the whole human scene', and he assigned 'no limits to the reinforcement which this royal journey may have brought to the health, the wisdom, the sanity and hopefulness of mankind'.[73] Small wonder that on Churchill's eightieth birthday, the whole royal family bought him a present of four silver wine coasters. 'You have been, and are, such an inspiration to our people', the queen mother wrote in congratulation, 'and we are all *very* proud of you' – a complete and conspicuous *bouleversement* from the

---

[71] *Churchill*, v, 303; *CV*, v, part 1, 1349; Rhodes James, *'Chips'*, 474; Moran, *Struggle for Survival*, 403, 484, 607; Pimlott, *The Queen*, 193–4; S. Bradford, *Elizabeth: A Biography of Her Majesty the Queen* (1996), 220–2, 226–7.

[72] Moran, *Struggle for Survival*, 404, 414, 450–1, 472, 547; *Churchill*, v, 763–5, 770–1, 822–4, 852, 874, 884, 886–7, 914, 942, 993.

[73] *Speeches*, VIII, 8487, 8567.

damning opinions she had entertained of him fifteen years before.[74]

But there was also serious and sensitive royal business with which Churchill as prime minister had to deal. Much of this concerned two familiar figures: the duke of Windsor, who remained a problem, and Lord Mountbatten, who had recently become one. The duke still wanted an official job; but there was nothing Churchill could do, try as he might (and he clearly did). He also wanted to attend Queen Elizabeth's coronation, but Churchill strongly and successfully advised against.[75] As for Lord Mountbatten: he was convinced that the marriage of his nephew to Princess Elizabeth meant the Mountbattens had become Britain's ruling house when the princess became the queen. But Churchill (strongly urged on by Queen Mary and Alan Lascelles) took the greatest exception to this idea, and the name of Windsor remained. The prime minister probably needed no encouragement, having taken against Mountbatten since 1945, partly because of his treatment of the princes in India, and partly because of his oft-repeated Labour sympathies. As a result, Churchill was less sympathetic to Mountbatten's determined wish to be first sea lord than he might once have been, and it was only towards the very end of his premiership that Churchill appointed him to the office from which his father had resigned forty years before.[76]

At the same time, a new royal reign, and a new royal generation brought with them new problems for Churchill. There was the question of televising the coronation, to which the cabinet and the queen were initially opposed, and which the prime minister thought would be too great a strain for the young monarch. Eventually, they were all forced to change their minds in response to public opinion. There was the problem of Princess Margaret, who wished to marry the divorced Peter Townsend: Churchill was initially favourable, believing 'the course of true love must always be allowed to run smooth'; but he was persuaded by his wife that this would be an error of judgement comparable to that of the abdication, and he threw his weight (and the cabinet's) against the scheme.[77] There was also the future of the queen mother: on the death of her husband, she inclined to retire into private life, but Churchill persuaded her otherwise, and even held out the prospect that she might become governor general of Australia. And there was the need to assuage the duke of Edinburgh, who had felt slighted when told that his wife had not taken his surname. At the very end of his

[74] *Churchill*, VIII, 1072–6.

[75] *Churchill*, VIII, 979; Ziegler, *Edward VIII*, 539–40, 549, 551; Bradford, *Elizabeth*, 184, 310–11, 343–4; Colville, *Fringes of Power*, 670, 675.

[76] *Churchill*, VIII, 672–3; Ziegler, *Mountbatten*, 502–3, 512, 523–4, 681–2; Pimlott, *The Queen*, 183–6; Bradford, *Elizabeth*, 176–8; Colville, *Fringes of Power*, 637, 641–2, 760.

[77] Pimlott, *The Queen*, 205–7, 218–20; Bradford, *Elizabeth*, 182–3, 204–5.

prime ministership, in March 1955, Churchill suggested to the cabinet that Philip might be created a prince of the United Kingdom, a proposal eventually carried through by Harold Macmillan two years later.[78]

By then, Churchill was well into his retirement, which had begun in April 1955. He had declined the dukedom which his sovereign offered him in his final audience, and he conspicuously refused to give 'advice', believing that the choice of his successor was a matter for the monarch alone. (In fact, of course, it was no such thing: Eden had for years been Churchill's acknowledged heir-apparent, and Churchill had advised George VI of that in June 1942.) And the queen not only attended his farewell dinner: she wrote to him in her own hand, thanking him 'with deep gratitude' for all his services as her first (and favourite) prime minister, a position in her affections that he has retained to this day. 'I had a lovely letter from her', Churchill told Lord Moran, 'eight pages in her own writing. It took me a whole morning to reply.'[79] Thereafter, sovereign and subject continued to correspond, he sent her copies of the *History of the English-Speaking Peoples*, he dined occasionally at Buckingham Palace, and the queen consulted him about the succession to Eden in 1957, when he recommended Harold Macmillan in preference to R.A. Butler on the grounds that he was the more decisive.[80]

The queen's affection for her first and favourite prime minister were fully displayed on his death in January 1965, when she behaved impeccably, and with great generosity and imagination. For it was at her instruction, and with parliament's acquiesence, that Churchill was given a state funeral – arrangements which represented a conspicuous reversal of the previous occasion, when parliament had had to petition the (extremely reluctant) Queen Victoria to accord a similar honour to Gladstone.[81] Setting aside all precedent and precedence, Elizabeth II attended in person (something even Victoria had not done for Wellington, and would never have dreamed of doing for the Grand Old Man) to mourn the passing of her greatest subject, as did almost the entire royal family – with the exception of the still-unforgiven duke and duchess of Windsor.[82] Appropriately enough, one of the most memorable images from that day was of the British monarch and her family

[78] *Churchill*, VIII, 722; Colville, *Fringes of Power*, 646; Bradford, *Elizabeth*, 275.

[79] *Churchill*, VII, 125; *Churchill*, VIII, 1123–8; Colville, *Fringes of Power*, 709; Bradford, *Elizabeth*, 228; Moran, *Struggle for Survival*, 653.

[80] Moran, *Struggle for Survival*, 710; Pimlott, *The Queen*, 258; Bradford, *Elizabeth*, 236; *Churchill*, VIII, 1177–8 1193–4, 1223, 1227, 1313, 1330–1, 1333.

[81] H.C.G. Matthew, 'Gladstone's Death and Funeral', *The Historian*, 57 (Spring 1998), 20–4; *Hansard*, fourth series, vol. LVIII, cols. 69, 80, 123–6, 265, 415; *Hansard*, fifth series, vol. 705, cols. 667, 679.

[82] *The Sunday Telegraph*, 31 January 1965.

gathered together in a royal tableau on the steps of St Paul's, saluting Churchill's coffin as it was carried away.

VI

As with many aspects of Churchill's public life and political career, his relations with British monarchs constitutes a rich and varied story, which unfolded at several different levels. There was a high rhetorical plane of history, drama, romance and sentiment, only equalled among British prime ministers by Disraeli. From this grandiloquent perspective, Churchill regarded successive sovereigns as national symbols and imperial icons, whose affairs he was proud to conduct, and whose encouragement, recognition and admiration he deeply cherished. At another level, and this was especially demonstrated in his instinctive feelings towards the duke of Windsor, the widowed Queen Elizabeth, the humiliated Prince Philip and the matrimonially troubled Princess Margaret, Churchill had a genuine sense of the loneliness, sadness and tragedy which was never far from the public pomp and glitter of the throne. And at yet a third level, of workaday politics and practical affairs, he often saw individual monarchs as flawed personalities, political opponents and tiresome nuisances, with inflexible attitudes, reactionary opinions and obscurantist instincts.

In practice, this meant that virtually everything was negotiable – and re-negotiable. For, as Churchill had earlier put it in his life of Marlborough, 'when kings forswear their oaths of duty and conspire against their peoples, when rival kings or their heirs crowd the scene, statesmen have to pick and choose between sovereigns of fluctuating values, as kings are wont to pick and choose between politicians according to their temporary servicableness'.[83] As the record shows, 'picking and choosing between sovereigns' was how Churchill spent much of his political life. Among British monarchs, his opinions of Edward VII, George V, Edward VIII and George VI all underwent serious and significant modification. Only Queen Victoria and Queen Elizabeth II seem to have been the beneficiaries of his unstinted admiration. And, of course, what was negotiable from Churchill's side was also negotiable from the monarchy's side: Edward VII and George V certainly changed their minds about Churchill, and so, even more significantly, did George VI and Queen Elizabeth, as initial alarm was replaced by 'temporary serviceableness' and eventually by lifelong admiration. For just as he came to modify his opinion of them in the light of events, so they in turn came to alter their opinion of him.

[83] *Marlborough*, I, 298.

Constitutional monarchy, like political activity, was very much the art of the possible.

But not everything was negotiable. Above all, the principle and practice of 'constitutional monarchy' was, for Churchill, inviolate. The crown was to be revered and respected as an institution, and individual sovereigns might be courted and flattered with Disraelian artifice, but 'the supremacy of parliament over the crown' was, for Churchill, the cardinal axiom of British political life, and of his political practice. As he put it in his *History of the English-Speaking Peoples*, the monarch was 'the instrument of parliament', the king was 'the servant of his people', and the Commons was 'the dominant institution of the realm'.[84] Accordingly, it was 'the duty of the sovereign to act in accordance with the advice of his ministers', and Churchill never wavered in this belief. To be sure, he was prepared to give way, throughout his career, on minor matters: the naming of ships in the royal navy, the employment of the duke of Windsor, his own attendance at the D-Day landings. But in all great matters – the personnel of politics, domestic statecraft, the grand strategies of war and peace – he was determined to prevail, and, as Philip Ziegler notes, 'it is hard to think of a single instance in which Churchill changed his views or his course of action on any important question in accordance with his perception of the wishes of the monarch of the time.'[85]

From one perspective, there was an extraordinary symmetry and completeness to Churchill's relations with the British monarchy. He began his public life at the end of the reign of one great queen, and he ended his public life at the beginning of what he felt sure would be the reign of another. 'I', he observed on her accession, 'whose youth was passed in the august, unchallenged and tranquil glories of the Victorian era, may well feel a thrill in invoking, once more, the prayer and the anthem, "God save the queen".'[86] So, indeed, it had been; and so, indeed, he did. But from another perspective, the serenity of these final years was late happening and hard won. Of course, and as befitted the grandson of a duke, he had never been a social revolutionary: even before 1914, one perceptive contemporary had opined that the 'whole tenor of his mind' was 'anti-radical'.[87] But in his early liberal, crusading years, he seemed on the side of radical reform to an extent which made successive sovereigns uneasy, and he also carried with him an accumulation of personal shortcomings which meant monarchs were disinclined to trust him – a hostile view which his misguided loyalty to

---

[84] *Speeches*, VI, 5821; *ESP*, II, 262.
[85] *Speeches*, VI, 5821; Ziegler, 'Churchill and the Monarchy', 198.
[86] *Speeches*, VIII, 8338.
[87] Vincent, *Crawford Papers*, 319.

Edward VIII seemed amply to vindicate. Only as he got closer to the British throne in the reigns of King George VI and Queen Elizabeth II, did he come to see virtues in them and, reciprocally, they in him. But there were also deeper trends and feelings at work. For as the first half of the 'terrible twentieth century' followed what he regarded as its uniquely dreadful course of 'woe and ruin', Churchill did become more socially and politically conservative, which meant he increasingly regarded the institution of monarchy as the best available antidote to the excesses of democracy, revolution, dictatorship, fascism and communism, by which the world seemed blighted. That the British crown remained, despite all this, stable and secure became, by contrast, a source of singular pride and gratification to him. It defied the course of history, and in his years of power and triumph, Churchill took great delight in helping and encouring it to become even 'stronger than in the days of Queen Victoria'. 'No institution', he told Lord Moran on the accession of Elizabeth, 'pays such dividends as the monarchy.' Small wonder that at his funeral, the queen's wreath bore the appreciative inscription 'In grateful remembrance: Elizabeth R.' For she, like her parents, had much to thank him for.[88]

[88] *Churchill*, VIII, 366, 1364; Moran, *Struggle for Survival*, 372.

CHURCHILL AND *THE GATHERING STORM*

By David Reynolds

CHURCHILL'S life was politics. His career as an MP ran, virtually unbroken, from 1900 to 1964 – almost the first two-thirds of the twentieth century. But although Churchill lived for politics, he lived by writing. Much of his income was earned as a journalist and author. At one end of the spectrum were scores of newspaper columns assessing contemporary events and politicians, summarising the plots of great novels, or just musing for money – as in 'Have You a Hobby?' or 'Are There Men in the Moon?' At the other extreme are large books such as the biographies of his father (1906) and of his martial ancestor, the first duke of Marlborough (1933–8), and his *History of the English-Speaking Peoples* (1956–8). Somewhere in between are autobiographical vignettes such as *The Malakand Field Force* (1898) and *My Early Life* (1930). But it is for his two sets of war memoirs that Churchill the historian is most remembered – six separate volumes on World War I (1923–31) and its aftermath, six more on World War II and its origins (1948–54).

J.H. Plumb observed that Churchill's historical work could be divided into two categories: 'formal, professional' histories and those dealing with 'contemporary events in which he himself was involved.'[1] Yet there is a sense in which, for Churchill, all history was autobiography. In July 1934, in an obituary of his much-loved cousin, 'Sunny', 9th duke of Marlborough, he wrote of 'the three or four hundred families which had for three or four hundred years guided the fortunes of the nation'.[2] Prominent among them, of course, were the Churchills, from the first duke via Lord Randolph to Winston himself. In his view, British history was a narrative of the deeds of great men (definitely men), and most of those men were intertwined with the saga of his own family. This approach to history and politics naturally privileges the significance of the individual and the uniqueness of events. By contrast, the thrust of most modern historiography has been to subsume the individual into

---

[1] J.H. Plumb, 'The Historian', in A. J. P. Taylor, *et al.*, *Churchill: Four Faces and the Man* (1969), 130. See also Maurice Ashley, *Churchill as Historian* (1968).

[2] Martin Gilbert, *Winston S. Churchill: Companion* (hereafter Gilbert, *CV*), v, part 2 (1981), 820. Like all students of Churchill, I am indebted to Martin Gilbert's volumes of biography and documents.

larger patterns (Marxism, the Annales school, the linguistic turn) or to emphasise the role of individual at the lower levels of society rather than through politics at the top.

Today, therefore, Churchill's philosophy of history is bound to seem somewhat outmoded. Yet his historical writings have been immensely influential, none more so than *The Second World War*, which between 1948 and 1954 was serialised in eighty magazines and newspapers worldwide, and went on to appear in hardback in fifty countries and eighteen languages.[3] Although Churchill was at pains not to describe his account as history, 'for that belongs to another generation', he expressed confidence that it was 'a contribution to history which will be of service to the future.'[4] Privately he was less diffident. He liked to say, on matters of controversy, that he would leave it to history but would be one of the historians. In the case of *The Second World War*, as Plumb observed, subsequent historians have moved down 'the broad avenues which he drove through war's confusion and complexity', with the result that 'Churchill the historian lies at the very heart of all historiography of the Second World War.'[5] At the beginning of the twenty-first century, how should this work be evaluated?

In this short essay, I shall confine myself to some reflections on the opening volume, *The Gathering Storm*, and particularly the first of its two books, entitled 'From War to War', which covers the period from 1919 to 1939. For it is in this volume – published in the United States in June 1948 and in Britain in October – that Churchill made perhaps his most enduring 'contribution to history', through his critique of appeasement in the 1930s. His aim was 'to show how easily the tragedy of the Second World War could have been prevented; how the malice of the wicked was reinforced by the weakness of the virtuous'. What he called 'this sad tale of wrong judgments formed by well-meaning and capable people' was intended to prove that the conflict was indeed 'The Unnecessary War'. His purpose, in short, was 'to lay the lessons of the past before the future'.[6] The Cassandra of the 1930s became the Thucydides of the 1940s.[7]

Before World War Two, 'appeasement', true to its French root, remained a neutral or even positive term, denoting the satisfaction of grievances by means of negotiation. Thereafter it became a term of

---

[3] John Ramsden, *'That Will Depend on Who Writes the History': Winston Churchill as His Own Historian*, Inaugural Lecture, Queen Mary and Westfield College, London, 22 October 1996, 12.

[4] Winston S. Churchill, *The Second World War* (hereafter *SWW*) (6 vols., 1948–54), I, vii.

[5] Plumb, 'The Historian', 149.

[6] *SWW*, I, vii–viii, 14, 270–1.

[7] Cf. D. C. Watt, 'Appeasement: The Rise of a Revisionist School?', *Political Quarterly*, 36 (1965), 198.

abuse, signifying peace at any price; likewise 'Munich' is now a synonym for betrayal. The supposed 'lessons' of appeasement have haunted postwar policymakers in America and Britain, be it Harry Truman over Korea in 1950, Anthony Eden during the Suez crisis of 1956, George Bush after Iraq invaded Kuwait in 1990, or the Blair government during the Kosovo war of 1999.[8] Of course, Churchill did not teach those lessons single-handed. Three Beaverbrook journalists, including Michael Foot, had already indicted Britain's leaders of the 1930s in the aftermath of Dunkirk – so successfully that their polemic against the *Guilty Men* sold 200,000 copies in its first six months.[9] Two other books also published in 1948 – *Munich, Prologue to Tragedy* by John Wheeler-Bennett and *Diplomatic Prelude* by Lewis Namier – took a similar line to *The Gathering Storm*. But Churchill's account of the interwar years was in a class of its own, selling *its* first 200,000 British copies in only two weeks.[10] Lengthy serialisation in *The New York Times*, *Life* magazine, and *The Daily Telegraph* (the latter running to forty-two extracts over two months) brought its principal themes to a huge audience. Nor was there anyone of comparable stature to defend appeasement. Britain's three premiers of the 1930s had all died discredited, without having written their memoirs – Ramsay MacDonald in 1937, Neville Chamberlain in 1940, and Stanley Baldwin in December 1947. Keith Feiling's official biography of Chamberlain, published in October 1946, did little to dispel the cloud of disapproval. What D. C. Watt has dubbed 'the Churchillian critique of appeasement' has held sway at a popular level for two generations.[11]

During that time, however, the historical documentation for the 1930s has changed dramatically. In the early 1970s, the official documents for the 1930s and World War Two became available at the Public Record Office under the new Thirty-Year Rule. Over the next decade a series of revisionist histories offered a more sympathetic account of the dilemmas faced by the appeasers. By the early 1980s, the interwar volume of Martin Gilbert's official biography, plus three massive companion volumes of documents, had provided much greater information about Churchill's views in the 1930s. And in the late 1990s, Churchill's original papers from the 1930s and 1940s were opened to

---

[8] Ernest R. May, *'Lessons' of the Past: The Use and Misuse of History in American Foreign Policy* (New York, 1973), 80–2; Anthony Eden, *Full Circle* (1960), 514–18 (where he uses the same image of a gathering storm); Alex Danchev, 'The Anschluss', *Review of International Studies*, 20 (1994), 97–101; David Reynolds, *Britannia Overruled: British Policy and World Power in the Twentieth Century* (second edn, 2000), 293.

[9] 'Cato', *Guilty Men* (reprint edn, 1998), xv.

[10] See Churchill College Archives Centre, Cambridge, Winston Churchill papers (hereafter CHUR), 4/24B, f. 334.

[11] Watt, 'Churchill and Appeasement', in Robert Blake and Wm Roger Louis, eds., *Churchill* (Oxford, 1993), esp. 199–201.

public inspection. Thus, from the vantage point of the early twenty-first century, historians can view appeasement, Churchill and *The Gathering Storm* from a new perspective. This essay, part of the larger project on the war memoirs, is a contribution to that reappraisal.

Given its historiographical impact, it is ironic that *The Gathering Storm* nearly did not appear. Churchill's basic contract was for five volumes, not six. Volume one was initially intended to run to the end of 1940 – a period eventually covered in two volumes. As late as January 1947, he envisaged only five chapters to take the reader from 1919 to the outbreak of war in September 1939. One chapter would survey the period 1919 to 1934, a second would deal with the rise of Hitler, 1931–8, and a third would examine British rearmament up to 1939. After a chapter devoted to Munich, one more, entitled 'The Interlude', would take the reader up to the outbreak of war.[12] It was not until Churchill began seriously to work on the interwar years during 1947 that the scope of this part of the book expanded dramatically, with outlines for eleven chapters, seventeen and even twenty-four chapters, before contracting down to the final twenty-one.

Self-evidently, five sketchy chapters about the appeasement era in a volume running to December 1940 would have had far less impact than the eventual first book of *The Gathering Storm*. Indeed the title itself, so evocative for Churchill's thesis, only emerged late in the day. Until October 1947, Churchill's working title was 'The Downward Path', for which he then substituted 'Toward Catastrophe'. Both of these seemed too negative to his publishers, particularly in the United States, given that the chapters were supposed to form the overture to his belated entry into Number Ten Downing Street. On 30 January 1948, just a few weeks before serialisation was to begin, Churchill was still canvassing suggestions for the title. It was his veteran literary agent, Emery Reves, who came up with the phrase 'The Gathering Storm'. This conveyed the sense of looming danger in a suitably 'crescendo' form.[13]

Why did the thrust of *The Gathering Storm* emerge relatively late in the day? There are, I think, three main reasons, each of them illustrative of Churchill the historian – the sources at his disposal, his method of writing and his sensitivity to the present.

As with most of his books since the biography of his father, Churchill employed a team of researchers. For *The Second World War*, this was an immensely distinguished team. Its anchor was William Deakin, a professional historian and Oxford don, who had particular responsibility

[12] See outlines in CHUR 4/74, f. 24 and CHUR 4/75, f. 1.
[13] CHUR 4/74, ff. 43, 61, and CHUR 4/24B, ff. 317–319; cf. Martin Gilbert, *Winston S. Churchill*, VIII (1988), 394–5.

for political and diplomatic matters. The naval side was handled by a retired officer, Commander Gordon Allen. For military affairs and high policymaking, Churchill used General Hastings Ismay, wartime military secretary to the cabinet, and General Sir Henry Pownall, who had been on the secretariat of the committee of imperial defence from 1933 to 1936 and was vice-chief of the imperial general staff in 1941. Ismay and Pownall were particularly well connected. The former was 'devilling' for Churchill even before he retired from the cabinet office in November 1946, while Pownall was a member of the advisory panel for the official military histories of the war, which gave him ready access to confidential material. Moreover, Churchill's prestige and connections also opened doors that would have been closed to ordinary historians.

In consequence, the source material for volume one is not simply Churchill's own documents from the period, as one might expect in the case of someone who was out of office. It also includes inside information of high quality on specific topics. For instance, on comparative air strengths in the 1930s, Pownall obtained statistical data from official contacts in France and the air ministry historical branch, while Churchill wrote direct to General Carl Spaatz, head of the Army Air Force in Washington, who had commanded the AAF in Britain in 1942. From half a dozen American agencies, Spaatz collated US data on German air strength.[14] To take another example, Churchill's account of Anthony Eden's resignation as foreign secretary in February 1938 drew on the diary of Oliver Harvey, Eden's private secretary, and on comments by several government ministers of the time. It was even checked by the cabinet secretary, Norman Brook, against the cabinet minutes. Consequently, Churchill was able to reveal for the first time that Eden's breach with Chamberlain occurred over policy towards the United States as well as Italy – ironically giving the world a far fuller account of this episode than Eden himself had done hitherto. In short, Churchill's indictment of appeasement was that of an outsider blessed with inside information. This was the case for the prosecution garnished with evidence from the defence.

The wealth of information that became available to Churchill is, I think, one reason why his account of the 1930s expanded so dramatically and why he found it difficult to control. A second reason is the way Churchill worked: he did not marshal that mass of information until late in the day. His preoccupation in 1946 and the first half of 1947

---

[14] See correspondence in CHUR 4/140A: the graph comparing French and German output of first-line aircraft, printed as appendix E of *The Gathering Storm*, was based on material provided via Pownall's friend, General Alphonse-Joseph Georges – *ibid.*, ff 23–32.

was the summer and autumn of 1940, when he was in power and Britain's fate lay in the balance. Meanwhile, his researchers were compiling essays on specific topics, using the official documents to which they had access as well as published sources such as the Nuremburg trials. At the same time, they were collating Churchill's own documents from the 1930s, particularly his speeches and correspondence with government ministers. These were printed as galleys at an early stage, allowing him to cut and paste lengthy quotation into his text. This was Churchill's standard method of writing his histories. After absorbing the material, he would start to cast it in his own mould, usually in lengthy late-night orations as he paced up and down his study at Chartwell – a pair of secretaries taking turns with the dictation, research assistants in attendance to give factual advice. He wrote, as he liked to say, 'from mouth to hand'.[15]

But this was an incremental process. Not only the documents but also Churchill's own text were produced as galley proofs: he preferred to revise from the printed page, often doing minor corrections in bed first thing in the morning. These galleys went through three, four or even five versions, with titles such as 'Almost Final', 'Provisional Final' and 'Final' (to which the caveat was added, in large type: 'Subject to Full Freedom of Proof Correction'). Since no publisher would tolerate such a costly method of editing, Churchill did this at his own expense (out of the munificent advances), using the Chiswick Press, a branch of the publishers Eyre and Spottiswoode.[16] The eventual book was set up in new type from those galleys by his publishers, often very late in the day. This, incidentally, helps explain the numerous printing errors in the British edition of *The Gathering Storm*, which had to be rectified at the last minute by two pages of corrections and then a further errata slip. Some of these errors were deeply embarrassing. On page fifty-six of the first edition we are told that the French army was 'the poop of the life of France'. That is corrected on the errata slip: 'For "poop" read "prop".'

Gradually Churchill's dictated narrative put flesh on his documentary skeleton. But it was a common complaint – from his researchers, his publishers and not least his wife – that the bones still tended to show through. With so much of the material emanating from others, and with political duties as leader of the opposition taking up a good deal of time, Churchill found it hard to get his mind round the whole book. It usually required a special vacation, paid for by his publishers, at which Churchill, plus secretaries and members of his research team, engaged in what was known as 'bulldozing' the final text. This entailed

[15] Robert Rhodes James, *Churchill: A Study in Failure* (Harmondsworth, 1973), 31.
[16] By June 1947 he already owed them over £1,400 – CHUR 4/24A, f.145.

pruning the quotations, or relegating them to the ever-swelling appendices, and ensuring that Churchill's own voice came through clearly. For the first volume, the bulldozing was done in the warmth and opulence of the Mamounia Hotel in Marrakesh between 11 December 1947 and 18 January 1948 (his wife stayed behind to enjoy the austerity of an Attlee Christmas). From Marrakesh, corrected galleys were sent almost daily to the Chiswick Press, and new proofs received with equal frequency. It was only at this late stage that the book took coherent shape.

As Churchill bulldozed the 1930s, he brooded on the 1940s. In mid-November, he received a message from Henry Luce, the owner of *Life* magazine, who was still unhappy that the mass of documents marred the 'architectural sense' and impeded 'analytical insight'. Churchill replied defensively that he had so far been assembling the material in chronological order and had not yet had time 'to read Book I through at a run'. This he said he would do at Marrakesh. The analytical point he intended to bring out was that 'in those years there happened exactly what is happening today, namely no coherent or persistent policy, even in fundamental matters, among the good peoples, but deadly planning among the bad. The good peoples, as now, drifted hither and thither, to and fro, according to the changing winds of public opinion and the desire of public men of medium stature to gain majorities and office at party elections.'[17]

Churchill had used the phrase 'The Unnecessary War' at least as early as October 1940. He deployed it publicly in a major speech in Brussels in November 1945.[18] So the basic theme was not new. But his conviction that the conflict had resulted, in large measure, from a failure of political leadership sharpened in 1946–8 amid the deepening Cold War. For Hitler, read Stalin (each engaged in 'deadly planning'); for Baldwin, read Attlee (those 'public men of medium stature'). In his 'Iron Curtain' speech at Fulton in March 1946 he insisted that there 'never was a war in all history easier to prevent by timely action', adding 'I saw it all coming and cried aloud to my own fellow-countrymen and to the world, but no one paid any attention.' And so, said Churchill, 'one by one we were all sucked into the awful whirlpool. We surely must not let that happen again.' The analogies were reiterated in his political speeches during 1948, at the same time as his account of the 1930s unfolded in newspaper articles and then in volume form. The Berlin crisis, he told a mass rally of 100,000 Tories in June 1948,

[17] Luce to Churchill, 18 Nov. 1947, and Churchill to Luce, 22 Nov. 1947, quoted in Gilbert, *Churchill*, VIII, 357–8.

[18] John Colville, *The Fringes of Power: Downing Street Diaries, 1939–1955* (1985), 278; Robert Rhodes James (ed.), *Winston S. Churchill: His Complete Speeches, 1897–1963* (hereafter Churchill, *Complete Speeches*) (8 vols., New York, 1974), VII, 7251, 16 Nov. 1945.

'raises issues as grave as those which we now know were at stake at Munich ten years ago. It is our hearts' desire that peace may be preserved, but we should all have learned by now that there is no safety in yielding to dictators, whether Nazi or Communist.'[19]

It was this political moral, painfully apt for contemporaries, that gave the first book of Churchill's war memoirs its emotional power. Several readers went so far as to liken the story to a classical tragedy.[20] The gathering storm, clearly discerned on the horizon by men of vision, was ignored by politicians of lesser stature. How does Churchill's account stand up to scrutiny fifty years on? How far was he aware of its deficiencies at the time? In addressing these questions within a brief compass, I shall focus on four main issues: leadership, defence, foreign policy, and domestic politics.

Who were these mediocre leaders, blind to the gathering storm? Not surprisingly, Churchill is kind to the Conservative government of 1924–9, in which he was chancellor of the exchequer. This is a period of 'very considerable recovery' at home and genuine 'distinction' in foreign policy, particularly thanks to the Treaty of Locarno. In 1929 'the state of Europe was tranquil, as it had not been for twenty years, and was not to be for at least another twenty'. Thereafter the rot set in. The prime minister from 1929 to 1935 was Ramsay MacDonald, but Churchill has little to say about him. In the book, MacDonald is a shadowy figure, 'brooding supinely' and in a state of 'increasing decrepitude' over a predominantly Tory government after 1931.[21]

In *The Gathering Storm* the culpable figures are MacDonald's successors as premier, Stanley Baldwin and Neville Chamberlain. (They were also the two Tory leaders who kept Churchill out of office during the 1930s.) The best Churchill can say for Baldwin is that he was 'the greatest Party manager the Conservatives ever had'; we are told that he 'took no active share in foreign policy' apart from his 'well-known desire for peace and a quiet life.'[22] Although Churchill did not write the famous index entry on Baldwin ('confesses putting party before country'), that summed up his sentiments. Whereas Baldwin was indicted for lethargy, political opportunism and indifference to foreign affairs; Chamberlain's crimes were hubris, illusions and mental rigidity. If Baldwin wanted to be left in peace, Chamberlain wanted to make peace. In dealing with Hitler, Churchill argues, this was folly of the highest order. He singles

[19] Quotations from Churchill, *Speeches*, VII, 7292–3 (5 March 1946) and 7671 (26 June 1948).

[20] For instance, Alfred Duff Cooper to WSC, 5 August 1948, CHUR 4/19; Sir Harold Butler, 'Mr Churchill and the Unnecessary War', *The Fortnightly*, 163, Oct. 1948, 227.

[21] *SWW*, I, 30, 52.

[22] *SWW*, I, 26, 187.

out Chamberlain's 'long series of miscalculations, and misjudgments of men and facts', though acknowledging that his 'motives have never been impugned'.[23] In Churchill's account, each man, for different reasons, wreaks appalling damage – from indolence or arrogance, they facilitated Hitler's resistible rise and thus an unnecessary war.

There is, however, a tension in Churchill's account. Baldwin was premier from 1935 to 1937, Chamberlain from 1937 to 1940. On Churchill's own admission, it was during the period 1931–5 that 'the entire situation on the Continent was reversed'. He says that 'once Hitler's Germany had been allowed to rearm without active interference by the Allies and former associated Powers, a second World War was almost certain'. (An earlier draft even used the word 'inevitable'.)[24] The years 1931–5 were the MacDonald era – hence Churchill's concern to represent Baldwin as 'the virtual Prime Minister' during that period.[25] But the main way in which he resolves the tension is to highlight a series of missed opportunities *after* 1935. In today's jargon, book one of *The Gathering Storm* is at times almost an exercise in counterfactual history.[26]

At the beginning of chapter eleven, for instance, he depicts 'a new atmosphere in England' in early 1936. The obvious breakdown of collective security and a general backlash against the Hoare–Laval pact dividing up Abysssinia had, he argued, created a cross-party consensus that was 'now prepared to contemplate war against Fascist or Nazi tyranny'. Yet the government stuck to its 'policy of moderation, half-measures and keeping things quiet'.[27] Critically, there was no reaction to Hitler's re-occupation of the Rhineland in March. In an early draft of the end of chapter thirteen, Churchill had written: 'Nothing could have stopped Hitler after the seizure of the Rhineland except a very serious war.' In the published text, however, this categorical judgement is heavily qualified: 'Many say that nothing except war could have stopped Hitler after we had submitted to the seizure of the Rhineland. This may indeed be the verdict of future generations. Much, however, could have been done to make us better prepared and thus lessen our hazards. And who shall say what could not have happened?'[28]

A second putative 'turning point' occurs at the end of 1936, where Churchill juxtaposes Baldwin's now notorious speech of 'appalling

[23] *SWW*, 1, 173–4, 255.
[24] *SWW*, 1, 52 and 148; cf. CHUR 4/85, f.4.
[25] *SWW*, 1, 94.
[26] It is worth noting that in 1931 Churchill contributed a long essay under the title 'If Lee Had Not Won the Battle of Gettysburg' to a collection entitled *If It Had Happened Otherwise*.
[27] *SWW*, 1, 147–8.
[28] CHUR 4/87, f. 65; cf. *SWW*, 1, 186.

frankness' to the Commons on 12 November and the crisis over Edward VIII's abdication the following month. Through the 'Provisional Semi-Final' version Baldwin's speech was placed as the climax of an earlier chapter on the loss of air parity from 1933 to 1936. This documented Baldwin's February 1934 pledge that Britain would keep abreast of Germany, his denials of Churchill's warnings that parity had been lost, his May 1936 'confession' that it had and, finally, his 12 November admission that, had he gone to the country on a rearmament platform, the outcome would have been certain defeat. In this form, the chapter had enormous power as a cumulative indictment of Baldwin. But at the 'Provisional Final' stage, Churchill sacrificed that in order to play up another turning point. He moved the November material into a later chapter on 1936–7, 'The Loaded Pause', and there followed it with a two-page account of the Abdication (previously a single sentence at the end of the draft on 'Air Parity'). In this treatment, Baldwin's 'appalling frankness' in admitting 'that he had not done his duty with regard to national safety because he was afraid of losing the election' is described as 'an incident without parallel in our Parliamentary history'. The impression produced on the House was 'so painful that it might well have been fatal' to Baldwin but for his adroit handling of the king's affair. Just at this moment, asserts Churchill, the cross-party forces for 'Arms and the Covenant' that he had been marshalling were on the verge of a breakthrough. But the contrast between Baldwin's shrewd judgement of public opinion and Churchill's pleas that the king be given time (to get over his infatuation) turned the tables for the two of them. Churchill wrote that the forces he had gathered on defence were 'estranged or dissolved' and that 'I was so smitten in public opinion that it was the almost universal view that my political life was ended.'[29]

Undoubtedly Baldwin did retrieve himself over the Abdication, but historian Paul Addison is surely right that Churchill greatly exaggerated the effect of the crisis on the 'Arms and the Covenant' movement. 'The reason why his campaign faltered after December 1936 was that 1937 saw a relaxation of Anglo-German tensions' that lasted until the Austrian Anschluss in March 1938.[30] Nevertheless, Churchill's interpretation has become widely accepted. Even more so has his version of what Baldwin told the Commons on 12 November. In *The Gathering Storm* Churchill's extracts from Baldwin's speech and his own commentary imply that Baldwin was referring to the 1935 election. In fact, as Baldwin's full text makes clear, he was referring to 1933–4, in the wake of the notorious 'pacificist' victory at the East Fulham by-

[29] *SWW* I, 169–71; cf. CHUR 4/81.
[30] Paul Addison, *Churchill on the Home Front, 1900–1955* (1992), 323.

election and was contrasting that with his success in gaining a mandate in 1935 on a clear, if cautious, platform for rearmament. All this was said by Baldwin in justification of his aphorism that 'a democracy is always two years behind the dictator'. Reginald Bassett suggested, just after *The Gathering Storm* appeared that Churchill was following a long line of writers who had quoted selectively and misleadingly from Baldwin's speech.[31] In fact, it is possible that Churchill was in their vanguard. As drafts make clear, the highly expurgated version of Baldwin's speech used in *The Gathering Storm* was taken verbatim from Churchill's June 1938 collection of speeches entitled *Arms and the Covenant*. There the editor, his son Randolph, had appended some of Baldwin's words on 12 November 1936 to Churchill's own 'locust years' speech the same day.[32] Ellipsis points in this text indicate two explicit omissions from Baldwin's words, but there are, in fact, three other unacknowledged gaps. Although proof copies of *Arms and the Covenant* do not survive in Churchill's papers, Winston made it clear to Randolph that 'I must have the final word in a matter which so closely concerns myself, upon what goes in or out.'[33] Whoever was responsible, this was an early and accessible version of the 'appalling frankness' speech, on which others may well have relied. In 1948 *The Gathering Storm* was following the pack hunting Baldwin, but *Arms and the Covenant* may have started them running a decade before.

Underpinning Churchill's account of the years 1936–8 is his hopeful estimate of potential German resistance to Hitler. Repeatedly he asserts or implies that a firmer stand by Britain and France would have destroyed Hitler's credibility and triggered a military putsch. This is evident in his treatment of the Rhineland crisis of 1936 and can be seen particularly in the key chapter about Munich. Churchill was confident that, if Britain and France had taken a tough line over Czechoslovakia, the German generals would have mounted a *coup* against Hitler. He took seriously their assertions to this effect at the Nuremburg trials and also under private interrogation, as relayed by Ismay from British military sources in Germany, particularly those of General Franz Halder, then army chief of staff. But readers of Churchill's draft questioned his interpretation. Sir Orme Sargent, the deputy under-secretary at the foreign office and critic of Munich in 1938, warned against 'overrating the possibility of an army revolt in September 1938 ... the generals were repeatedly planning revolts; but at the last

[31] R. Bassett, 'Telling the Truth to the People: The Myth of the Baldwin "Confession"', *The Cambridge Journal*, II, 1 (Oct. 1948), 84–95, especially 95, note 1. See also Keith Middlemas and John Barnes, *Baldwin: A Biography* (1969), 969–73.

[32] *SWW*, I, 169; cf. CHUR 4/81, f.175, and *Arms and the Covenant*, 385–6.

[33] WSC to Randolph, 3 April 1938, Chartwell Trust papers, CHAR 8/598, ff. 1–2 (Churchill College, Cambridge).

moment they drew back, either because the situation was too favourable for Germany, or because it was so unfavourable that they could not as patriots play into the hands of the enemy'.[34] From inside Churchill's research team, Deakin also advised him not to 'put too much store on Halder's account', while Pownall said he had found no corroborative evidence in the foreign or cabinet office records and warned that 'Halder, as you know, is apt to "shoot a line".'[35] In response, Churchill softened his tone. The phrase 'We now know for certain what was happening on the other side' became 'We may now look behind the brazen front which Hitler presented to the British and French governments.' Echoing Sargent, he added the qualification that 'the generals were repeatedly planning revolts, and as often drew back at the last moment for one reason or another'. He also acknowledged: 'It was to the interest of the parties concerned after they were prisoners of the Allies to dwell on their efforts for peace.' But he retained a lengthy version of the generals' story and noted that it 'has been accepted as genuine by various authorities who have examined it. If it should eventually be accepted as historical truth, it will be another example of the very small accidents upon which the fortunes of mankind turn.' He summed up 'The Tragedy of Munich' as follows: 'Hitler's judgment had been once more decisively vindicated. The German General Staff was utterly abashed ... Thus did Hitler become the undisputed master of Germany, and the path was clear for the great design.'[36]

Here is an excellent example of Churchill's principles of interpretation: contingency not determinism, an emphasis on individuals rather than broad forces, and the ostensible deference paid to 'history' while seducing future historians. Of course, Churchill's counterfactuals remain imponderable, but it is a tribute both to his vision and his craftsmanship that many of his turning points are the ones that scholars still ponder.[37] Although *The Gathering Storm* had not ended historical debate – far from it – Churchill was eminently successful in shaping the agenda.

[34] Sargent to WSC, 15 Dec. 1947, CHUR 4/141A. f. 126. Sargent was also drawing on the comments of his colleague Ivone Kirkpatrick, who had served in the Berlin Embassy in 1933–8.
[35] Memos by Pownall [20 Sept. 1947], and Deakin, undated [early 1948], in CHUR 4/91, ff. 98, 120–1.
[36] *SWW*, I, 243–6, 250; cf. CHUR 4/91, f. 113.
[37] For instance, Hitler's most recent biographer highlights the importance of the Rhineland occupation in 1936 for the Führer's domestic position and, while admitting it is 'an open question' whether the 'ill-coordinated' plotting in 1938 'would have come to anything', argues that the 'legacy of Munich was fatally to weaken those who might even now have constrained Hitler', Ian Kershaw, *Hitler* (2 vols., 1998, 2000), I: 589–91, II: 123–5.

In shaping it, but not setting it in stone. If we look at Churchill's treatment of appeasement, we can see how *The Gathering Storm* is at odds with the revisionism of historians writing after the archives became open in the early 1970s.

On fundamental issues of defence and diplomacy, Churchill was, of course, essentially right. In the early 1930s he repeatedly urged that it was folly for the victors either to disarm or to allow Germany to rearm while German grievances had not been resolved. His whistle-blowing about the pace of German air rearmament after 1933 helped galvanise the government into belated action over air defence and his lurid warnings about Hitler's intentions were amply vindicated by the unfolding of events. The first book of *The Gathering Storm* documents Churchill's public statements about Hitler and his secret intelligence about German rearmament, often leaked by anxious officials, validating both against evidence from postwar sources. The official biography develops these themes with rich detail. But there is more to say on these matters. Air rearmament was not the totality of defence issues, nor the Nazi threat the sum of 1930s diplomacy.

It is now clear that Churchill was not so much a lone voice calling for rearmament in the 1930s but one of a number of actors – in office, officialdom, the military and parliament – engaged in a complex bureaucratic battle to shift the government from its early ignorance and complacency about the growth of the Nazi airforce. The leaks to Churchill were only a facet of this struggle, in which, for instance, Chamberlain shared Churchill's priorities more than Baldwin's. Yet even today, and certainly in the 1930s, reliable evidence is lacking for the growth of Hitler's Luftwaffe during its early years. Even numbers of aircraft, where the data exists, are an insufficient guide. What matters are serviceable front-line planes, in other words combat aircraft for which the Luftwaffe had fuel, spare parts and trained pilots to keep in the air in time of war. On these criteria, Richard Overy, a historian of the German war economy, has argued that Churchill exaggerated German potential, for instance predicting in September 1935 a total of 2,000 first-line aircraft by October 1936 and possibly 3,000 a year after that. In fact, says Overy, the figure was less than 3,000 even in September 1939. In any case, the statistics were not used at the time as precision weapons but rather as bludgeons to create alarm and thus provoke action. Churchill admitted as much in *The Gathering Storm*. 'I strove my utmost to galvanise the Government into vehemence and extraordinary preparation, even at the cost of world alarm. In these endeavours no doubt I painted the picture even darker than it was.'[38]

---

[38] R. J. Overy, 'German Air Strength 1933 to 1939: A Note', *Historical Journal*, 27 (1984), 465–71, esp. note 5; *SWW*, I, 180.

Churchill and others were partly victims of German disinformation, spread assiduously by General Erhard Milch and staff in the air ministry. But their exaggerations about the potential of the Luftwaffe were reinforced by exaggerated fears about bombing itself. During the course of the Second World War, 147,000 people were killed or maimed in the whole of the United Kingdom as a result of aerial bombardment.[39] But when Churchill addressed the Commons in November 1934 he predicted that, in seven to ten days of intensive bombing, at least 30,000 to 40,000 Londoners would be killed or maimed and that, 'under the pressure of continuous air attack', at least three or four million people would flee the metropolis for the surrounding countryside. In July 1936, he was even more alarmist. As part of the delegation of senior MPs to see Baldwin, his estimates for bomb tonnage and casualty rates implied figures of 5,000 dead and 150,000 wounded from a single all-out raid on London.[40] Churchill was not alone in such fears. What Uri Bialer has called 'the shadow of the bomber' hung over British life throughout the 1930s. Writing in 1966, Harold Macmillan recalled that 'we thought of air warfare in 1938 rather as people think of nuclear warfare today'. That was not mere popular paranoia, stirred up by H. G. Wells, Bertrand Russell, and the like. In October 1936 the Joint Planning Sub-Committee of the Chiefs of Staff estimated that 20,000 casualties might be expected in London in the first twenty-four hours of an air attack, rising within a week to around 150,000.[41]

As Wesley Wark has shown, the exaggerations of German air strength and of the potency of bombing, to which Churchill contributed, had a counter-productive effect on the government. Having underestimated the German air threat in 1933–6, Whitehall swung to the opposite extreme in 1936–8. The fear of German airpower was much in the minds of both the chiefs of staff and Chamberlain himself as they debated whether to take a stand over Czechoslovakia. In reality the German air staff had concluded that they could not deliver a knock-out blow against Britain. But, as Chamberlain told his cabinet after his second visit to Hitler in September 1938 (and only his second round-trip in a plane), as he flew back up the Thames toward London 'he had imagined a German bomber flying the same course, he had asked himself what degree of protection they could afford to the thousands of homes which he had seen stretched out below him, and he had felt that we were in no position to justify waging a war today in order to prevent a war hereafter'.[42]

---

[39] Basil Collier, *The Defence of the United Kingdom* (1957), 528.
[40] Winston S. Churchill, *Arms and the Covenant* (1938), 172–3; Gilbert, *CV*, v, part 3, 273–4.
[41] Harold Macmillan, *Winds of Change, 1914–1939* (1966), 575; Uri Bialer, *The Shadow of the Bomber* (1980), 130.

The frenzied mid-1930s debate about the 'air menace' therefore helped galvanise RAF modernisation, but it also induced diplomatic paralysis. Moreover, it diverted attention from the other two services, particularly the army – a consequence deplored at the time by none other than Henry Pownall, then an army bureaucrat![43] A British Expeditionary Force for France and Belgium was low on Churchill's list of priorities. When he spoke of his 'Grand Alliance' with France, he meant 'the Union of the British Fleet and the French Army, together with their combined Air Forces'. Or, as he put it in the early 1930s, 'Thank God for the French Army.'[44] It is also worth noting that, in contrast with his passion for air rearmament, Churchill was slow to support peacetime conscription. Although this issue was popular with many local Conservative associations during 1938 and was pushed strongly by dissident MPs such as Leopold Amery, Churchill did not speak out on the matter and only signed two of the five Commons motions about national service introduced between July 1938 and April 1939. At late as 18 April 1939, after Hitler had devoured Czechoslovakia and Britain had guaranteed Poland, Churchill was not among sixty-five MPs (many of them Tories, including his son-in-law Duncan Sandys) who demanded 'immediate acceptance of the principle of the compulsory mobilisation of the man, munition, and money power of the nation'. Compulsory national service had socialistic undertones and ran against national custom, but Churchill's reticence also reflected his preoccupation with the air and sea, not the land. He wrote in a newspaper article in May 1938, 'if our Fleet and our Air Force are adequate, there is no need for conscription in time of peace. No one has ever been able to give a satisfactory answer to the question: "What do you want conscription for?" '[45]

As Donald Cameron Watt has observed, Churchill's rearmament campaign 'never focused on the issues that might have made an impact on German military opinion – military arms production, conscription, a Continental commitment'.[46] Air rearmament had a bias towards isolationism – the defence of the United Kingdom. Greater resources

[42] Wesley K. Wark, *The Ultimate Enemy: British Intelligence and Nazi Germany, 1933–1939* (Oxford, 1986), ch. 3; Cab 42 (38), 24 Sept. 1938, CAB 23/95 (Public Record Office, Kew).

[43] Pownall blamed 'Air Panic', whipped up by Churchill and others, for the July 1934 cutback in funds for the army expansion programme. See Martin Gilbert, *Winston S. Churchill*, v (1976), 553 note.

[44] Both of these remarks are quoted in *SWW* I, respectively 179 and 59.

[45] N.J. Crowson, *Facing Fascism: The Conservative Party and the European Dictators, 1935–1940* (1995), 158–63; cf. 'Future Safeguards of National Defence', *News of the World*, 1 May 1938, in Michael Wolff, ed., *The Collected Essays of Sir Winston Churchill* (4 vols., Bristol, 1976), I, 402.

[46] Watt, 'Churchill and Appeasement', 204.

for the army would have implied a continental strategy, projecting British power across the Channel. In all this, of course, Churchill was broadly at one with Chamberlain, most politicians and public opinion. That is why in May 1940 there were only 10 British divisions alongside 104 French, 22 Belgian and 8 Dutch on the Western Front. Such were the ghosts of the Somme and Passchendaele that in 1934 MacDonald had decreed that the words 'Expeditionary Force' not be used in public statements or even official documents. As the military critic Basil Liddell Hart wrote of the Western Front of 1914–18, 'It was heroic, but was it necessary? It was magnificent, but was it war?'[47] Churchill agreed that, even if Britain had to fight, a repeat of Flanders Fields would indeed be an unnecessary war. What he does *not* say about rearmament in *The Gathering Storm*, therefore points us on to his equivocations about mass invasion of the continent in later volumes of memoirs. And his refrain, 'Thank God for the French Army' – which only voiced the unspoken assumptions of most policymakers – reminds us that he, like they, never imagined the collapse of the Western Front in 1940. In short, one might argue that Churchill's warnings against appeasement in the 1930s played a part in helping win the Battle of Britain, but they did nothing to avert the prior disaster of the Battle of France.

On foreign policy, as on defence, Churchill's retrospective concentration on Germany (informed by the events of 1940) distorts the diplomacy of the 1930s and, at times, his own part in it.

Since the revisionism of the 1970s, it is a commonplace of historical scholarship that British policymakers discerned a potential three-front threat in the 1930s. The menace of German airpower at home was reinforced by Japan's challenge to Britain's substantial interests in China and Southeast Asia and by Italy's threat to the Eastern Mediterranean and the Suez lifeline to India. Japan was, in fact, the main concern in the early 1930s, after its invasion of Manchuria, and this prompted the beginnings of British rearmament. Although the revival of German power, especially in the air, took precedence after Hitler gained power in 1933, in 1936–7 it was the combination of Mussolini's empire-building in Ethiopia and the outbreak of the Spanish Civil War that preoccupied ministers and focused their attention on the Mediterranean. Not until 1938, with first the Austrian Anschluss and then the Czech crisis, did Germany in Europe return to centre-stage. But policymakers could not ignore the fact that, from July 1937, Japanese and Chinese forces were locked in a major war across eastern China.

In *The Gathering Storm*, however, Churchill's eyes are fixed on Berlin. After a couple of pages on the Manchurian crisis in chapter five, there is virtually nothing about events in Asia. Only from a minute by

[47] Brian Bond, *Liddell Hart: A Study of His Military Thought* (1976), 68 and 85.

Churchill when first lord of the admiralty in February 1940, printed in an appendix, does one learn that Japan had 'for two and a half years been engaged in a most ruinous war in China'. The almost total omission of the Far East from the volume was noted by Denis Kelly, one of Churchill's junior research assistants, very late in the day, on 8 January 1948. At his suggestion a brief reference to Japan's signature in 1936 of the Anti-Comintern Pact was inserted in chapter twelve. Asked for his advice, Deakin suggested on 31 January that the Japanese story should be dealt with as 'an introduction to their entry into war' in 1941. 'All right', Churchill agreed, and the matter was relegated to volume three.[48]

Although there is more reference to Mediterranean affairs in *The Gathering Storm*, they do not bulk large. To a considerable extent, as Robert Rhodes James observed thirty years ago, this mirrors Churchill's perspective in the 1930s. Warning the Commons about the real priorities as the Abyssinian crisis deepened in October 1935, Churchill pointed to German rearmament: '*There* is the dominant factor; *there* is the factor which dwarfs all others.'[49] Contrary to many League enthusiasts, notably Eden, Churchill was not keen to make Italian aggression a major moral and political issue. In Europe, Mussolini (about whom Churchill continued to make complimentary references in public) was a potential bulwark against German expansion. Churchill endorsed the Stresa agreement of April 1935, which committed Britain, France and Italy to maintaining the independence of Austria. On the other hand, Churchill could see the dangers to the League's credibility if its council in Geneva decided on half-hearted sanctions against Mussolini, which then failed. That could irreparably damage the League's role in containing Germany. At the height of the furore over the Hoare–Laval Pact, Churchill was vacationing in Spain and North Africa. 'Looking back', he wrote in *The Gathering Storm*, 'I think I ought to have come home', speculating that he might have been able to marshal the anti-government forces and bring down 'the Baldwin régime'. More likely, as historian Graham Stewart has observed, his speeches and correspondence at the time suggest that he (and many in the government) was genuinely undecided as to whether 'Geneva or Stresa represented the best hope of containing Germany.' Keeping away from Westminster allowed him to stay on the fence.[50]

The Spanish Civil War merits only a brief discussion in chapter twelve of *The Gathering Storm*. There Churchill presents the two sides as

---

[48] *SWW*, I, 67–9, 168, 598; cf. CHUR 4/141B, ff. 311–13.
[49] Rhodes James, *Churchill*, 328–9.
[50] *SWW*. I, 144; cf. Graham Stewart, *Burying Caesar: Churchill, Chamberlain and the Battle for the Tory Party* (1999), 243.

equally barbarous and states: 'In this quarrel I was neutral.' His main point is to endorse the official policy of non-intervention, on the grounds that, 'with all the rest they had on their hands the British Government were right to keep out of Spain.'[51] In the early months of the Civil War, however, Churchill definitely leaned towards Franco and 'the Anti-Red' forces, as he often called them. 'I am thankful the Spanish Nationalists are making progress', he told his wife in September 1936, adding that it would be 'better for the safety of all if the Communists are crushed'. The following April he admitted to the Commons that, despite his attempts to remain neutral, 'I will not pretend that, if I had to choose between Communism and Nazi-ism, I would choose Communism.'[52] Churchill, it should be remembered, remained a visceral anti-Bolshevik. Although he did not agree with many of the Tory right that Nazi Germany might be used to contain Bolshevism, it is possible that in 1936-7, with Hitler less menacing after the Rhineland crisis, Churchill's sense of priorities may temporarily have wavered. In February and April 1936, Popular Front governments came to power with Communist support in Spain and then France. In Spain, the election began the descent to civil war; in France, the ensuing rift between left and right seemed, at times, to presage something similar. Reiterating the need for Britain and France to keep out, he hinted in an article in August 1936, of deeper fears. A 'revivified Fascist Spain in close sympathy with France and Germany is one kind of disaster. A Communist Spain spreading its snaky tentacles through Portugal and France is another, and many may think the worse.'[53] It has often been observed that Churchill's lack of ideological zeal about Italy and Spain distanced him from many of his potential allies on the centre and left who supported the League. It is also possible that at times in 1936-7, he was uncertain about the greatest international dangers. Not until 1938-9, with Hitler on the march again and Franco in the ascendant, did he state clearly that a Fascist victory in Spain would be more dangerous to the British Empire.

On the other side of the diplomatic fence, Churchill tended to exaggerate the potential for a 'Grand Alliance' against Germany. This is a familiar point and can be discussed more briefly. With regard to France, it remains a matter of debate how far British appeasement was the reason or the pretext for French inertia in the 1930s. Churchill, as usual, includes qualifying passages that carefully straddle this divide. 'More than once in these fluid years French Ministers in their ever-

---

[51] *SWW*, I, 167.

[52] Gilbert, *Churchill*, v, 785; Churchill, *Speeches*, vi, 5850.

[53] See Rhodes James, *Churchill*, 406-9, quotation from 407; cf. David Carlton, *Churchill and the Soviet Union* (Manchester, 2000), 50-61.

changing Governments were content to find in British pacifism an excuse for their own. Be that as it may', he adds, 'they did not meet with any encouragement to resist German aggression from the British.' And in characteristically counter-factual mode, he leaves the reader with the impression that, over the Rhineland and on other occasions, British resolve could have tipped the balance. Yet most historians of the period tend to locate relations with Britain in a complex of factors – political, economic and military – that shaped French policy.[54]

On the Soviet Union, Churchill plays up signs of Soviet readiness to intervene in the Czech crisis of 1938. Again this issue remains a matter of controversy, but such evidence as has been gleaned from the Soviet archives strongly suggests that Stalin did not intend to take independent action to save Czechoslovakia and that he had not decided what to do if the French honoured their treaty obligations, thereby bringing his own into play. Churchill again registers the necessary qualifications, notably on Soviet good faith, but the weight of his account in chapters sixteen and seventeen is on the 'astonishing' degree of 'indifference – not to say disdain' displayed by British and French leaders towards the Soviet Union. For this, he adds in an allusion to the Nazi-Soviet Pact, 'we afterwards paid dearly'.[55] In support of his theme, he highlights a public declaration by Maxim Litvinov, the Soviet foreign minister, at the League of Nations and also private assurances made to him by Ivan Maisky, Stalin's ambassador in London, which Churchill passed on to the Foreign Office. (At an earlier stage, Churchill had a whole draft chapter entitled 'The Maisky Incident'.) Churchill also wrote of the 'intimate and solid friendship' between the Soviet Union and the Czech state, arguing that Stalin felt 'a very strong desire to help' the Czechs. This, he suggested, stemmed largely from 'a personal debt' felt to President Eduard Benes because the latter had forwarded intelligence of German contacts with the Soviet military, which triggered Stalin's purges in 1937. In the original draft Churchill accepted unequivocally that there was a genuine plot: 'This was in fact the great military and Old-Guard-Communist conspiracy to overthrow Stalin, and introduce a regime based on a pro-German policy.' Deakin persuaded Churchill to replace 'in fact' with 'a part of' and 'great' with 'so-called'. Deakin also proposed a qualification that the information supplied by Benes was probably planted by Soviet intelligence, in the hope that transmission by the Czechs would make it more credible to the paranoid Stalin, but

---

[54] *SWW*, I, 151; cf. Anthony Adamthwaite, *Grandeur and Misery: France's Bid for Power in Europe, 1914–1940* (1995), 222–31.

[55] *SWW*, I, 239–40; cf. Igor Lukes, *Czechoslovakia between Stalin and Hitler: The Diplomacy of Edvard Beneš* (Oxford, 1996), chs. 4 and 7; Zara Steiner, 'The Soviet Commissariat of Foreign Affairs and the Czechoslovakian Crisis in 1938: New Material from the Soviet Archives', *Historical Journal*, 42 (1999), 751–79.

Churchill relegated the qualification to a footnote and added that
it was 'irrelevant'. Even after Deakin's editing, this anecdote (which
Benes had told Churchill in 1944) added immensely to what Churchill
called 'the salient fact for the purposes of this account', namely
'the close association of Russia and Czechoslovakia, and of Stalin and
Benes'.[56]

In contrast with later volumes of the memoirs, the United States
does not bulk large in *The Gathering Storm*. It is, however, striking that
one of Churchill's most trenchant criticisms of Chamberlain occurs
over his handling of President Roosevelt's offer in January 1938 to
convene an international conference to explore the basis of a general
peace settlement. This cut across Chamberlain's plans for bilateral
negotiations with Hitler and Mussolini, so the prime minister asked
Roosevelt to delay his initiative. A few days later, pressed by Eden, he
invited the president to go ahead. It is unlikely that Roosevelt had
anything substantial in mind when he made his offer. But Churchill
asserted: 'We must regard its rejection – for such it was – as the last
frail chance to save the world from tyranny otherwise than by war.'
That Chamberlain, he went on, in mounting incredulity, 'should have
possessed the self-sufficiency to wave away the proffered hand stretched
out across that Atlantic leaves one, even at this date, breathless with
amazement'. Here, transparently, the Cold War context of *The Gathering
Storm* shows through. After the intimate wartime alliance, after lend-
lease and the Marshall Plan, it was indeed hard to recall the depths of
suspicion entertained in 1930s Britain about American isolationism.
Chamberlain's 1937 aphorism, that it was 'always best and safest to
count on nothing from the Americans except words', was then an
axiom in most of Whitehall and Westminster. In a way Churchill did
not intend, he was right to say about British handling of the Roosevelt
initiative: 'One cannot to-day even reconstruct the state of mind which
would render such gestures possible.'[57]

Together with his counterfactuals, Churchill's tendency to simplify the
international scene in the 1930s – reducing several storm clouds into
one – is a central weapon in his attack on British appeasement. But the
clarity of Churchill's indictment derives not just from his simplification of
events abroad. One of the most notable features of book one of *The
Gathering Storm* is what he *doesn't* say about politics at home.

The 1930s are now conventionally dubbed Churchill's 'wilderness
years'. He used that phrase on the last page of *The Gathering Storm*,

---

[56] *SWW*, I, 224–6; cf. Deakin and WSC notes on CHUR 4/90, f. 45.
[57] *SWW*, I, 196–9; cf. David Reynolds, *The Creation of the Anglo-American Alliance, 1937–
1941: A Study in Competitive Co-operation* (1981), 16–23, 31–2, 297.

where he referred to 'eleven years in the political wilderness', but it was popularised by Martin Gilbert's book *Winston Churchill: The Wilderness Years* and the related eight-part TV series shown on both sides of the Atlantic in 1981–2.[58] Historian Alastair Parker has, however, questioned the appropriateness of this term, arguing that in the 1930s Churchill tempered his criticism of the Government's foreign policy because of his persistent hopes of returning to office.[59] As recent historians of the Tory party have shown, the politics of the 1930s were more fluid than our impression of 'the era of Baldwin and Chamberlain' now suggests. However it may look in retrospect, therefore, Churchill did not expect to stay on the backbenches for more than a decade. Little of this emerges in *The Gathering Storm*.

Churchill's campaign against the government's India policy in the early 1930s seems, in retrospect, to be a quixotic flourish by an incorrigible diehard. But it is now clear that much of the Tory party was unhappy about the proposed devolution and that in early 1931 and again in mid-1934 the Government was in serious danger over its India Bill. Had Samuel Hoare, then spoken of as a future premier, not successfully covered up his manipulation of evidence to the Select Committee on India in 1934, Churchill might well have succeeded in his hope of evicting Baldwin and joining a reconstituted national government led by Austen Chamberlain. Yet, although the India Bill dominated British politics in 1933–5, filling 4,000 pages of Hansard with over fifteen million words, it is hardly mentioned in *The Gathering Storm*. To do so would have detracted from Churchill's focus on Germany. It would also have signalled Churchill's political motives, encapsulated in the celebrated Commons exchange when Leo Amery characterised Churchill's India policy with the Latin tag, 'Fiat iustitia ruat caelum.' Translate, demanded Churchill, whereupon Amery responded, to gales of laughter: 'If I can trip up Sam, the Government is bust.'[60]

A new chapter opened in the summer of 1935, with the India Bill passed and Baldwin now prime minister. Churchill eagerly anticipated that the autumn election would produce a smaller majority for the national government, more attention by Baldwin to the Tory right and,

[58] Gilbert also used *The Wilderness Years* as the title for the 1981 volume of documents on 1929–35 that accompanied his official biography. In 1994, however, Sir Martin observed that the phrase now seemed to him 'less apposite' because, as the 1930s wore on, Churchill 'became a kind of one-man unofficial opposition', backed by a 'Cabinet' of former colleagues and civil servants, many of whom fed him information about Britain's defence weakness. Thanks to them, 'his wilderness years had been fully inhabited', Martin Gilbert, *In Search of Churchill* (1994), 109, 135.

[59] R.A.C. Parker, *Churchill and Appeasement* (2000), xi, 65, 261–2.

[60] See Stuart Ball, *Baldwin and the Conservative Party: The Crisis of 1929–1931* (1988); Stewart, *Burying Caesar*, esp. chs. 4–6, Amery quotation from 179.

in consequence, a cabinet post for himself, ideally the admiralty. He alludes to these hopes in *The Gathering Storm*, but represents his exclusion from office after the election as providential. '[N]ow one can see how lucky I was. Over me beat the invisible wings.' He takes the same line when relating how Baldwin passed over him for the new post of minister for the co-ordination of defence in March 1936. Although again admitting disappointment, Churchill wrote: 'This was not the first time – or indeed the last – that I have received a blessing in what was at the time a very effective disguise.'[61]

At the time, however, Churchill's passion for office was intense. On 8 March, the day after Hitler occupied the Rhineland, he called on Neville Chamberlain, then chancellor of the exchequer. According to Chamberlain's diary Churchill said 'he was in a very difficult position' because Stanley Baldwin did not propose to announce the name of the new minister until after the Commons debate on the Rhineland. Churchill said he 'wanted to make a "telling" (I understood in the form of a fierce attack on S.B.) speech if he were ruled out from the post, but not if there were any chance of its being offered him'. Chamberlain, who privately regarded this inquiry as 'an audacious piece of impertinence', declined to give any sign. On 10 March Churchill pulled his punches in the Commons, making little reference to the Rhineland while offering a broad and, in Chamberlain's words, 'constructive' survey of the defence scene. His reward, however, was the appointment of Sir Thomas Inskip on 14 March.[62]

For the remainder of Baldwin's premiership Churchill acknowledged, albeit bitterly, that he had no chance of office. But when Neville Chamberlain succeeded Baldwin in May 1937, Churchill's hopes revived and this again affected his handling of foreign policy. Rearmament was now gaining momentum, Hitler was relatively quiet, and Churchill persuaded himself that the government was moving towards his policy of arms and the covenant. Then came Eden's resignation as foreign secretary in February 1938, mainly over conversations with Italy but also over Chamberlain's handling of Roosevelt's recent initiative. In *The Gathering Storm* Churchill devotes a whole chapter to Eden's departure as a major turning point. This begins with a stark statement of policy differences between Chamberlain and Eden. It ends with one of the most vivid purple passages in *The Gathering Storm*, when Churchill recalls

---

[61] *SWW*, I, 141, 157.

[62] Parker, *Churchill and Appeasement*, 82–5. Interestingly, Baldwin had used a similar tactic during the crisis over the Hoare-Laval pact the previous December, pre-empting a possible assault from Austen Chamberlain, the Tory elder statesman and backbench critic, by hinting that Austen might succeed Samuel Hoare at the Foreign Office. Once the parliamentary crisis had passed, the post was then offered to Eden. See Crowson, *Facing Fascism*, 58–65.

receiving the news of Eden's resignation while at Chartwell on the evening of 20 February. Throughout the war, he tells his readers, he never had any trouble sleeping, even in the darkest days of 1940. But that night 'sleep deserted me. From midnight till dawn I lay in my bed consumed with emotions of sorrow and fear', thinking of this 'one strong, young figure standing up against long, dismal drawling tides of drift and surrender'. But now, said Churchill, 'he was gone. I watched the daylight slowly creep in through the windows, and saw before me in mental gaze the vision of Death.'[63]

Early drafts of this chapter, however, lacked the stark introduction and conclusion. One version opened with a passage of somewhat faint praise of Eden, later moved to page 190, and ended with Churchill's speech to Commons after Eden's resignation. In the book, this appears in the next chapter. Churchill's reworkings made the episode more dramatic. One of Churchill's readers, Lord Vansittart, who had been Eden's permanent under-secretary until December 1937, questioned Churchill's polarity between Eden and Chamberlain. Vansittart argued that the former was more concerned about Italy than Germany ('the *real* issue') and that, in consequence, the resignation was mistimed: Eden 'played his one big card at the wrong moment'.[64] Privately Churchill may have shared some of these reservations. The story of the sleepless night is not unique to *The Gathering Storm*: Churchill told it at least twice in private in 1945–6. But when he did so at Yalta the reason he gave for his sleeplessness was subtly different. 'I was too excited', he told Eden. 'It was a grand thing to do, but I never felt it was done in the right way. More could have been made of it.'[65] In fact, Churchill was often scathing about Eden in private during the 1930s. 'I think you will see what a lightweight Eden is', he told his wife in January 1936, after Eden was appointed foreign secretary. And in February 1940 Churchill went so far as to say 'he would rather have Chamberlain than Eden as Prime Minister by eight to one'.[66]

In the light of recent research, the whole Churchill–Eden–Chamberlain triangle in 1938 looks very different from Churchill's account, written, it should be remembered, after Eden had served for most of the 1940s as Churchill's wartime foreign secretary and then as his

[63] *SWW*, I, 201; drafts of chapter fourteen in CHUR 4/88.

[64] Vansittart to WSC, 10 Nov. 1947, CHUR 4/141A, f. 102.

[65] Lord Moran, *Winston Churchill: The Struggle for Survival, 1940–1965* (1968), 261; cf. Halifax, diary, 7 Mar. 1946, Hickleton papers, A 7.8.18 (Borthwick Institute, York). Back in 1943, Halifax recorded, Churchill also 'waxed eloquent over Anthony's resignation in 1938; said that he had staged it badly and hadn't made any effort to work with all the powerful factors (such as Winston!) who would have co-operated' (Diary, 23 May 1943, A 7.8.12.)

[66] WSC to Clementine, 11 Jan. 1936, Gilbert, *CV*, V, part 3, 11; Cecil H. King, *With Malice toward None: A War Diary*, ed. William Armstrong (1970), 22.

deputy leader in the postwar opposition. In 1938 Churchill viewed Eden's resignation from the foreign office as a shock, but not a mortal blow to his hopes of working with Chamberlain. Although abstaining in the opposition's vote of censure, Churchill was also the fourth Tory MP to sign a round-robin expressing continued support for Chamberlain and his policy.[67] In the summer of 1938 he still believed that a satisfactory agreement could be reached over the Sudetenland. As for his relations with Eden, the two men kept their distance from each other. The former Foreign Secretary, over twenty years Churchill's junior and icon of the Tory left not the right, was reluctant to associate himself with Churchill, now widely seen as one of yesterday's men. Eden was also trying to avoid political isolation and muted his criticisms to make himself credible for renewed office when Chamberlain was forced to broaden his government.

It was not until after Munich that Churchill's opposition to Chamberlain became unqualified. Again he abstained in the Commons, but this time only after being dissuaded from actually voting against his own leader. By contrast, both Eden and Leo Amery, the other leading critic of Chamberlain, were almost persuaded by the premier's final speech in the Munich debate to vote with the government rather than abstain, and they made conciliatory noises in private to Number Ten. Churchill did nothing of the sort this time, unlike February. In fact, he dramatised his opposition by sitting ostentatiously in the Commons chamber while the votes were counted. His ringing denunciation of Munich as 'a total and unmitigated defeat' contrasted with Eden's more tempered criticisms.[68] While Eden continued to pull his punches during 1938–9, Churchill eclipsed him as the most trenchant critic of appeasement. The government U-turn in March 1939 and the guarantees to Eastern Europe were seen as vindication of Churchill not Eden. In September 1939 a top job for Churchill was essential if the government were to seem serious about the war. He was given the admiralty and a seat in the new war cabinet. Eden, by contrast, although a former foreign secretary, could be fobbed off with a non-cabinet portfolio at the dominions office.

In retrospect, it was the end of his 'wilderness' decade. But throughout the 1930s, Churchill had agitated for office, both from frustrated ambition and from frustrated conviction, amply justified after 1939, that he could make a difference. His problem was tactical: was criticism or cooperation the best route back? Under both Baldwin and

---

[67] N.J. Crowson, 'Conservative Parliamentary Dissent over Foreign Policy during the Premiership of Neville Chamberlain: Myth or Reality?', *Parliamentary History*, 14 (1995), 322–3.

[68] Crowson, 'Conservative Parliamentary Dissent', 326–7. More generally see Parker, *Churchill and Appeasement*, chs. 8–10, and Stewart, *Burying Caesar*, chs. 11–13.

Chamberlain, the prophetic voice was often muted. At times, book one of *The Gathering Storm* is almost history with the politics left out.

Churchill's self-image of apolitical rightness in *The Gathering Storm* grated on some contemporaries. Lord Halifax, successor to Eden as foreign secretary, remarked to Chamberlain's aggrieved widow: 'I fancy the main purpose of the book is not only to write history, but, also, to "make a record" for W.S.C.' In a particularly nasty review, entitled 'Churchill's "Mein Kampf" ', Michael Foot, the Beaverbrook journalist and co-author of *Guilty Men*, wrote of Churchill clothing his 'personal vindication in the garb of history ... In 500 pages Churchill hardly allows himself one admission of weakness or false judgment on his own part.' Foot added: 'The whole book, of course, is vastly more enjoyable and instructive than Hitler's *Mein Kampf*. But in personal conceit and arrogance there is some likeness between the two.'[69]

As I have indicated in this essay, Churchill had indeed written a political memoir. His propensity for counterfactuals, his isolation of the German air threat from the mass of international problems facing British governments in the 1930s, and his simplification of the politics of that decade were all exercises in self-vindication. I have also tried to show how, despite his disingenuous disclaimer, this war memoir represented 'history'. The documents at his disposal, the stature he had attained as war leader and the lessons he drew from the past for the future all helped give his words an extra authority.

There was another reason for that authority – one worth dwelling on in conclusion since the thrust of this essay may seem to have belittled Churchill's achievement in *The Gathering Storm*. The most significant counterfactual in book one is Churchill's claim that Britain would have been wiser to fight Hitler in September 1938 over Czechoslovakia rather than a year later over Poland. At the end of the chapter entitled 'Munich Winter', he devoted three pages to this question.[70] Churchill had to acknowledge the core of the retrospective case for appeasement, namely that the extra year allowed Britain to modernise the RAF with Hurricanes and Spitfires and deploy the essential Chain Home Radar system. During the drafting he prepared an essay on how the Battle of Britain would have gone if fought a year earlier, in which he was forced to conclude: 'As the Battle of Britain was won on a very narrow margin in 1940 it may be argued that it might have been lost if fought in 1939.'[71] In consequence, perhaps, he dropped this little setpiece from

[69] Halifax to Anne Chamberlain, 13 April 1948, Hickleton papers, A 4.410.18.4; Michael Foot, 'Churchill's "Mein Kampf" ', *Tribune*, 8 Oct. 1948, 7.

[70] *SWW*, I, 218, 263–5.

[71] CHUR 4/92, f. 119.

the book and recast the air material. In the book he emphasised that, despite the danger of air raids on London, there was 'no possibility of a decisive Air Battle of Britain' until Hitler had occupied France and the Low Countries and thereby obtained bases in striking distance of southeast England. Churchill also insisted that the German army was not capable of defeating the French in 1938 or 1939. 'The vast tank production with which they broke the French Front did not come into existence till 1940.' His conclusion, therefore, was that 'the year's breathing-space said to be "gained" by Munich left Britain and France in a much worse position compared to Hitler's Germany than they had been at the Munich crisis.' This was the greatest 'what if' in *The Gathering Storm*. Although its force was diminished by Churchill's cascade of counterfactuals and by his exaggeration elsewhere of the potency of airpower and of the Luftwaffe, most military historians would now agree with his verdict: 1938 was the time for confrontation, not negotiation.[72] On the big issue, Churchill was, quite simply, right.

We should remember, however, that Churchill was not against appeasement *per se*. Occasionally in *The Gathering Storm* he does use the word in a pejorative sense: ' "Appeasement" in all its forms only encouraged their aggression and gave the Dictators more power with their own peoples.' But this is one of only a handful of explicitly negative references.[73] Moreover, when setting out some 'principles of morals and action which may be a guide in the future', he argues that those seeking 'peaceful compromise' are 'not always wrong. On the contrary, in the majority of instances they may be right, not only morally but from a practical standpoint.' The follies Churchill describes in *The Gathering Storm* are essentially those of men not methods. As his conduct of wartime relations with Stalin shows, he was not averse to negotiating with dictators. He returned from Yalta in February 1945 momentarily hopeful that the agreements would stick. 'Poor Nevil[l]e Chamberlain believed he could trust Hitler', he told his ministers. 'He was wrong. But I don't think I'm wrong about Stalin.'[74] Even when these agreements broke down, his line was not war but negotiation from strength. His address at Fulton in March 1946, now indelibly known as the Iron Curtain speech, was actually entitled 'The Sinews of Peace'. And when in December 1950, at the critical moment of the Korean war, Prime Minister Clement Attlee promised that there would be no appeasement, Churchill set out his own position to the Commons: 'Appeasement in itself may be good or bad according to the cir-

[72] *SWW*, 1, 265; cf. Williamson Murray, *The Change in the European Balance of Power, 1938–1939: The Path to Ruin* (Princeton, 1984), ch. 7.

[73] *SWW*, 1, 194; cf. pp. 261, 271, 372, 381.

[74] Hugh Dalton diary, 32: 28 (23 Feb. 1945) (British Library of Political and Economic Science, London).

cumstances. Appeasement from weakness and fear is alike futile and fatal. Appeasement from strength is magnanimous and noble and might be the surest and perhaps the only path to world peace.' His efforts as prime minister in 1951–5 for a new 'summit' to achieve détente, analysed by John Young, were a continuation of this philosophy, for which he now used the term 'easement'.[75]

By then, however, the forces arrayed against him were too strong. These included the foreign office, the Eisenhower administration and the Kremlin, not to mention his own stroke in June 1953. But there was yet another reason for his failure. As I noted at the start of this essay, Churchill lived a double life as politician and writer. In *The Gathering Storm* he transformed the fluid politics of the 1930s into enduring history. But during his second premiership Churchill again strove to make history as actor not author. By then, however, the 'lessons' of appeasement had become too strong. The images of Baldwin and Chamberlain, of the Rhineland and Munich, had become part of Western culture. And for that *The Gathering Storm* was, in large part, responsible. In the 1950s, one might say, Churchill was a prisoner of history – his own history of the 1930s. It proved easier to make history than to unmake it.

[75] Gilbert, *Churchill*, VIII, 574; John Young, *Winston Churchill s Last Campaign: Britain and the Cold War, 1951–1955* (Oxford, 1996), esp. 8–10, 323–4.

CHURCHILL AND THE AMERICAN ALLIANCE

By John Charmley

THE influence of Churchill's account of the appeasement years on the public mind has long been recognised and has been rehearsed here by David Reynolds. Equally influential in moulding the present view of the past has been the account of the Anglo-American alliance given by Churchill in *The Second World War*. One healthy change that the twenty-first century might bring is a less romanticised and more realistic account of the so-called special relationship. Like all good revisionism, this essay will attempt to clear away some of the rich Churchillian detritus, before trying to trace some of the outline of a different version of events. Such, however, is the artistry of the Churchillian version, and so strong the need of the British to believe it, that only the boldest of seers would wager on the chances of it being dislodged in the near future.

Churchill was, of course, himself half-American, one of a number of products of what one historian has termed the 'gilded prostitution' of the 1870s when American heiresses fulfilled the dynastic ambitions of their parents by marrying into the British aristocracy. In his early manhood there was a vogue for what was called 'Anglo-Saxonism', stimulated by America's aggression against the Spanish Empire.[1] In 'The White Man's Burden', Kipling welcomed his fellow Anglo-Saxons to the responsibilities of imperialism. The British colonial secretary, Joseph Chamberlain, himself married (at the third time) to an American, looked forward to a partnership of the Anglo-Saxon races. But this fashion proved transient. The experience of working with the Americans at the end of the First World War, and more especially of the moralising of Woodrow Wilson and the return of America into isolation, ensured that for most of the interwar period, a quite different attitude obtained. This is captured nicely in a protest made by the cabinet secretary, Sir Maurice Hankey, to Balfour in 1927: 'Time and time again we have been told that, if we made this concession or that concession, we should secure goodwill in America. We have given up the Anglo-Japanese Alliance. We agreed to pay our debts and we have again and again made concessions on this ground. I have never seen any permanent results follow from a policy of concession. I believe we are less popular and more abused in America than ever before, because they think us

[1] John Charmley, *Churchill's Grand Alliance* (1995), 3 and references given there.

weak.[12] So, when Neville Chamberlain wrote that 'It is always best and safest to count on nothing from the Americans except words',[3] he was reflecting a common assumption of his generation of politicians, and one that was not always unspoken.

How different has been the rhetoric of British leaders since 1945. To a very large extent this change was wrought by Churchill. We can discern the early signs of this in *The Gathering Storm* when in the best Whig fashion he used hindsight to distort the reality of events in early 1938 by making Roosevelt's fatuous offer of an international conference into a great lost opportunity. Viewed through the lenses of the Second World War, the idea that an American alliance in 1938 might have helped to prevent the war did not look as ridiculous as it appeared in 1938 when Chamberlain rightly commented that there was everything to be said for Churchill's idea of the grand alliance – until you examined it.[4] Churchill, having thus early established the centrality of the American alliance to any sensible British policy, goes on to delineate the steps by which, once prime minister himself, he was able to woo America, bring her into the war, and forge therein an alliance of the most intimate nature. From this far from bald but convincing narrative it would be impossible to guess that what had happened was that the appeasement of Germany had been followed by the appeasement of the United States.

It is a mark of the success of the Churchillian version of events that even the application of the loaded word appeasement to Anglo-American relations should cause hackles to rise. The Churchillian grand narrative disguised the reality of British decline by portraying it as a passing of the torch to another branch of the English-speaking peoples. Any twenty-first century revisionism will have to deal not only with the literary power of Churchill's Anglo-American alliance, but also the psychological need that it filled. After all, why question an account of a relationship that most British prime ministers have described as 'special'; surely they cannot all be wrong? To this there are two answers. Firstly, those prime ministers who have subscribed to the idea of the special relationship have, by so doing, underwritten their own importance and that of the United Kingdom, which is the main reason why it has had such resonance in post-war British politics. Secondly, not all prime ministers have, in fact, gone along with the Churchillian version. Eden, who of course suffered from the reality of Britain's declining power in 1956, and Edward Heath who saw another path for Britain

[2] British Library, Balfour Papers, Add. MS. 49704, Hankey to Balfour, 29 June 1927.
[3] Birmingham University Library, Neville Chamberlain Papers, NC 18/1/1032, Neville to Hilda Chamberlain, 19 December 1937.
[4] John Charmley, *Churchill: the end of glory* (1993), 330–3 and references there.

to follow, declined to join in the Americanophilia, as did the laconic Clement Attlee. An additional problem in revising the Churchillian narrative lies in the feelings of Americanophilia naturally generated in generations of British historians who have reason to be grateful to American archives and American funding. This has not led to an uncritical approach to the Anglo-American relationship, but it has, perhaps, generated a tendency to see it as essentially benign for Britain. This all serves to disguise what might be clearer to the future revisionist, which is that A.J.P. Taylor may well have been right when he called the 1939–45 conflict 'the war of the British Succession'.

It would take an effort of revisionism beyond imagination to argue that the Anglo-American alliance was unnecessary. Churchill's own line of defence against accusations of appeasement tended along this line, with the addition that he seldom sacrificed anything of importance and obtained, in return concessions of great value.[5] This is certainly the impression left on any reader of *The Second World War*. Difficult though it has proved to break away from the Churchillian version of the war, a less sanitised version of the Anglo-American alliance suggests what the outlines of such an attempt might be in this area. In the confines of a short essay it is possible to do only two things: the first is to subject some of the key elements in the Churchillian canon to critical scrutiny; and the second is to examine more sceptically the implication that no very heavy price was paid by the British for American co-operation.

Churchill liked to imply that America's eventual entry into the war was the product of his prolonged and ardent wooing; cause and effect are not, however, as clear as this. When Churchill rallied his colleagues behind the policy of staying in the war despite the collapse of France, the argument that America's entry into the conflict was imminent was crucial. Indeed, David Reynolds cites it as one of the 'wrong reasons' for Churchill adopting the 'right policy'.[6] Wrong though he was, Churchill undoubtedly believed what he told the cabinet; the problem is that he continued to hold this belief for the next eighteen months, during which America repeatedly declined to enter the war. This certainly presented Churchill the historian with a problem, not least since during that period Britain made a number of concessions to the United States; but he was equal to the challenge and created one of his most effective myths. In *The Second World War*, the period between the fall of France and Pearl Harbor is portrayed as one in which America edged closer and closer to entering the war. Any concessions

[5] Charmley, *Churchill's Grand Alliance*, chapter 8, for examples.
[6] D. Reynolds, 'Churchill and the British "Decision" to fight on in 1940: Right Policy, Wrong Reasons', in *Diplomacy and Intelligence During the Second World War*, ed. R. Langhorne (1985), 147–67.

made by Britain were nothing more than what was demanded if that process was to gather momentum, and they were more than justified by that 'most unsordid act', lend-lease. This is an interesting version of events, but hardly definitive.

The historian who claims to divine truly Roosevelt's intentions between May 1940 and December 1941 is brave to the point of self-delusion. Roosevelt made and unmade sense from day to day; he was a politician who erected ambiguity and ellipsis into an art form. These were qualities Churchill scarcely discerned, and ones his literary style was unable, in any event, to portray. Churchill's bold, swift narrative was filled with Macaulayesque characters, and in it, FDR became the soldier of freedom. Roosevelt's admirers were naturally delighted with this portrait and saw no reason to question it. His Republican opponents had their own reasons for finding it acceptable, because it confirmed the views of those who had always suspected that Roosevelt had dragged America into the war on Britain's coat-tails. In the absence of any demand for a more nuanced version of Roosevelt, it took a good deal of time for one to emerge.[7] Alongside the firm lines of the older portraits, the lineaments of another Roosevelt have emerged clearly enough to hazard a few generalisations. This Roosevelt is also an opportunist, but about means rather than ends. His objectives remain fluid enough to irritate historians who wish to pin him down, but they are discernible in the sort of broad outlines Roosevelt himself indulged in. His ultimate commitment was to the creation of a world safe for America and Roosevelt saw no reason why the application of liberal and democratic principles on a global scale should not achieve that objective. This Roosevelt shared Churchill's commitment to the defeat of the evils of fascism, but he was flexible about how that would be achieved. For a long time he hoped that Britain would be able, in Churchill's plangent phrase, to 'finish the job' if America provided the 'tools'; American entry into the war might be necessary, or it might not be, either way, Roosevelt kept his options open and Churchill's hopes as high as he dared. He was not, however, committed to many of the things for which Churchill and the British were fighting. Roosevelt had no time for the British Empire or for imperialism on the British model; he was equally opposed to the sort of autarchic trading system the British had created for their Empire since 1932. These things were obstacles to the sort of world Roosevelt wanted, and between 1940 and 1945 he did his best to use Britain's dependence upon America to

---

[7] For the traditional version from the pro-FDR camp, see J.M. Burns, *Roosevelt: The soldier of Freedom* (NY, 1970) and J.P. Lash, *Roosevelt and Churchill* (1976); on the critical side, Harry Elmer Barnes, *Perpetual War for Perpetual Peace* (1953). For a more nuanced view see Warren Kimball, *The Juggler* (Princeton, 1992).

remove them. Churchill's Roosevelt is a paladin of freedom whose eventual failure at Yalta could be partially forgiven as it was redeemed by his earlier actions. He was a fit partner for Churchill and the inheritor of the white man's burden. Concessions made to such a figure in the name of hastening America's entry into the war were not only forgivable, they were laudable.

Churchill himself was prepared to make a virtue out of necessity. As he told General de Gaulle in early 1944: 'Look here! I am the leader of a strong, unbeaten nation. Yet every morning when I wake my first thought is how I can please President Roosevelt, and my second is how I can conciliate Marshall Stalin.' Why, he asked, did de Gaulle's first thought appear to be how he could snap his fingers at the British and the Americans.[8] De Gaulle had already given the definitive reply to Churchill's question back in November 1942, namely that it was his task to look after French interests, not those of other Powers. As Eden later sadly commented, if de Gaulle had seemed 'contumacious, especially to our American allies, perhaps we should have learnt from it. Some of the faults of later years might have been avoided if we had shown more of the same spirit.'[9] The historian of the twenty-first century might find this comment more resonant than his predecessors have done. Were Anglo-American war aims as identical as Churchill thought? Was America's participation in the war so conditional that it depended upon a drip-feed of concessions from the British? Was Britain's role in the war after 1941 as glorious as the Churchillian legend would have it, or was she, in effect, squeezed by her allies for their own ends?

The Churchillian grand narrative avoids the need for such questions by implying a connection between British concessions and America's involvement in the war. It is difficult to establish such a direct connection. It is clearly not impossible to argue that the bases for destroyers deal, lend-lease and the Atlantic Charter were all milestones on the road to war, since that was exactly what Churchill did, but other interpretations are possible and may more plausibly be linked with the more nuanced picture of Roosevelt with which the twenty-first century will replace the heroic simplicities of Churchill's portrait. In essence the president was establishing American hemispheric hegemony and securing for his country what Lord Curzon would have called a *glacis*, that is a buffer zone of security. Perhaps, as some have argued, Roosevelt's decision to allow American destroyers to convoy British ships was a provocative move to create an 'incident' that would precipitate America's entry into the war. However, since this had not

[8] Martin Gilbert, *Winston S. Churchill*, VII (1986), 646.
[9] Lord Avon, *The Eden Memoirs, volume II. The Reckoning* (1965), 250.

happened by December 1941, such a hypothesis neither confirms nor denies Churchill's narrative thrust. What is undeniable is that it was Hitler's actions rather than those of Churchill that actually brought America into the war. Still, for a mythologist of Churchill's capacity and skill, *post hoc* and *propter hoc* were easily elided, especially since it could be asked whether Britain had actually conceded anything of importance in return for such an excellent result.

The triumph of the Rooseveltian world order has made the formulation of such a question as problematic as answering it. Its values have become hegemonic in western societies, and most of us take its precepts for granted: free trade, anti-imperialism, the transcendence of the values of democracy and of toleration, these truths we hold as self-evident. That the war helped their progress, and that Britain helped win the war that achieved this result, we take as a legitimate source of pride. This is, perhaps, Whig history with a vengeance. The British were fighting not to create the commonwealth of the reign of Elizabeth II, and a modern, progressive, multi-cultural society, but to preserve the empire of Victoria and the values which it represented and held dear. We may now hold such things cheap and abhor imperialism. We may feel that empire was a doomed cause and rightly so, and feel little grief at its passing; nor do we pronounce elegies for the end of imperial preference. We do not regret the decline and fall of the old social order with its inequalities and its indefensible hierarchies, its prejudices and its conservatism. None of this should blind us to the fact that for those who were fighting the war to defend the world they knew and loved, there was indeed a price exacted for the American alliance. Men such as the secretary of state for India, Leo Amery, and the colonial secretary, Lord Lloyd, saw America as a rival as well as an ally. For them, as for many of their ilk, the concessions demanded by Washington were not easily distinguished from extortion. Will the historian of the twenty-first century allow more space for their version of the Anglo-American relationship before Pearl Harbor?

When Churchill renewed his plea to Roosevelt for more destroyers at the end of July 1940, the president's agreement was conditional on long leases on the British bases in the Caribbean. Eden described it as a 'grievous blow at our authority and ultimately ... at our sovereignty'.[10] That stout imperialist and ally of Churchill's, Lord Lloyd, accused the Americans of resorting to gangster tactics.[11] The professional diplomats had, however, already come up with the excuse that would underpin every other concession that Britain would make: 'the future of our

---

[10] Public Record Offce, London, Prime Minister's Papers, PREM. 3/476/10, Eden minute, 29 December 1940.

[11] Charmley, *Churchill's Grand Alliance*, 430.

widely scattered Empire is likely to depend upon the evolution of an effective and enduring collaboration between ourselves and the United States.'[12] This platitude was not accompanied by any query about whether the United States wanted to underwrite the British Empire. In fact, in return for bases described by Roosevelt as 'of the utmost importance to our national defence',[13] the British received out of date destroyers, and far from the fifty promised, by the end of January 1941, only two of them had turned up. To argue that the concession on the British side was only symbolic is both to underrate the importance of symbol and to attribute a late twentieth-century consciousness to men born in the reign of Queen Victoria.

The second item in the Churchillian catalogue, lend-lease, seems less in need of the aid of the word symbolic; without it Britain could not have stayed in the war. The 'most unsordid act' actually had a good deal of shoddiness about it. Writing a year before Pearl Harbor, Churchill revealed his own unspoken assumptions when he told Roosevelt that he believed 'you will agree that it would be wrong in principle and mutually disadvantageous in effect if, at the height of this struggle, Great Britain were to be divested of all saleable assets so that after victory was won with our blood ... we should stand stripped to the bone'.[14] Roosevelt did not agree in the slightest. His secretary of state, Cordell Hull, had spoken about using 'American aid as a knife to open up that oyster shell, the empire';[15] and that was precisely what the Roosevelt administration attempted to do. Even Churchill bridled at Roosevelt's proposal to send a destroyer to Simonstown to pick up the last of Britain's gold reserves,[16] and although he finally decided not to protest formally, he did not dissent from Beaverbrook's view that the Americans had taken advantage of Britain's situation to 'exact payment to the uttermost for all they have done for us.'[17] It was entirely legitimate for the Americans to promote their national interests in this way, as it was for them to force the British to sell off their overseas assets at bargain-basement prices to obtain lend-lease; whether it is accurate to portray the process as one of 'mixing together' might well be questioned more by the twenty-first century than it has been thus far.

The notion of Roosevelt pursuing a policy of his own devising that was compatible with British interests only up to a point is strengthened

---

[12] PRO, War Cabinet Memoranda, Cab. 66/10, WP(40)276, 18 July 1940.
[13] E. Roosevelt (ed.), *The Roosevelt Letters*. III (1953), Roosevelt to David Walsh, 22 August 1940, 329–30.
[14] W. Kimball (ed.), *Churchill and Roosevelt: the Complete Correspondence* (hereafter: *Churchill–Roosevelt Correspondence*) (Princeton, 1984) I, Churchill to Roosevelt, 7 December 1940, 108.
[15] Kimball, *The Juggler*, 49.
[16] PRO, PREM. 4/17/1, Churchill minute, fos. 93–4.
[17] PREM. 4/17/1, Beaverbrook memorandum, fos. 104–6.

by the Atlantic Charter. Such has been the success of the new order of which the Charter was the harbinger in the postwar era that it is difficult to recapture just how radical it was. One of the anxieties of the Roosevelt administration in the summer of 1941 was that with the entry into the war of the Soviet Union, the British would enter into commitments that would prejudice the creation of the sort of world order America wanted.[18] The Atlantic Charter, so lauded in the official Churchillian version of the Anglo-American relationship, came as a bolt out of the blue at the time. British historians, struck either by its now platitudinous nature, or by Churchill's version of it, have shown a lack of curiosity about its origins. These lie in Roosevelt's determination to avoid the fate of Woodrow Wilson. He was well aware of the allegations of his opponents that American aid was simply subserving British imperial interests; the Charter was the answer to them. Article 3, which provided for 'the right of all peoples to choose the form of government under which they live', struck at the very heart of imperialism. Churchill's declaration that it did not apply to the British Empire was unilateral in nature, and there is no sign that the Americans agreed with him, even if it was hardly politic to say so. Article 4, providing for all nations to have 'access of equal terms to the trade and to the raw materials of the world', was the pure doctrine of Hull's free trade beliefs and ran directly counter to the economic beliefs of the party upon whose support Churchill's premiership rested.

Churchill's justification for signing up to the Charter followed the usual lines. After explaining away the exemptions he claimed for the Empire, Churchill argued that nothing much had been conceded; in return, the president had promised to become 'more provocative' towards Germany, which surely heralded a swift American entry into the war.[19] By the end of August Churchill was telling Roosevelt of the 'wave of depression' created in Britain by his own repeated statements to the American press that the Atlantic meeting was not the prelude to America's entry into the war. It may be that Roosevelt's comments were made for domestic purposes and that the impression he had left on Churchill at the conference was the correct one, but to assume this to be the case because of the assumption that Roosevelt was moving America towards war, is to go down a perilous road. That, of course, does not mean that Roosevelt's remarks to Churchill might not have reflected his own views, but it suggests caution about assuming that it was so because Churchill's portrait of Roosevelt demands that it should have been so. Roosevelt was well aware of the part Churchill's leadership

---

[18] Charmley, *Churchill's Grand Alliance*, 32–3, 36–7.

[19] Franklin D. Roosevelt Library, Private Secretary's File, Safe File, Atlantic Charter (1), Box 1, Churchill to Harry L. Hopkins, 29 August 1941.

played in keeping Britain in the war and he wanted to do nothing to jeopardise it. Roosevelt's actions in late 1941 certainly lend themselves to the Churchillian version of events, namely that he was becoming more and more provocative with a view to creating an incident with Germany that would bring America into the war; but they might also be read as efforts to bolster Churchill and to keep the British in the war.

If the historian of the twenty-first century might approach Churchill's narrative of the prelude to America's entry into the war with a more sceptical eye, asking questions about the compatibility of Anglo-American objectives, and taking more account of those who thought a real price was being paid to Washington for aid that could have been had more cheaply, then he will have to admit, nonetheless, that Churchill's claims for influence over the direction of allied grand strategy in 1942 stand up to scrutiny. The Mediterranean strategy was undoubtedly his brain-child, which no doubt accounts for the controversy it has generated over the years. But those who would use it as yet another stick with which to beat Churchill will have to take into account the fact that it succeeded for reasons that were also unconnected with him. Churchill's own explanation, couched in terms of the role his relationship with Roosevelt allowed him to play, is only part of the story. Had there been no more to it then, after General Marshall's visit to London in March 1942, the western allies would have found themselves preparing for an invasion of France. But Churchill's agreement to Marshall's plans had come only because of a conviction that they were impossible to implement – as proved to be the case. The Alliance, and the Americans, needed an operation in 1942, and since most of the available troops were British and in North Africa, that effectively dictated the main theatre of operations. The Anglo-American failure to clear to the Germans out of Tunisia before May precluded a cross-Channel invasion in 1943, which then gave Churchill's preferred strategy a prolonged lease of life. However, for all Churchill's claims for the influence that he gained through his relationship with Roosevelt, he was unable to persuade the Americans of the merits of continuing with a campaign in the Adriatic for 1944.

Was it, however, true that even in return for America's agreement to the Mediterranean Strategy in 1942 and 1943, Churchill surrendered nothing of great value? An answer to this requires us to go beyond the tramlines laid down in *The Second World War*. One of the great differences between Churchill's account of the war and that given in the other great personal account of it, de Gaulle's *Mémoires de Guerre*, is that where the latter is largely an account of the political struggle to determine the future of France, Churchill's concentrates upon the war itself. When Eden attempted to engage Churchill in serious debate in late 1942 about the future of British foreign policy, he received the discouraging response that he hoped that such 'speculative studies will be entrusted to those on whose hands time hangs heavy', commending to him the recipe of Mrs Glass for jugged hare – 'First catch your hare'.[20] It could be argued that too much should not be built upon such a remark, except for the fact that throughout the war the foreign secretary, Anthony Eden, found it impossible to get Churchill to engage in serious planning for the postwar era. To set against that a few musings by Churchill to his private secretary in 1940, and his appointment of his son-in-law, Duncan Sandys, to a postwar planning committee, smacks of special pleading. One could simply dismiss Eden's complaints had they been made once or twice, but they are a constant refrain throughout the war.

Eden told his colleagues in 1942 that the absence of any 'guiding principle' for British foreign policy was a 'grave weakness'. Both of Britain's main allies treated the vagueness of British policy with suspicion; America and Russia naturally suspected imperialist ambitions were being hidden from them, whilst the European governments in exile were 'puzzled by an apparent inability on our part to give them the kind of lead, to provide for them the kind of focus, which they have come to realise they must have if they are to survive'.[21] The argument that Britain had no alternative to following what America and the Soviet Union wanted is more convincing applied to 1945 than it is in 1942. Indeed it was this consciousness of a limited window of opportunity that prompted Eden to try to persuade Churchill to map out a vision for British foreign policy; it might have to be deviated from, but without such a vision the danger of drifting into the American slipstream was only too apparent.

Churchill's refusal to enage in such a debate does not mean that he had no thoughts. As he told Eden in response to his 'Four power plan', his thoughts rested 'primarily in Europe – the revival of the glory of Europe, the parent continent of the modern nations and of civilisation'; unfortunately 'the war has prior claims on your attention and mine.'[22] Moreover, when it came to the 'greatest' problems, intimate cooperate with America would be necessary, and it was upon that that his heart was set.[23] Nor were his hopes here modest ones. If one characteristic of Whig history is the tracing of clearer lines between the past and present than actually existed, another is the airbrushing out of inconvenient facts. The speech that Churchill gave on the hills of old

    [20] PREM. 4/100/7, M.461/42, Churchill to Eden, 18 October 1942.
    [21] PREM. 4/100I7, WP(42)516, 'The Four Power Plan', Eden memorandum, 8 November 1942.
    [22] PREM. 4/100/7, M.461/42, Churchill to Eden, 18 October 1942.
    [23] PREM. 4/100/7, M.474/2, Churchill to Eden, 21 October 1942.

Missouri on 5 March 1946 is usually known by the title of its striking metaphor, 'the Iron Curtain' speech, but it is in fact entitled the 'Sinews of Peace'. Although posterity has focused upon its message about the Iron Curtain, the main theme of the speech was the renewal of a plea for Anglo-American unity. That plea had been made in a major speech Churchill had given at Harvard in September 1943, but which fails to get any mention in the war memoirs. There Churchill made it plain that when he talked about 'unity' he meant 'union'. Churchill advocated the healing of the breach made in the reign of George III and looked forward to an Anglo-American union with a common legal system and a common currency.[24] That this did not happen should not disguise from us Churchill's hope that it would, or the price it exacted in terms of having an independent British foreign policy. No where was this price heavier than in it was in Anglo-French relations.

Churchill shared Eden's view that British interests demanded the restoration of French power, not least as a counterweight to possible Soviet 'preponderance';[25] indeed, it was partly to that end he had built up General de Gaulle. However, Churchill's pursuit of the American special relationship served to wreck Britain's relations with de Gaulle, and with it short circuited any attempt to evolve a constructive policy towards the future organisation of Europe. There was little point Churchill having inchoate ideas about a 'Council of Europe' if the effect of his American policy was to prevent their execution. Indeed, following my leader where Washington was concerned landed the British in a good deal of hot water, before pouring the cold remnants over plans for European unity. De Gaulle's policy of asserting France's interests regardless of Anglo-American feeling had brought American enmity from the moment he irritated Cordell Hull by occupying the islands of St Pierre and Miquelon in 1941. Those anti-Vichy French exiles who had fallen out with de Gaulle (or never been in with him) tended to wash up on the shores of the New World where they provided the state department with a colourful collection of anti-Gaullist rumours. The state department was never sure whether de Gaulle was a crypto-fascist (he was a general after all) or a Communist pawn, but they were clear, as was Roosevelt, that the Allies should have as little truck with him as possible.[26] This meant, in practice, not just keeping him out of Operation TORCH, but co-operating with the Vichy collaborationist, Admiral Darlan.

The crisis caused by the Darlan affair is absent from Churchill's

---

[24] *The Times*, 7 September 1943.

[25] M. Kitchen, *British Policy towards the Soviet Union during the Second World War* (1986), 151, quoting Churchill to Sir Alexander Cadogan, 2 April 1943.

[26] On all of this see, J. Charmley; 'British Policy towards General de Gaulle, 1942–1944' (Oxford D. Phil, thesis, 1982).

account of the war, but at the time it raised a storm of protest. Progressive opinion in Britain and America reacted very badly to it, with Attlee warning about the reaction of the Labour movement, and Eden of its effect on Anglo-Soviet relations.[27] Churchill, however, preferred to go along with Roosevelt, who opined that the French were a 'very silly people' and that de Gaulle 'really did not know what the opinion of France is or who represents France'.[28] The result was that the Western allies ended up setting up Darlan as the *chef d'état* of a French North Africa that owed allegiance to Marshal Petain, whilst Churchill, in a secret session of the House of Commons, excoriated de Gaulle as 'one of those Frenchmen who have a traditional antagonism against the English'.[29] Whatever the truth of that observation, Churchill and Roosevelt's treatment of de Gaulle ensured that he would indeed have such an antagonism. The assassination of Darlan on Christmas Eve 1942 provided a way out of a situation that was damaging relations between Britain and Russia as well as with de Gaulle, but again, Churchill chose to follow Roosevelt's policy of promoting General Giraud as Darlan's replacement, rather than breaking with the Vichy regime in North Africa; indeed, much to the fury of the Gaullists, the Americans even brought in fresh Vichy collaborationists such as Marcel Peyrouton to help run what was, in effect, an American puppet government in North Africa. In May 1943, Churchill even agreed, at Roosevelt's behest, that the time had come to break with de Gaulle, although the announcement of a union between the Gaullists and the forces of the American-backed General Giraud prevented this.

Roosevelt seemed to class France along with 'Spain and Italy as a Latin power with no great future in Europe', but in Eden's eyes Britain should have no truck with such a view. If Britain was to contain Germany after the war then a strong and friendly France was 'indispensable for our security whether or not the United States collaborates in the maintenance of peace on this side of the Atlantic'. This meant doing 'everything to raise French morale and promote French self-confidence'. There were, he told Churchill in July 1943, points beyond which 'we ought not to allow our policy' to be governed by the Americans: 'Europe expects us to have a European policy of our own, and to state it.'[30] Churchill had already made it clear that he did not propose to 'allow our relations with the United States to be spoiled through our proposed patronage of this man ... whose accession to

---

[27] PRO, Foreign Office General Correspondence, Series 371/32144/Z9714 for sheafs of protests. See also Cab. 66/32, WP(42)576, Eden memorandum, 11 December 1942.

[28] PRO. Avon Papers, FO 954/29 part II, Oliver Lyttelton's record of a meeting with Roosevelt, November 1942.

[29] Gilbert, *Churchill VII*, 277–78.

[30] PRO. FO 371/36301/Z8225, draft memorandum, 12 July 1943 by Eden.

power in France would be a British disaster of the first magnitude.'[31] Eden thought that the deliberate snubbing of de Gaulle by the Americans and by Churchill 'would make him a national hero' inside France, as well as fatally damaging Anglo-French relations.[32] Churchill would have none of this. He was not, he told Eden, willing to 'mar those personal relations of partnership and friendship ... between me and President Roosevelt ... by which... the course of our affairs has been most notably assisted' for a 'budding Fuhrer' like de Gaulle.[33] Although Eden was able to prevent this hostility from actually leading to a breakdown in Anglo-French relations, he could not prevent the damage caused by de Gaulle's conviction that as long as Churchill had anything to do with it, Britain would put the American alliance before her commitments to Europe.

The danger in this line was pointed out to Churchill by his old friend, Duff Cooper, who was appointed as ambassador to the French Committee of National Liberation in late 1943, when he asked him on the eve of D day whether he could be sure that 'having sacrificed ... [French] friendship and the hegemony of Europe out of friendship to the United States', the latter would not retreat into isolationism.[34] The answer, of course, was that he could not, but that did not prevent him from continuing to alienate de Gaulle at every opportunity. At a famous meeting with the general on 4 June 1944, Churchill made unambiguously plain his preference for America and Roosevelt over Europe and de Gaulle. Despite assurances to the general from both Eden and Bevin that Churchill's views were purely personal, the Frenchman had already drawn his own conclusion that Britain preferred being an American client state to trying to lead Europe.[35] Duff Cooper argued passionately that Britain would 'emerge from this war with greater honour than any other country' and that the 'leadership of Europe' awaited her if she would only take it.[36] In May, and again in December 1944, he advocated Britain taking the lead to organise a Western European Union, only to be frustrated because Eden thought it might displease the Soviets whilst Churchill thought that the Americans would not like it.[37]

Churchill's record of deferring to the American dislike of de Gaulle continued right down to his refusal to recognise any French Provisional

[31] FO 371/36047/Z6026, Churchill to Eden, 23 May 1943.
[32] *The Reckoning*, diary entry, 8 July 1943, 397.
[33] PREM. 3/181/8, Churchill draft paper, 13 July 1943.
[34] FO 37/42134/Z3307, Cooper to Churchill, 25 April 1944.
[35] Charmley, *Churchill's Grand Alliance*, 569–70 for the various sources for this conversation.
[36] John Charmley, *Duff Cooper* (1986), 186–187.
[37] Charmley, *Churchill's Grand Alliance*, 539–540 for the references.

government until Roosevelt himself suddenly, and without consulting Britain, decided to do so in October 1944. It damaged British interests in both a short and a long-term way. In the first instance it helped prevent Churchill from actually doing anything effective about his ideas about a 'Council of Europe'. In the second place it encouraged a belief that there was a dichotomy between constructive engagement with Europe and the special relationship. Constructive engagement with Europe was not possible because it would mean transgressing American policy towards de Gaulle, and it was also unnecessary because Britain's continuance as a Great Power depended upon America not upon her relationship with Europe. Churchill may have indulged in 'Morning thoughts' and after-dinner conversations about Europe, he certainly wished to see it as one of 'regional councils' of the United Nations, but Roosevelt wanted no 'regional councils', so naturally he got his way on that, as he did on policy towards France.

One of the other areas where Churchillian deference to Roosevelt exacted its price was in British policy towards the USSR, a topic on which the views of the twenty-first century might well differ from those prevailing hitherto. Any attempt to argue, as Eden did, for a constructive engagement with Soviet Russia is likely to founder on the reality of the Cold War. In its hindsight both Eden's eagerness to offer Stalin his 1941 frontiers, and Churchill's belief that Stalin was a man of his word, can be made to look very like appeasement.[38] It may well be that there never was any chance of Anglo-Soviet relations avoiding the freezer, but Eden's attempt to win Stalin's goodwill by granting his demand for a recognition of the frontiers of June 1941 was not without its merits. In the first place, as Eden himself pointed out, if the war was to be won it was highly likely that it would because Soviet troops were already in possession of the territory lost in 1941, and since the Western Allies would be unable to take it from the Soviets, they might at least have whatever benefits might accrue from such a recognition before it became inevitable.[39] There was naturally a good deal of suspicion of British intentions on the Soviet side, and these were hardly likely to be dispelled by a British refusal to recognise the 1941 frontiers, especially if that were to be followed by no 'Second Front' in Europe until 1944. However, unfortunately for Eden, Churchill was in America when his proposals came through. Roosevelt's confidant, Sumner Welles later called Eden's proposed treaty a 'Baltic Munich', and stigmatised Russian demands as 'indefensible from every moral standpoint and equally indefensible from the standpoint of the future

---

[38] Most recently here see D. Carlton, *Churchill and the Soviet Union* (2000).
[39] *The Reckoning*, 295–297.

peace and stability of Europe'.[40] This exaggeratedly moral outburst avoided addressing Eden's assertion that if German military power was destroyed 'Russia's position on the Continent will be unassailable'. As Rab Butler put it: 'our refusal to concede their claim to certain territories in Central Europe – the future of which without them we are unable to influence – will tend to maintain that atmosphere of suspicion which has for so many decades affected Anglo-Soviet relations';[41] and so it proved.

For all Churchill's interest in forging a special relationship with Roosevelt and the Americans, the evidence suggests that Roosevelt's interest lay in trying to create one with Stalin. Roosevelt's own belief was that the Soviet system was evolving in a manner favourable to his own plans. It was, he thought, 'increasingly true that the Communism of twenty years ago has practically ceased to exist' and that the 'current system is more like a form of the older socialism'.[42] He told Churchill in March 1942 that 'I think I can personally handle Stalin better than either your Foreign Office or my State Department. Stalin hates the guts of all your top people. I think he likes me better, and I hope he will continue to do so.'[43] Roosevelt's concept of the United Nations had no place in it for Churchillian regional councils, it depended rather upon Stalin co-operating in a single global organisation with the 'Four Policemen' controlling its activities. Churchill's acceptance of that model in August 1943 at Quebec marked, in the words of William H. McNeill, the surrender 'of whatever hopes he once had of pursuing an independent postwar policy. Instead of 'relying on Britain's own strength and the support of a friendly and consolidated Europe, Churchill decided to pin his hopes upon America'.[44] That Roosevelt's hopes were pinned on Stalin emerges from any study of the last two years of the war that can steer between the Scylla of the Churchillian version and the Charybdis of Cold War hindsight.

By mid-1943, Roosevelt had decided that he needed a bilateral meeting with Stalin, something that shocked Churchill who tried to persuade him against the idea.[45] Roosevelt had been advised by ambassador Joseph Davies that Stalin distrusted Churchill as an old-fashioned imperialist, and Roosevelt, with his invincible belief in himself, thought that he might, face to face, be able to persuade the Soviet leader to try to achieve his territorial objectives without, in the process,

[40] FDR Library, A.A. Berle Papers, diary, Welles to Berle, 4 April 1942.
[41] PRO. FO 945/25, SU/42/26, Butler to Eden, 13 March 1942.
[42] Charmley, *Churchill's Grand Alliance*, 33.
[43] *Churchill–Roosevelt Correspondence*, I, Roosevelt to Churchill, 18 March 1942, 421.
[44] William H. McNeill, *America, Britain and Russia 1941–1946* (1953), 323.
[45] *Churchill–Roosevelt Correspondence*, II, Churchill to Roosevelt, 28 June 1943, 283–284.

offending 'democratic public opinion.'[46] At Tehran, Roosevelt exerted himself to reassure Stalin that America was not going to gang up with the British, telling him that America would not fight him over the future of Poland, and assuring him that whatever Churchill thought, there would be an invasion of France in 1944. In language calculated to appeal to Stalin's realism, Roosevelt told him that the essential thing over Poland was to make Soviet claims in a way which did not upset western opinion, especially his own Polish-American voters. In return, Stalin responded warmly to Roosevelt's ideas for a global United Nations, with both of them rejecting Churchill's view that such a body should be organised on a regional basis. They also agreed on the insignificance of France in a future Europe and on the possible disposal of the French and Italian colonial Empires.[47] The two men even joined in having a little fun at Churchill's expense, teasing him about the future of Germany and suggesting that its entire general staff should be taken out and shot. It was little wonder that Churchill should later have said that it was at Tehran that he had realised for the first time 'what a small nation we are. There I sat with the great Russian bear on one side of me with paws outstretched, and on the other side the great American buffalo, and between the two the poor little English donkey who was the only one ... who knew the right way home.'[48] That last comment did him far more honour than he deserved. In fact, far from Churchill's wooing of Roosevelt paying off in terms of increased influence on American policy, the last eighteen months of the war witnessed both a diminution in British influence and growing signs of stress.

Here the twenty-first century historian may have to part company with the rhythms of the Churchillian grand narrative. An investigation of the internal politics of the Roosevelt administration after the election victory in November 1944, and a study of Anglo-American divergences over Greece and Italy, might reveal a story different in tone and content from the one with which we are familiar. Harry Hopkins had warned Lord Halifax before Roosevelt's re-election in November that the British might well be better off with a Republican victory. The Republicans would 'give you a free hand in India, in Europe and in the Middle East. You will have no embarrassing insistence on this or that in Saudi Arabia and all the other places where you have been accustomed to having your own way. It won't be like that with Roosevelt after the elections.'[49] Nor was it. As Halifax noted in December, there was a

[46] Elizabeth Kimball Maclean, 'Joseph P. Davies' (Ph.D. thesis, University of Michigan, 1986, p. 340, citing Davies' diary, 13 May 1945).
[47] See Charmley, *Grand Alliance*, 78–80 for detailed argument on this theme.
[48] John W. Wheeler-Bennett, *Action This Day* (1967), 96.
[49] FO 371/38550/AN4451, Michael Wright letter, 14 November 1944.

real 'desire for a brand new 100% American foreign policy'.[50] This manifested itself in protests against the reactionary nature of British policy in Greece and Italy, It was all very well for Churchill to protest (in the case of Greece) 'we have a right to the President's support',[51] but that did not make it forthcoming. As Harry Hopkins warned, whilst the administration wanted a 'strong Britain', they 'had ideas of their own on many question which might differ from ours and were not going to be an amenable junior partner. At best, Britain could hope to be 'America's outpost on the European frontier, the sentinel for the New World.'[52] This is not to imply that Anglo-American relations were heading for a breakdown, but it is to question the assumption that Britain gained great influence in Washington as a result of Churchill's deference to the president.

Instead of the real picture, an increasingly assertive America whose policy was unamenable to British guidance, Churchill provides us with an artistically more satisfying conclusion to his story of the Anglo-American alliance. The tragedy in the title of volume six of the war memoirs is, of course, Roosevelt's refusal to heed Churchill's advice after Yalta and to take a firm stand against Soviet designs in Eastern Europe. Argument will always rage over Roosevelt's actions at Yalta, but there seems no reason to disagree with the interpretation that it was essentially an attempt to fudge a settlement in a climate where too much clarity would only expose divisions within the Grand Alliance. As for Churchill's self-proclaimed prescience, there was not much sight of it either before or immediately after the conference. For all his wooing of Roosevelt, the president refused to have a pre-Yalta bilateral meeting with Churchill and preferred to set himself up as the mediator between the British imperialists and the Soviet Communists. His own summary of his policy towards Stalin can hardly be bettered: I think if I give him everything I possibly can and ask for nothing from him in return, noblesse oblige, he won't try to annex anything and will work with me for a world of democracy and peace.'[53] This may, as the president's enemies allege, be a sign of his naïveté, but equally it reflected his belief that he, and he alone, could find a way to give Stalin what he wanted without breaking the Grand Alliance. Moreover, if Roosevelt was naïve, Churchill was no better, returning from Yalta declaring that Stalin was a man who could be trusted.[54] As the signs multiplied, at least in British eyes, that things might not be so optimistic,

[50] FO 371/38551/AN4618, Halifax to Foreign Office, 10 December 1944.

[51] *Churchill–Roosevelt Correspondence*, III, Churchill to Hopkins, 10 December 1944, 451.

[52] FO 371/38550/AN4451, Michael Wright letter, 14 November 1944; Charmley, *Grand Alliance*, pp. 117–118.

[53] F. Harbutt, *The Iron Curtain* (1986) p. 42.

[54] *Churchill–Roosevelt Correspondence*, III, Churchill to Roosevelt, 5 April 1945, p. 613.

Eden concluded that British policy was a 'sad wreck'.[55] Although gloomy, that was not a bad summary. Because of the onset of the Cold War and its effect on the historiography of the period from 1945 to 1947, it is easy to anticipate events and forget that for much of that period the British were anxious about America's refusal to help them against the Soviet, as well as indignant at America's refusal to bail them out financially except at a price. In short, the dividends from Churchill's policy were minimal. The argument that American participation in NATO contradicts such a conclusion is only tenable on the assumption that the British influenced American policy in that direction. For that, as for so many of the assumptions behind the myth of the Special Relationship, evidence is wanting. America came into the Cold War for her own reasons, not because the British persuaded her to do so.

Such, in brief, are the outlines of an alternative version of the Anglo-American alliance. The chances of it winning acceptance should not be rated highly. The Churchill myth was benign in a way that the British needed, and that need shows no sign of ending. It provided them with a gentle and even generous way of stepping down from power and accepting American leadership. When the Cold War came it was easy, as Churchill's memoirs showed, to ignore the 'sad wreck' of the hopes of 1945 and to construct a straight line between 1941 and the Truman doctrine. Churchill himself contributed another step on the road with his Iron Curtain speech, which everyone could conveniently forget had met with a largely hostile reception when it had been given. Parts of the Churchill myth even became true over time. With the decline of empire and the creation of the welfare state the British polity did become more liberal and democratic in tone, and the influence of American popular culture added a new dimension to the Anglo-American relationship. Of course, as Churchill belonged to the class, which saw most to deplore in these developments, it was not surprising that some of its members viewed his achievement with ambiguous feelings.

Churchill resembles Disraeli in many respects, not least in leaving behind a protean legacy that allowed his successors to link an unimagined future with his imagined past. The American illusion allowed the British ruling elite to pretend, to themselves and to their electorate, that Britain was a great power. The costs and consequences of that we live with today; some will welcome it, others not, but we cannot pretend to a neutrality on that part of the Churchillian legacy. More than that, by encouraging the belief that the road to power lay through Washington, Churchill's myth encouraged British statesmen, including himself during his peacetime premiership, to neglect Europe

[55] *The Reckoning*, p. 525.

in favour of the special relationship. This ignored the lessons to be drawn from the fact that twice in one generation Britain had found Europe so important that she had had to stake her imperial might on its freedom. Those voices raised in the first half of the 1940s to argue that Britain should take advantage of the unique position she had won in Europe to lead its unification were ignored in favour of Churchill's grander narrative. A more measured appreciation of the successes and failures of the American alliance might have encouraged a more realistic politics about Europe. Still, we should not complain too loudly. Churchill may have written history the way it ought to have been, but at least he paid it some regard and great respect – which is more than some of our modern politicians do.

CHURCHILL AND THE TWO 'EVIL EMPIRES'

By David Carlton

Introduction

When, on 22 June 1941, Nazi Germany invaded the Soviet Union, Winston Churchill's public response was immediate and unambiguous: in a broadcast to the nation he proclaimed that 'any man or state who fights on against Nazism will have our aid ... It follows, therefore, that we shall give whatever help we can to Russia and the Russian people.' He also referred to his own past as an opponent of Communism: 'I will unsay no word that I have spoken about it, but all this fades away before the spectacle which is now unfolding.'[1] This seminal broadcast has cast a long shadow both backward and forward from 1941 in its effect on how most historians and biographers have seen Churchill's attitude to the two principal dictatorships of the twentieth century.

Looking backward, the following assumptions have tended to be made:

- that Churchill's celebrated hostility to the early Bolshevik state was largely shaped, as in 1941, by strategic calculations centring on British national interest – with the Soviet leaders condemned above all for withdrawing Russia from the common war against Wilhelmine Germany.
- that Churchill was clear once Adolf Hitler had come to power in Germany that the Soviet Union must be courted as a potential ally and that he never wavered from this conviction until, after many vicissitudes, the Soviet Union finally acquired this status as a result of Nazi Germany's attack upon it in June 1941.
- that Churchill's obsessional hostility to Nazi Germany meant that after becoming prime minister in May 1940 he never contemplated a compromise peace with the state that for him represented the sole embodiment of the threat to create a 'new dark age'.

Looking forward from 1941, the following assumptions about Churchill have also tended to command broad support:

[1] *The Times*, 23 June 1941.

- that Churchill had confidence in the Soviets' ability to stand up to the German invasion; attempted sincerely to work in a co-operative spirit with Josef Stalin during the remainder of the war; and, despite some inevitable differences, looked forward to a postwar world built on the Anglo-Soviet 'Percentages Agreement', on the Yalta Declaration and on other agreements reached among the big three.

- that Churchill's criticisms of the Soviet Union and of Communism made at Fulton, Missouri, in March 1946 were offered more in sorrow than in anger and were aimed at creating an Anglo-American framework for 'containment' of any further Communist expansionist designs rather than at a confrontation with Moscow over East European developments that had already taken place beyond the 'Iron Curtain'.

- that Churchill's last premiership (1951–55) was marked by a sincere bid to achieve a lasting *détente* with the Soviets – especially after Stalin's death in March 1953; and that his desire for summitry, unimaginatively blocked by President Dwight Eisenhower and by some members of the British cabinet, farsightedly pointed the way to the eventual ending of the Cold War a quarter of a century later.

Here a challenge will be offered to these various assumptions in the expectation that historians in the twenty-first century will prove increasingly ready to look at a Churchill largely shorn of mythology. And the thesis will be advanced that Churchill, despite tactical trimming, was an adamantine enemy of the Soviet Union from its birth until his retirement in 1955; and that his desire to confront Nazi Germany, though genuine enough, amounted for him to no more than a second-order crusade.

Intervention

Churchill, in common with other British ministers in David Lloyd George's coalition government, reacted to the Bolshevik Revolution of 1917 by supporting collective Allied intervention in order to try to force Russia back into war against Germany. This in practice meant backing the white forces led by A. V. Kolchak, Anton Denikin, and others. But once the struggle with Germany had ended in November 1918 the main reason for British intervention appeared to Lloyd George and most of his colleagues to have ended, although there was uncertainty about how precipitately to withdraw from Russia. At this point Churchill's role became crucial. According to one traditionalist historian, Roland Quinault:

The British troops in Russia became Churchill's direct responsibility when he was appointed Secretary of State for War [and Air] in January 1919. He immediately decided to withdraw the British troops stationed at Murmansk and insisted that all British troops in Russia should abstain from active operations against the Bolsheviks. By the end of 1919 Churchill had reduced the number of British troops in Russia from 40,000 to 2,000. However, he wanted to 'protect as far as possible those who had compromised themselves in the common cause of the Allies and of Russia herself', and he authorised the despatch of surplus stocks of munitions to the anti-Bolshevik forces.

Churchill's hostility to the Bolsheviks stemmed first and foremost from their desertion of the Allies. There is little evidence to support Lloyd George's allegation that Churchill's 'ducal blood revolted against the wholesale elimination of Grand Dukes in Russia'.[2]

This treatment is, however, open to challenge. For it glosses over the fact that Churchill was thought by Lloyd George and other leading colleagues, including Chancellor of the Exchequer Austen Chamberlain, to have been an extremist on the subject of Russia. Churchill was in their eyes during 1919 and 1920 frequently guilty of pursuing his own agenda, namely that of seeking to expand rather than to contract the British presence in Russia and of wanting to eliminate the Bolshevik experiment for ideological reasons. As he put it in a public speech on 11 April 1919: 'Of all the tyrannies in history, the Bolshevist tyranny is the worst, the most destructive, and the most degrading. It is sheer humbug to pretend that it is not far worse than German militarism.'[3] Churchill's colleagues seem not to have endorsed this line and certainly they were not minded to prolong British intervention on ideological grounds alone. On 29 July 1919, for example, Lloyd George called in the war cabinet for early withdrawal from Archangel and Murmansk but Churchill said that 'he was very sorry to be associated with such an operation'. Lloyd George responded that 'it was a mistake to treat the present operations as though they were a campaign against Bolshevism' and claimed that the war cabinet had accepted the view that 'it was not our business to interfere in the internal affairs of Russia'. And he even singled out Churchill for criticism in front of his colleagues, saying:

If the Allies had decided to defeat Bolshevism, great armies would have been required. The small British force in Russia had not been sent there for this purpose. It was true that one member of the

[2] Roland Quinault, 'Churchill and Russia', *War and Society*, 9 (1991), 103.
[3] *The Times*, 12 Apr. 1919.

Cabinet had always urged this policy, but he himself [Lloyd George] had always protested against it.[4]

The war cabinet backed the prime minister and hence troops were withdrawn from Archangel and Murmansk against Churchill's wishes. The latter continued, however, to plead for support for Denikin in the South. Again Lloyd George moved against him – sending this harsh letter of reprimand on 22 September 1919:

> I wonder whether it is any use my making one last effort to induce you to throw off this obsession, which if you will forgive me for saying so, is upsetting your balance ... The reconquest of Russia would cost hundreds of millions. It would cost hundreds of millions more to maintain the new Government until it had established itself. You are prepared to spend all that money, and I know perfectly well that is what you really desire. But as you know that you won't find another responsible person in the whole land who will take your view, why waste your energy and your usefulness on this vain fretting which completely paralyses you for other work?[5]

Even after this Churchill continued to rail, often in public, against the line of his own colleagues well into 1920. But Lloyd George, sorely tried, chose not to dismiss him. Rather he and his entourage began privately to deride him. On 16 January 1920, for example, the prime minister told Sir Henry Wilson, the chief of the general staff, that 'Winston has gone mad.'[6] And on the following day Frances Stevenson, the prime minister's secretary and mistress, recorded in her diary: 'He [Churchill] has arrived [in Paris] simply *raving* because of the decision of the Peace Conference with regard to trading with Russia, which absolutely and finally ruins his hopes of a possible war in the East. At times he became almost like a madman.'[7]

The extent to which Churchill 'lost his balance' on the subject of the early Soviet Union is, then, too little recognised. But one historian who stands out as an exception is Clive Ponting. He has collected some of Churchill's wilder utterances in this early phase:

> He told the House of Commons ... 'Bolshevism is not a policy; it is a disease. It is not a creed; it is a pestilence.' This image of Bolshevism as a disease was one of Churchill's favourites. In the *Evening News* in

[4] War cabinet minutes, 29 July 1919, CAB 23/11, Public Record Office [hereafter PRO].

[5] Lloyd George to Churchill, 22 Sept. 1919, Churchill Papers, in Martin Gilbert, *Winston S. Churchill: Companion*, IV (1977) 869.

[6] Diary of Henry Wilson, 16 Jan. 1920, in *ibid.*, 1004.

[7] *Lloyd George: A Diary by Frances Stevenson*, ed. A.J.P. Taylor (1971), 197.

July 1920 he wrote of 'a poisoned Russia, an infected Russia, a plague bearing Russia'...

The Bolsheviks were also a 'league of failures, the criminals, the morbid, the deranged and the distraught'. In a speech in the Connaught Rooms in April 1919 they were a 'foul combination of criminality and animalism'. Animals were another favourite source of imagery. In a speech in Dundee in November 1918 Bolshevism was described as 'an animal form of Barbarism' and its adherents were 'troops of ferocious baboons amid the ruins of cities and the corpses of their victims' although the 'bloody and wholesale butcheries and murders [were] carried out to a large extend by Chinese executioners and armoured cars'. Again in a speech at the Mansion House in February 1919 he spoke of the 'foul baboonery' of Bolshevism ... although a month later the Bolsheviks were portrayed as vampires.[8]

The singularity of this language, at least in a British context, is surely what is so striking. It suggests that Churchill's approach to the Soviet Union was fundamentally different from that of other leading figures, however conservative, in the British political elite. The question at issue, therefore, is whether he ever really changed.

Churchill in the wilderness: responding to Nazi Germany

One viewpoint – broadly shared also by Martin Gilbert, William Manchester and many other historians – has been succinctly presented by Quinault:

Churchill's attitude to Communist Russia changed after Hitler's accession to power in Germany. This development convinced Churchill that Britain and France should seek a rapprochement with Soviet Russia. In July 1934, after warning about German rearmament, Churchill welcomed the pacific tone recently adopted by [Maxim] Litvinoff, the Soviet Commissar for Foreign Affairs. After Hitler's remilitarisation of the Rhineland in 1936, [Maurice] Hankey [the cabinet secretary] noted that, 'In view of the danger from Germany' Churchill had 'buried his violent anti-Russian complex of former days'. Churchill told Ivan Maisky, the Soviet envoy in London, that Hitler was the greatest threat to the British Empire and that he wanted therefore to rebuild the entente of the First World War between Britain, France and Russia. Churchill interpreted Stalin's purges as a 'lurch to the right' by a regime which had reason to fear

[8] Clive Ponting, *Churchill* (1994), 229–30.

German aggression. Consequently, he had no wish for Britain and France to support a Nazi crusade against Soviet Communism.

Events in 1938 increased Churchill's desire for cooperation with the Soviet Union. After the Anschluss with Austria, Churchill declared that although he detested Russia's form of government, it should not be shunned by Britain ... But Chamberlain responded to the new crisis over Czechoslovakia by seeking an understanding with Hitler, rather than with Stalin. After Chamberlain's visit to Hitler in September 1938, Churchill observed that the premier's fundamental mistake had been his refusal to take Russia into his confidence.[9]

All this is, however, a great oversimplification. First, Churchill's initial response to the appointment of Hitler as German chancellor was to favour a British retreat into isolation. On 14 March 1933, for example, he stated in the House of Commons; 'I hope and trust that the French will look after their own safety, and that we shall be permitted to live our life in our island ... without again being drawn into the perils of the Continent of Europe. But if we wish to detach ourselves, if we wish to lead a life of independence from European entanglements, we have to be strong enough to defend our neutrality.'[10] If he did not favour at this stage any alliance with France, we may be sure that the thought of alliance with the Soviet Union would have been wholly repugnant to him. For as recently as 17 February 1933 he had addressed the Anti-Socialist and Anti-Communist Union in these terms:

> I hope we shall try in England to understand a little the position of Japan, an ancient state with the highest state sense of national honour and patriotism and with a teeming population and a remarkable energy. On the one side they see the dark menace of Soviet Russia. On the other the chaos of China, four or five provinces of which are actually now being tortured, under Communist rule.[11]

Secondly, Churchill did not use language about Hitler and the Nazis in their first years in power that was in any way comparable to that with which he had assailed the Bolsheviks in their early years. For example, he wrote of the Führer as late as 1935: 'We cannot tell whether Hitler will be the man who will once again let loose upon the world another war in which civilization will irretrievably succumb, or whether he will go down to history as the man who restored honour and peace of mind to the great Germanic nation and brought it back serene,

---

[9] Quinault, 'Churchill and Russia', 107. See also, for example, Martin Gilbert, *Prophet of Truth: Winston S. Churchill, 1922–1939* (1976) *passim*; and William Manchester, *The Caged Lion: Winston Spencer Churchill, 1932–1940* (1988), *passim*.

[10] *Hansard*, 14 Mar. 1933, CCLXXV, col. 1820.

[11] *The Times*, 18 Feb. 1933.

helpful and strong, to the forefront of the European family circle.'[12]

Finally, we need to recognise that any moves Churchill did make towards a rapprochement with the Soviets were cautious in character and subject to reversal. It is true that between 1934 and mid-1936 he did speak in public along lines that suggested possible Soviet involvement in collective security arrangements designed to check Germany and he even had some private meetings with Soviet Ambassador Maisky. But he was careful not to propose an Anglo-Soviet alliance and he did not endorse France's alliance with Moscow.

In the summer of 1936, however, he seems to have had second thoughts about the desirability of even limited British association with the Soviets. For he became greatly agitated by the outbreak of the Spanish Civil War and hoped fervently that General Francisco Franco would defeat the 'Red'-leaning government. Moreover, he came to believe that the Soviets had a considerable measure of responsibility for creating the polarised situation in Spain. On 5 November 1936, for example, he vigorously condemned Soviet 'intrigues' there as 'insensate folly'. He elaborated:

> so far as I have been able to ascertain, there is practically no doubt that an enormous influence in creating revolutionary conditions in Spain was the most imprudent and improvident action of Soviet Russia. I say that it would be quite impossible for the free nations of the western world to interest themselves in the fate of Russia, let alone make incursions on her behalf, if she continues to present herself in this guise. It would be a crime to call upon French or British soldiers, or upon the good peoples of these two countries, to go to the aid of such a Russia.[13]

And Churchill was not even apparently unwilling to rule out that Nazi Germany might have to be utilised as a counter against 'such a Russia'. For on 4 August 1936 he was sent a private letter by an intimate friend, General Sir Hugh Tudor, who argued as follows:

> The situation in Europe certainly seems to be getting worse. Spain is a new complication. If the rebels win the Fascist group will be strengthened in Europe, and Spain may line up with Italy and Germany.
>
> If the red Government wins Bolshevism will come very near us. With Spain Bolshie, France half Bolshie, and Russia subsidising our communists are we going to line up with them and Russia?
>
> I know how important even vital our friendship with France is, but I feel many in England would rather make a strong western pact

---

[12] Winston S. Churchill, *Great Contemporaries* (1937), 203.
[13] *Hansard*, 5 Nov. 1936, cccxvii, col. 318.

with Germany and France and let Germany settle Russia and Bolshevism in her own way. No doubt Germany would *eventually* be stronger after defeating Russia but in the meantime we and France would have time to get our defences right; and it would take years before Germany would be in a position to make war again, nor do I suppose she would want to having got a satisfactory expansion. Even Germany cannot like war.

Russia deserves what is coming to her, as she will never stop undermining capitalistic governments in every way she can. If she is left alone, in 10 years or so she will be the strongest power on earth and *she* may want to take in India and may be a more dangerous enemy than Germany.[14]

Churchill's remarkable reply read:

I have, as you divine, been much perturbed in my thoughts by the Spanish explosion. I feel acutely the weight of what you say ... I am sure it represents the strong and growing section of Conservative opinion, and events seem to be driving us in that direction.[15]

This surely is proof that the traditional view of Churchill's attitude to the 'two evil empires' in the 1930s is oversimplified. And more evidence is to be found in 1937, when Churchill told the House of Commons that 'I will not pretend that, if I had to choose between Communism and Nazi-ism, I would choose Communism.'[16]

By 1938–39, it is true, Churchill had returned to the line that the Soviets should be courted with a view to using them to contain Germany. In the meantime, however, Franco had won the Civil War in Spain and Neville Chamberlain had taken over as prime minister without offering Churchill a cabinet post. Had these matters gone otherwise maybe Churchill would have found himself in the camp of the 'appeasers' of Germany rather than working with the British Left for an arrangement with Moscow.

The 'Finest Hour'

'Churchill [on becoming prime minister on 10 May 1940] at once defined British war aims, or rather he laid down a single aim: the total defeat of Hitler and the undoing of all Germany's conquests.'[17] This,

[14] Tudor to Churchill, 4 Aug. 1936, Churchill Papers, in Martin Gilbert, *Winston S. Churchill: Companion*, v (1982) 306–7.
[15] Churchill to Tudor, 16 Aug. 1936, *ibid.*, 313.
[16] *Hansard*, 14 Apr. 1937, cccxxii, col. 1063.
[17] A.J.P. Taylor *et al.*, *Churchill: Four Faces and the Man* (1969), 36.

according to A.J.P. Taylor in 1969, was Churchill's unwavering approach to the Second World War. And this version of history still commands widespread acceptance. But the war cabinet minutes and Neville Chamberlain's diary point to a more complicated reality.

What is now known is that at the time of Dunkirk, Churchill seemingly agreed with his colleagues Chamberlain (the lord president of the council) and Lord Halifax (the foreign secretary) that a settlement with Germany was desirable in principle, provided that satisfactory terms could be obtained. The essential point was, in Halifax's words, that 'matters vital to the independence of this country were unaffected'. There was certainly no insistence, as Taylor supposed, on 'the total defeat of Hitler and the undoing of all Germany's conquests'. On the contrary, Churchill himself stated that he would not object in principle to negotiations 'if Herr Hitler was prepared to make peace on the terms of the restoration of German colonies and the overlordship of Central Europe'. And at one point he went even further. For, according to the war cabinet minutes, he said on 26 May 1940 'that he would be thankful to get out of our present difficulties, provided we retained the essentials of our vital strength, even at the cost of some cession of territory'.[18] That he had in mind cession of British territory is made clear in Chamberlain's diary entry for 27 May, in which he recorded that the prime minister had told his colleagues that 'if we could get out of this jam by giving up Malta and Gibraltar and some African colonies he would jump at it'.[19]

This does not mean, however, that Churchill and Halifax were in complete agreement. But what actually divided them was apparently a rather narrow point: whether and when acceptable peace terms might be on offer. Halifax conceded that the matter was 'probably academic' but he nevertheless favoured accepting a French proposal jointly to invite neutral Italy to try to discover how severe Hitler's terms might be. For the foreign secretary was conscious that if the war continued, 'the future of the country turned on whether the enemy's bombs happened to hit our aircraft factories'. According to the war cabinet minutes, 'he was prepared to take the risk if our independence was at stake, but if it was not at stake he would think it right to accept an offer which would save the country from avoidable disaster'. Churchill, on the other hand, thought that Germany, with France on the point of collapse, would not at this juncture be willing to make such an offer; and he was concerned that it would have a deplorable effect on national morale if it became known that a fruitless bid for such an offer had

[18] War cabinet minutes, 26, 27, and 28 May 1940, CAB 65/13, PRO.
[19] Neville Chamberlain Diary, 26 May 1940, in Clive Ponting, *1940: Myth and Reality* (1990), 107.

been made. Chamberlain then found a formula acceptable to both Halifax and Churchill. According to the war cabinet minutes, he said: 'While he thought that an approach to Italy was useless at the present time, it might be that we should take a different view in a short time, possibly even a week hence.' He then proposed framing a reply to the French, 'which, while not rejecting their idea altogether, would persuade them that now was the wrong time to make it'.[20]

The French disregarded this advice from London and appealed to Benito Mussolini to act as mediator on their behalf. But he refused. It must therefore remain a matter for speculation whether, if Mussolini had acted otherwise, Hitler, given that his primary interest had always lain in the East, would have offered the kind of terms that Churchill's war cabinet could have accepted. As it was, the Battle of Britain went ahead. And when its outcome proved sufficiently favourable to the British to allay their worst fears the war cabinet had no difficulty in uniting on the policy of continued unambiguous prosecution of the war.

An admirable 'revisionist' verdict on all this has been offered by historian David Reynolds:

> there can be little doubt that, contrary to the mythology he himself sedulously cultivated, Churchill succumbed at times to the doubts that plagued British leaders in the summer of 1940 ... The Churchill of myth (and of the war memoirs) is not always the Churchill of history. Scholars working on the 1930s and World War II have long been aware of this discrepancy, but it deserves to be underlined in view of the dogged rearguard action fought by popular biographers and television producers. Contrary to national folklore, Churchill did not stand in complete and heroic antithesis to his pusillanimous, small-minded political colleagues. British leaders in the 1930s and World War II all faced the same basic problem of how to protect their country's extended global interests with insufficient means at their disposal. The various policies they advanced are not to be divided into separate camps – appeasers and the rest – but rather on different points of a single spectrum, with no one as near either extreme as is often believed. This is true of the Chamberlain era; it is also true ... in 1940. In private Churchill often acknowledged that the chances of survival, let alone victory, were slim. He also expressed acceptance, in principle, of the idea of an eventual negotiated settlement, on terms guaranteeing the independence of the British Isles, even if that meant sacrificing parts of the empire and leaving Germany in command of Central Europe ...

[20] War cabinet minutes, 28 May 1940, CAB 65/13, PRO.

This is not in any sense to belittle Churchill's greatness. On the contrary. My contention is that the popular stereotype of almost blind, apolitical pugnacity ignores the complexity of this remarkable man and sets him on an unreal pedestal.[21]

What we may, therefore, conclude for our purposes is that Churchill was not so very inflexible concerning Nazi Germany in 1940 any more than he had been in 1936–37. This needs to be borne in mind as we return to a study of his attitude towards the Soviet Union in the aftermath of Barbarossa.

From Barbarossa to Potsdam

Churchill's famous broadcast of 22 June 1941 gave the impression, which has largely endured, that he welcomed the Soviet Union as an ally and was willing to disregard past differences. In private, however, Churchill spoke at times in terms that would have shocked most of those who listened to his broadcast. On the previous evening, for example, he had told his private secretary, John Colville, that 'Russia will assuredly be defeated'. So his offer of aid may have amounted to little more than posturing. Or, as he put it to Colville, 'if Hitler invaded Hell he would at least make a favourable reference to the Devil!' Then on the next day he privately 'trailed his coat for [Stafford] Cripps [the British ambassador in Moscow], castigating Communism and saying that the Russians were barbarians'. He added, according to Colville, that 'not even the slenderest thread connected Communists to the very basest type of humanity'.[22]

All of this suggests that in June 1941 Churchill had by no means

[21] David Reynolds, 'Churchill and the British "Decision" to Fight On in 1940', in *Diplomacy and Intelligence during the Second World War*, ed. Richard Langhorne (Cambridge, 1985), 165–6. See also David Carlton, 'Churchill in 1940: Myth and Reality', *World Affairs*, 161 (1993–4), 97–103.

[22] John Colville, *The Fringes of Power: Downing Street Diaries, 1939–1955* (1985), 404–5. A decade later Colville recalled that Churchill had declared in the presence of various guests at Chequers, including Cripps, Lord Salisbury, Anthony Eden, Sir John Dill (the chief of the imperial general staff) and Gilbert Winant (the American ambassador): 'I will bet anybody here a Monkey [£500] to a Mousetrap [a sovereign] that the Russians are still fighting and fighting victoriously, two years from now' Martin Gilbert, *'Never Despair': Winston S. Churchill, 1945–1965* (1988), 550. But there appears to be no contemporary documentation supporting this claim; and Colville's published diary does not refer to it. Apart, however, from the chance that Colville's memory may have played him false, there is also the possibility that in the presence of so many witnesses Churchill did not feel able to say that the Soviets would 'assuredly be defeated' lest his 'defeatism' become widely known. Thus his wholly private words to his Private Secretary, as recorded in the latter's contemporary diary, surely give us a much better guide to his real expectations.

changed his mind about the evil that the Soviet Union represented and that he did not expect or perhaps even desire to see the Soviets among the victors at the end of the Second World War. What he actually anticipated was that the Americans would soon join the war and that the Soviets would soon leave it. Then the Anglo-American combination would proceed to defeat Germany and be able to reconstruct the entire European continent on liberal-capitalist lines. His optimism was naturally reinforced in December 1941 when Hitler capriciously declared war on the United States. But it was to be cruelly dispelled during 1942 and 1943 as a result of the Soviets' great military victories on the Eastern Front.

Churchill probably never fully recovered from the blow that came with the realisation that the Soviets would be a principal victor in the 'good' European war he had backed so volubly in 1939. His son Randolph recalled a conversation with Harold Macmillan:

> He [Macmillan] described how in Cairo in 1943 Churchill suddenly said to him late one night: 'Cromwell was a great man, wasn't he?' 'Yes, sir, a very great man.' 'Ah,' he said, 'but he made one terrible mistake. Obsessed in his youth by fear of the power of Spain, he failed to observe the rise of France. Will that be said of me?' He was of course thinking of Germany and Russia.[23]

Churchill was, however, clear by 1943 that, with the Soviets and the Americans now being Britain's allies, the war against Germany would be fought to a finish. But for him this crusade was by no means enough to give him a sense of true fulfilment. Hence he was soon seen by many of his intimates to be devoting at least as much of his attention to frustrating Soviet designs, real or imaginary, as to defeating Germany. One of his obsessions concerned the fate of Greece: in order to save her from Communism he entered into a bilateral negotiation with Stalin during 1944 involving the ruthless abandonment of Romanians, Bulgarians and anti-Communist Russian prisoners-of-war. But none of this was based on a genuine desire to co-operate with the Soviets but was driven by hatred and fear on Churchill's part. In this he undoubtedly differed from most members of the British elite.[24]

Another episode that indicated how eager Churchill was, well before Nazi Germany's final collapse, to frustrate Soviet designs, as he saw them, concerns Spain. This little-known drama surprisingly does not feature in either Churchill's own war memoirs or in Gilbert's authorised biography. It began on 16 October 1944, when Britain's retiring

---

[23] Randolph S. Churchill, *Winston S. Churchill*, II (1967), 283.
[24] On the attitude of the British elite in this period see Martin H. Folly, *Churchill, Whitehall and the Soviet Union, 1940-1945* (Basingstoke, 2000).

ambassador in Madrid, Lord Templewood (formerly Sir Samuel Hoare), with all the authority of an ex-foreign secretary, urged in a memorandum sent to the foreign office that the British, American and Soviet governments send a warning to Franco that Spain must reform its internal regime or face economic sanctions.[25] Foreign Secretary Anthony Eden found this idea attractive and, to Churchill's fury, asked that the matter be raised in the war cabinet. By 4 November Clement Attlee, Labour's leader, was taking the same line. He feared, he stated in a memorandum, that Britain was in danger of being regarded as the Franco regime's sole external supporter among the victors and he accordingly urged a change of direction: 'We should use whatever methods are available to assist in bringing about its downfall. We should, especially in the economic field, work with the United States and France to deny facilities to the present regime.'[26] That both Washington and Paris, given the left-wing mood then prevailing in both capitals, would have been willing to co-operate was of course not in doubt.

Churchill's first response was to confront Eden privately. The prime minister had, above all, been dismayed by a foreign office draft intended for despatch to the US government which had argued that 'if the present unsatisfactory position is allowed to crystallise we may therefore eventually be faced with a new Spanish civil war as the only means of getting rid of the present regime'.[27] This seemed to him to amount to the promotion of Communism. He accordingly drafted a candid minute for his foreign secretary, dated 10 November, which tells us something of his contempt for the foreign office and much about his fear of Europe-wide Communism at a time when most observers would have assumed that he would be concentrating on the defeat of Germany and Japan. First, he stated: 'I am no more in agreement with the internal government of Russia than I am with that of Spain, but I certainly would rather live in Spain than Russia.' He then argued that economic sanctions would not lead to a benign transition to a more liberal order in Spain. He added: 'What you are proposing to do is little less than stirring up a revolution in Spain.' He then set the matter in the wider European context:

Should the Communists become masters of Spain we must expect the infection to spread very fast through Italy and France ... I was certainly not aware that the Foreign Office nursed such sentiments...
I can well believe that such a policy as you outline would be hailed with delight by our Left Wing forces, who would be very glad

[25] Llewellyn Woodward, *British Foreign Policy in the Second World War* (5 vols., 1970–76), IV, 30.
[26] Attlee memorandum, 4 Nov. 1944, WP(44)622, CAB 66/57, PRO.
[27] Draft telegram, 9 Nov. 1944, FO 371/39671/C15949, PRO.

to see Great Britain in the Left Wing of a doctrinal war. I doubt very much, however, whether the Conservative Party would agree once the case was put before them, and personally I should not be able to seek a fleeting popularity by such paths. I should of course be very glad to see a Monarchical and Democratic restoration, but once we have identified ourselves with the Communist side in Spain which, whatever you say, would be the effect of your policy, all our influence would be gone for a middle course.[28]

This minute also deserves to be considered in the context of the British domestic scene. For maybe the prime minister intended it to be understood by Eden as a preliminary to a possible resignation threat. Certainly it should not be forgotten that the House of Commons in 1944 still had a clear majority of Conservative MPs who had been elected in 1935 and who had shown little sympathy for the Left in the Spanish Civil War.

Eden, however, was defiant and made clear his resentment at Churchill's charging the foreign office with having Communist sympathies. In an unusually pompous minute dated 17 November the foreign secretary replied:

It was certainly not my desire to provoke or to precipitate a revolution in Spain ... You also raised in your minute the general question of opposition to Communism. I hope I have satisfied you that it is far from Foreign Office intention to foster Communism in Spain. I think I ought to add that Foreign Office policy has never tended towards fostering Communism anywhere else ...[29]

Matters came to a head at a meeting of the war cabinet on 27 November. Decisive to the outcome was Attlee, who was now evidently reluctant to confront Churchill. Perhaps tabling a memorandum had been sufficient for his purposes, which may have been to appear to be broadly in step with Labour party thinking. At all events, the cabinet minutes recorded him as having 'expressed his entire agreement with the action proposed by the Prime Minister'.[30] This amounted to no more than the despatch to Franco of a hostile message which indicated that Spain would not be allowed to participate in the peace negotiations nor to join the future United Nations. Thus Churchill had frustrated those who favoured economic sanctions and who wanted, in his words, to 'make suggestions to the [US] State Department to beat up the Spaniards'.[31]

[28] Churchill minute no. M1101/4 to Eden, 10 Nov. 1944, FO 371/39671/C16068, PRO.
[29] Eden to Churchill, 17 Nov. 1944, FO 371/39671/C16068, PRO.
[30] War cabinet minutes, 27 Nov. 1944, CAB 65/48, PRO.
[31] Churchill minute no. M1254/4 to Eden, 31 Dec. 1944, PREM 8/106, PRO.

There were limits, however, to what Churchill could achieve in Europe as a whole. For it had become obvious to him by 1943 at the latest that any all-out anti-Soviet crusading on his part would henceforth have to be in a joint partnership with the president of the United States. But during the closing stages of the war he was compelled to see that neither Franklin Roosevelt nor Harry Truman was minded to confront the Soviets. On this matter Averell Harriman was eventually to reflect perceptively:

> It is important to remember that we still had a war to win in the Pacific; our military plans called for a massive redeployment of American troops from Europe to the Far East. I am not persuaded that by refusing to withdraw from the Elbe we could in fact have forced the Russians to allow free elections, and the establishment of freely elected governments, in Eastern Europe...
>
> There was no way we could have prevented these events in Eastern Europe without going to war against the Russians ... But I cannot believe that the American people would have stood for it, even if the President had been willing, which he was not.[32]

Churchill's sense of frustration was further compounded in July 1945 when during the Potsdam Conference he had to hand over the premiership to Attlee following Labour's landslide election victory.

Advocating a US nuclear ultimatum to Moscow

In opposition Churchill seemed to have expected that as an *eminence grise* he would gradually be able to steer both Attlee and Truman on matters relating to the Soviet Union. Immensely encouraged by the emerging East–West tension and by signs of increasing American robustness, he accordingly risked his reputation in March 1946 at Fulton with his dramatic warning about Communism. He also called for a special relationship between the United States and the British Empire, which would enable the two countries 'to walk forward in sedate strength'.[33] This sounds like an endorsement of the containment policy which, at George Kennan's suggestion, the Truman administration was about to adopt towards the Soviet bloc. But Churchill had a hidden agenda during the early Cold War years: he actually favoured not containment but a confrontation with Moscow before the Americans lost their A-bomb monopoly.

As early as the Potsdam conference in July 1945 Sir Alan Brooke,

---

[32] W. Averill Harriman and Elie Abel, *Special Envoy to Churchill and Stalin, 1941–1946* (New York, 1975), 479.

[33] *The Times*, 6 Mar. 1946.

the chief of the imperial general staff, had noted the delight with which Churchill had received the news that the Americans had successfully tested an atomic bomb: 'He had at once painted a wonderful picture of himself as the sole possessor of these bombs and capable of dumping them where he wished, thus all-powerful and capable of dictating to Stalin.'[34] Of course he had to know that only the Americans were actually going to possess these weapons in the immediate postwar years but this was a mere detail: for he seems to have assumed that, whether as prime minister or as leader of the opposition, he would be able to persuade the Americans to do his bidding.

By 8 August 1946 he was confiding to his doctor, Lord Moran, what he envisaged:

> We ought not to wait until Russia is ready. I believe it will be eight years before she has these bombs. America knows that fifty-two per cent of Russia's motor industry is in Moscow and could be wiped out by a single bomb. It might mean wiping out three million people, but they [the Soviets] would think nothing of that.[35]

And gradually he made his views known to an ever larger circle.

Among those he approached were Conservative politicians Macmillan, Eden and Robert Boothby. To Eden, for example, he wrote in September 1948:

> I have felt misgivings and bewilderment ... about the policy of delaying a real showdown with the Kremlin till we are quite sure they have got the atomic bomb. Once that happens nothing can stop the greatest of all world catastrophes.[36]

And overseas leaders canvassed included J.C. Smuts of South Africa and Mackenzie King of Canada. According to King's diary entry for 25 November 1947, Churchill 'thought America would, as indeed she should, tell the Russians just what the United States and the United Kingdom were prepared to do in meeting them in the matter of boundaries, seaports etc., but let them understand that if they were not prepared to accept this, their cities would be bombed within a certain number of days'.[37]

The Americans were also of course aware of what Churchill proposed. He wrote, for example, to General Dwight Eisenhower on 27 July 1948 urging that the West should use its possession of overwhelming force

[34] Arthur Bryant, *Triumph in the West* (1959), 373–4.
[35] Lord Moran, *Winston Churchill: The Struggle for Survival, 1940–1965* (1966) 315.
[36] Churchill to Eden, 12 Sept. 1948, Churchill Papers, in Gilbert, '*Never Despair*', 422.
[37] *The Mackenzie King Record*, IV: *1947–1948*, eds. J.W. Pickersgill and D.F. Forster (Toronto, 1970), 236–7.

to compel them not merely to quit Berlin and all Germany but to retire entirely to within their own borders: failure to do this would make a third world war inevitable.[38] And US ambassador in London Lewis Douglas reported in the same sense to his government:

> You probably know his [Churchill's] view, that when the Soviets develop the atomic bomb, war will become a certainty . . . He believes that now is the time, promptly, to tell the Soviet that if they do not retire from Berlin and abandon East Germany, withdrawing to the Polish frontier, we will raze their cities. It is further his view that we cannot appease, conciliate, or provoke the Soviets; that the only vocabulary they understand is the vocabulary of force; and that if, therefore, we took this position they would yield.[39]

Only once, however, did Churchill risk advancing his views in public. This was at the Conservative party conference held in Llandudno in October 1948. He declared that 'the Western nations would be far more likely to reach a lasting settlement, without bloodshed, if they formulated their just demands while they had the atomic power and before the Russians had it too'. 'We ought', he proclaimed, 'to bring matters to a head and make a final settlement.' He added: 'We ought not to go jogging along improvident, incompetent, waiting for something to turn up, by which I mean waiting for something bad for us to turn up.'[40] Much of the British public and media may not have grasped that this amounted to a call for a threatened immediate military 'showdown'. But *The Times* at least saw the point and did not minimise the risks involved. Its editorial contained this passage:

> it is extremely unlikely that just the threat of the bomb would make Russia consent to a settlement on western terms. No great and proud nation will negotiate under duress: Britain and the United States have rightly refused to do so in the case of Berlin. It is unreasonable to suppose that Russia will willingly negotiate on the division of the world under threat of nuclear bombardment.[41]

After this Churchill showed considerable restraint in public. And even in private Churchill's approach was soon to change with the successful testing of a Soviet atomic bomb in 1949. For his own country, unlike as yet the United States, was now vulnerable to atomic retaliation.

[38] Churchill to Eisenhower, 27 July 1948, Churchill Papers, in Gilbert, *'Never Despair'*, 422.

[39] *Papers Relating to the Foreign Relations of the United States, 1948*, III: *Western Europe*, United States Department of State (Washington, DC, 1974), 90–1.

[40] The full text of Churchill's speech at Llandudno is in *Winston S. Churchill: His Complete Speeches, 1897–1963*, ed. Robert Rhodes James (8 vols., New York, 1974), VII, 7707–17.

[41] *The Times*, 11 Oct. 1948.

All the same, he never entirely abandoned his belief in the case for precipitating a 'showdown'. As late as 4 May 1954 Moran reported him as having said:

> The danger is that the Americans may become impatient. I know their people – they may get in a rage and say: ... Why should we not go it alone? Why wait until Russia overtakes us? They could go to the Kremlin and say: 'These are our demands. Our fellows have been alerted. You must agree or we shall attack you.' I think if I were an American I'd do this. Six years ago in my Llandudno speech I advocated a show-down. They had no bombs then.[42]

All of this surely calls into question Sir Michael Howard's verdict on Churchill at the time of Fulton:

> Churchill was no cold warrior. Wary as he had been of Soviet ambitions and objectives, he had gone to extreme lengths – in the eyes of some, too extreme – to conciliate his wartime ally. He had established – so he believed – a warm relationship with Marshal Stalin. He was sensitive to the security needs of the Soviet state. Most of all, he had a deep respect and affection for the Russian people and a grateful recognition for all they had suffered in the common cause.[43]

As for Churchill's view during the immediate postwar years as to the relative demerits of the two 'evil empires', we find him saying in a public meeting in New York on 25 March 1949:

> We are now confronted with something which is quite as wicked but much more formidable than Hitler, because Hitler had only the Herrenvolk stuff and anti-Semitism. Well, somebody said about that – a good starter, but a bad stayer. That's all he had. He had no theme. But these fourteen men in the Kremlin have their hierarchy and a church of Communist adepts whose mercenaries are in every country as a fifth column.[44]

Advocating summitry

By the time Churchill returned to the premiership in October 1951 the Soviets had successfully tested an atomic bomb of their own and this inevitably meant that even he, as leader of a country now vulnerable

---

[42] Moran, *Winston Churchill*, 545.

[43] Michael Howard, 'Churchill: Prophet of Détente', in *Winston Churchill: Resolution, Defiance, Magnanimity, Good Will*, ed. R. Crosby Kemper III (Columbia, Missouri, 1996) 177–88.

[44] *Complete Speeches*, VII, 7800.

to nuclear bombardment, could no longer plausibly call for decisive 'showdown' with the ultimate enemies of civilisation in Moscow; and in any case Truman would on past form have been unimpressed. The rest of Churchill's time in politics was thus, on this reading, to be a sad anticlimax.

Many historians, however, do not favour this interpretation. For they believe that Churchill in the 1950s became something of an optimist about the Soviets – particularly in the aftermath of Stalin's death. Hence, he called for an early summit in order to explore with the 'new look' leaders in Moscow the prospects for *détente* – an approach frustrated mainly by Cold War Americans. Gilbert, for example, has written:

> On 6 April [1955] Churchill resigned. A decade [*sic*] of seeking amelioration with the Soviet Union, and a summit to set in train a wider negotiated détente, was over. It had been his last, his most sustained, and least successful foray into international affairs.[45]

In urging summitry, however, Churchill was probably motivated primarily either by a desire to hang on to office or to leave office in a spectacular fashion rather than by a genuine belief in any change in Moscow. Historian John Young was at one time tempted to offer an explanation along these lines (though at a later date he seems to have become more inclined to take Churchill's protestations of sincerity at face value):

> The Prime Minister may not have sought détente purely in order to make a reputation as a great peace-maker, but there was a degree of vanity behind his interest in easing tensions with Russia and this blinded him to some of the problems with his policy – particularly the reaction his ideas would have on [Konrad] Adenauer's policy in Germany and on the French government's efforts to secure EDC [the European Defence Community] … After mid-1953 he claimed that it was the hope of reaching a *modus vivendi* with Moscow that kept him in office, but it is difficult to know whether this was a reason or a rationalization for remaining as premier.[46]

Even less complimentary to Churchill was the contemporary verdict of Sir Evelyn Shuckburgh of the foreign office. He wrote in his diary on 24 July 1953:

[45] Martin Gilbert, 'From Yalta to Bermuda and Beyond', in *Churchill as a Peacemaker*, ed. James W. Muller (Cambridge, 1997), 332.

[46] John W. Young, 'Cold War and Détente with Moscow', in *The Foreign Policy of Churchill's Peacetime Administration, 1951–1955*, ed. John W. Young (Leicester, 1988), 75. The note of scepticism is missing in John W. Young, *Winston Churchill's Last Campaign: Britain and the Cold War, 1951–55* (Oxford, 1986).

The more I think of it, the more I disapprove of W.S.C. fostering this sentimental illusion that peace can be obtained if only the 'top men' can get together. It seems an example of the hubris which afflicts old men who have power, as it did Chamberlain when he visited Hitler. Even if you do believe in the theory, surely you should keep this trump card in your hand for emergency and not play it out at a time when there is no burning need, no particularly dangerous tension (rather the reverse) and your opponents are plunged in internal struggles and dissensions. It is hard to avoid the conclusion that W.S.C. is longing for a top-level meeting before he dies – not because it is wise or necessary but because it would complete the pattern of his ambition and make him the father of Peace as well as of Victory. But it would do no such thing unless he were to make concessions to the Russians which there is no need to make, in return for a momentary and probably illusory 'reduction of tension'. After that splendid achievement he would die in triumph and we should all be left behind in a weaker position than before.[47]

Moreover, a minute sent by Churchill to Eden in December 1953 has come to light which Gilbert did not use in his authorised biography and which surely serves to show what an unreconstructed anti-Soviet Churchill privately remained even in his final years in office. He feared that the French would refuse to ratify the EDC project (intended to permit West German rearmament) and that as a consequence the vexed Americans might redeploy their forces in Europe to peripheral areas. He accordingly wrote:

We are all agreed to press EDC through. President Eisenhower rejects the idea that if it continues to be indefinitely delayed an arrangement can be made to include a German army in NATO. It must be EDC or some solution of a 'peripheral' character. This would mean that the United States would withdraw from France and occupy the crescent of bases from Iceland, via East Anglia, Spain, North Africa, and Turkey, operating with atomic power therefrom in case of war. The consequence would be a Russian occupation of the whole of defenceless Germany and probably an arrangement between Communist-soaked France and Soviet Russia. Benelux and Scandinavia would go down the drain. The Americans would probably declare atomic war on the Soviets if they made a forcible military advance westward. It is not foreseeable how they would deal with a gradual, though rapid and certain Sovietisation of western Europe à la Czechoslovakia. It is probable that the process would be gradual so that Sovietisation would be substantially effective

[47] Evelyn Shuckburgh, *Descent to Suez, 1951–56* (1986), 91–2.

and then war came. Thus we should certainly have the worst of both alternatives.

If the United States withdraws her troops from Europe, the British will certainly go at the same time. The approach of the Russian air bases and the facilities soon available to them west of the Rhine would expose us, apart from bombing, rockets, guided missiles etc, to very heavy paratroop descents. We must have all our available forces to garrison the Island and at least go down fighting.

The French should realise that failure to carry out EDC (unless they can persuade the United States to try the NATO alternative) would leave them without any American or any British troops in Europe, and that a third World War would become inevitable. It would be conducted from American peripheral bases, and as the Russian armies would be in occupation of Western Europe all these unhappy countries would be liable to be American strategic bombing points. Whatever happens Great Britain will continue to resist until destroyed. In three or four months or even less after the beginning of atomic war the United States unless out matched in Air Power will be all-powerful and largely uninjured with the wreck of Europe and Asia on its hands...[48]

These are not the words of a serious pioneer of *détente*. For with great certitude they depict the Soviets as unreformable creatures of tireless aggression. In fact they represent the convictions of the visceral anti-Soviet that Churchill had never ceased to be since the first days of the Bolshevik Revolution. In short, his anti-Nazi phase, for which ironically he will always be principally remembered, was for him something of a digression, however necessary, in his extraordinarily long career. Thus, once the Battle of Britain had been won and the Americans had entered the war, the struggle to defeat Germany became for him no more than a second-order crusade. For in his own eyes at least the contest with Soviet Bolshevism was what gave his political life the greatest continuity and meaning.[49]

[48] Churchill to Eden, 6 Dec. 1953, PREM 11/618, PRO.
[49] This paper is based on a much longer study, namely David Carlton, *Churchill and the Soviet Union* (Manchester, 2000). I am grateful to its publisher, Manchester University Press, for permission here to draw on material and arguments which first appeared there.

CHURCHILL AND THE EAST–WEST DETENTE

By John W. Young

AS with many aspects of his career, Churchill's attitude towards
the Soviet Union and Communism has generated considerable
debate.[1] The same statesman who urged war on the Bolshevik
regime in 1919 – likening it to 'troops of ferocious baboons' or 'a
culture of typhoid'[2] – also urged co-operation with Stalin in the
1930s; he spent his last years in office calling for a summit meeting
to reduce Cold War tensions, having himself stirred up those tensions with the 1946 Fulton Speech, where he coined the term 'Iron
Curtain'. Where one historian has concluded that 'ideologically-
based anti-Sovietism and anti-Communism were Churchill's most
abiding obsession for some forty years', placing emphasis on the
rhetoric of the intervention period[3]; another historian recognises that
Churchill's language never reached such intensity again, that
he sought to work with Stalin despite the latter's purges and that
even the Fulton Speech praised the Soviet war effort, welcoming
'Russia to her rightful place among the leading nations of the
world'.[4]

Few will doubt that Churchill genuinely detested Communism. By
aiming at the destruction of monarchy, aristocracy, parliamentary
democracy and private property, as well as the British Empire, its
ideology was directed against all that he cherished. But there is a debate
about whether ideological differences made Churchill 'obsessive' in his
anti-Communism or whether he was capable of a more subtle approach
to the subject. This essay concentrates on his pursuit of a summit in
the 1950s and argues that, in fact, his desire for détente was quite
consistent with his anti-Communism. However, once the USSR had
the atomic bomb, he realised that Communism was most safely
undermined, not by war but by diplomacy, trade and security agree-

[1] I am grateful to the British Academy for providing financial support for the research
that led to this article.

[2] Martin Gilbert, *Winston S. Churchill*, IV (1975), 227 and 257.

[3] David Carlton, *Churchill and the Soviet Union* (Manchester, 2000), 200 and see 201–2 for
the emphasis on 1919–20.

[4] Ian S. Wood, *Churchill* (2000), chapter 4; and, for the Fulton Speech, Randolph S.
Churchill, *The Sinews of Peace* (1948), 93–105.

ments that would 'infiltrate' the Soviet bloc and eventually dissolve totalitarianism from within.[5]

Churchill and the USSR before 1950

As his political life developed, and particularly after 1929, Churchill increasingly focused on foreign, imperial and defence issues. He had a view of international affairs that best fits within the 'realist' school of analysis: countries are involved in a struggle for power in an anarchic environment; under the logic of the 'balance of power', the weak must band together if the strong are to be resisted; and alliances and armed forces are a better guarantee of survival than international law or organisations. His complaint against the appeasers in the 1930s was not that they negotiated with Hitler but that they did so from a position of weakness, that they 'neither prevented Germany from rearming, nor did they rearm themselves in time ... and they neglected to make alliances'.[6] Yet Churchill also believed that certain groups of countries could share a common outlook, hence his interest in co-operation with the 'English-speaking' Dominions, in European unity and in a 'special relationship' with America. He believed in promoting trade links as a way to ensure peace, he favoured active diplomacy and, partly because he believed in the balance of power, he was ready to respect the sphere of influence of rival states – so long as they did not impinge on Britain's. In December 1950 he even declared that, while 'Appeasement from weakness and fear is ... fatal. Appeasement from strength is magnanimous ... and might be the surest way to peace.'[7] This may seem to be at odds with his dislike of totalitarianism, but in fact it was not in contradiction to it, because, alongside his *realpolitik*, Churchill also had a faith in humanity that told him that repressive regimes could not last forever.

Where the USSR was concerned Churchill's realism led him to accept, by the 1930s, that it would exist for some time and was an essential component in any anti-German balance of power. Roland Quinault has argued that this was consistent with Churchill's view of

---

[5] I first made the case that Churchill accepted 'the division of Europe in the short-term whilst hoping eventually to see a withering away of Soviet Communism' in *Winston Churchill's Last Campaign* (Oxford, 1996), quote from vi–vii; but I was deeply indebted to two earlier works: Kenneth Thompson, *Winston Churchill's World View* (Baton Rouge, 1983); and S. J. Lambakis, 'The Soviet Union and Churchillian Diplomacy' (Ph.D. thesis, Catholic University of America, 1990).

[6] Martin Gilbert, *Winston S. Churchill*, v (1976), 999.

[7] Robert Rhodes James (ed.), *Winston S. Churchill: His Complete Speeches, 1897–1963* (8 vols., New York, 1974), 8143.

Russia since before the 1917 revolution; that he had a 'persistent belief that Russia was a major and essential element in the international community . . .' and 'always regarded Russia as a natural ally of Britain and other powers who wished to check German ascendancy in Europe'.[8] His dealings with the USSR during the Second World War are still the focus of much debate. In his memoirs, written as the Cold War began, he naturally portrayed himself as a tough opponent of Stalin, an approach some historians have followed.[9] But others argue that Churchill's military strategy for most of the war was not well geared to limiting Soviet influence at the end of it.[10] Two of the most detailed studies of wartime policy towards the USSR see him as uncertain in his overall approach: for Martin Kitchen, the prime minister genuinely sought a good working relationship with Stalin, underestimated the revolutionary content of Soviet policy and, even in 1945, wavered over taking a firmer stand; while for Martin Folly, Churchill was quite prepared in the last months of the war to talk sharply to the Soviets' when he felt agreements were being broken, but at the Potsdam summit in July he was 'hardly . . . uncompromising'. In particular the prime minister looked positively on Stalin's desire for a warm-water port, giving the Soviets access to the world's oceans.[11]

The most controversial of Churchill's wartime dealings with Stalin was the so-called 'percentage deal' of October 1944, the essence of which was that Britain preserved Greek independence of Moscow while the Soviets gained predominance in Romania and Bulgaria. As John Charmley has argued, the 'percentage deal' was no aberration but an attempt to secure a deal on spheres of influence in Europe that would restrain Stalin's ambitions and provide the basis for Britain and the USSR to work together after the war.[12] Faced by a deteriorating position in the Balkans, and with the US unwilling to engage in such divisions of territory, the prime minister put his faith in secret diplomacy, a head-to-head meting and a spheres of influence arrangement that fitted his *realpolitik*. Such an approach was to be revived by him when he returned to the premiership in 1951. Indeed, in 1953 Churchill was even to recall the October 1944 visit to Moscow as 'the highest level

[8] Roland Quinault, 'Churchill and Russia', *War and Society*, 9 (1991), 99.

[9] For example, Richard G. Kaufman, 'Winston Churchill and the art of statecraft', *Diplomacy and Statecraft*, 3 (1992), 175.

[10] The thesis is best argued in T. Ben-Moshe, *Churchill: Strategy and History* (1992) or in John Charmley, *Churchill's Grand Alliance* (1995), chapters 3–14.

[11] Martin Kitchen, *British Policy towards the Soviet Union in the Second World War* (1986); Martin Folly, *Churchill, Whitehall and the Soviet Union* (2000), quote from 164.

[12] Charmley, *Grand Alliance*, 102–3. For other discussions of this episode see P.G.H. Holdich, 'A Policy of Percentages?' *International History Review*, 9 (1987), 28–47; and John Kent, *British Imperial Strategy and the Cold War* (Leicester, 1993), 23–33.

we ever reached' in Anglo–Soviet relations.[13] In the meantime, however, after losing office in the very midst of the Potsdam conference, Churchill was to become known, not for his desire to co-operate with the Soviets, but for urging resistance to them.

In the aftermath of the war Anglo-Soviet relations quickly became strained, not least over spheres of influence in the Near East. By November 1945 Churchill was advocating an alliance with America because the 'fact that ... the English-speaking world is bound together, will enable us to be better friends with Soviet Russia ... that realistic state.'[14] Four months later Churchill made his Fulton Speech, with its condemnation of the 'Iron Curtain' and its call for a 'special relationship between the British Commonwealth ... and the United States'. Although the image of the Iron Curtain became part of Cold War rhetoric, the logic of the speech was typical of Churchill's established outlook on the world: the Soviets were a threat, but 'there is nothing they admire as much as strength' and an Anglo-American alliance was necessary to deter them. But at the same time he spoke of his 'strong admiration ... for the valiant Russian people', advocated 'frequent and growing contact with them' and hoped that Western strength would pave the way for an East–West 'settlement'.[15] Over the following few years Churchill supported the unity of the West under American leadership, particularly with the Marshall plan and Atlantic alliance, while also referring to hopes of an East–West settlement. But he had radically different views, even in his own mind, about how to bring such a settlement about.

With the diplomatic breakdown between the USSR and the Western allies in late 1947, and especially during the dangerous months of the Berlin blockade, Churchill privately pressed an idea that had been forming in his mind for some time. Concerned that America's atomic monopoly would not last and fearful that the Cold War must at some point become hot, he wanted to force Stalin to accept a 'reasonable' settlement by threatening the USSR that – if they did not accept such a settlement – they would be subjected to nuclear attack. This was a dangerous twist to the logic of 'negotiation from strength' but Churchill avoided stating it baldly in public and he was far from being alone in such ideas. Various Americans advocated a pre-emptive strike against the USSR, if only to avoid a worse conflict later, and one air force general was sacked in 1950 for publicly urging this. Fortunately President Truman never accepted such logic. In London the idea of a showdown

[13] Lord Moran, *Winston Churchill: The Struggle for Survival* (1966), diary entry of 24 February 1953.
[14] Martin Gilbert, *Winston S. Churchill*, VIII (1988), 166–7.
[15] Churchill, *Sinews of Peace*, 93–105.

was contemplated by, among others, the chiefs of staff, Harold Mac-millan and even the philosopher – and later anti-nuclear campaigner – Bertrand Russell.[16] 'Either we must have a war against Russia before she has the atom bomb', Russell once told an audience of schoolboys, 'or we will have to lie down and let them govern us.'[17]

Return to power, 1950–2

Even as he was privately contemplating a 'showdown' Churchill's speeches were developing in parallel an alternative, long-term strategy for securing victory in the Cold War. At the Party conference in October 1948, a few months into the Berlin blockade he spoke against 'false hopes of a speedy ... settlement with Soviet Russia' and came the closest he ever did in public to urging a 'showdown'; but he also hoped that, if the USSR could be opened to 'the ordinary travel and traffic of mankind', then it could lead 'the spell of ... Communist doctrines to be broken.'[18] And in 1949, in New York, he said that the Kremlin 'feared the friendship of the West' because 'free and friendly intercourse' with the outside world would destroy Communism.'[19] 'Contacts and trade', Martin Gilbert has written, 'these were the twin tracks of Churchill's search for a way to ease the East–West divide.'[20] With the end of the US atomic monopoly later that year, and the growing danger thereafter of a Soviet nuclear strike on Britain, the desirability of a 'showdown' became less attractive and it was the alternative ideas, of opening contacts with the Soviets as the way to break down the Iron Curtain, which came to the fore in Churchill's thinking. This was most noticeable in his February 1950 election address in Edinburgh, where he called for a 'parley at the Summit', which would be 'a supreme effort to bridge the gulf between the two worlds, so that each can live their life ... without the hatreds of the Cold War'. It was the first time the word 'summit' had been used to describe an East–West leaders' meeting and (like 'Iron Curtain') it soon became part of popular vocabulary. But it would be wrong to contrast the messages of Edinburgh and Fulton: just as the earlier speech had praise for Stalin and hoped for a settlement of differences, so the later one condemned Soviet expansionism and emphasised the importance of the US nuclear arsenal

---

[16] Young, *Last Campaign*, 23–28.
[17] Caroline Moorehead, *Bertrand Russell* (1992), 469.
[18] Randolph S. Churchill, *Europe Unite* (1950), 409–24.
[19] Randolph S. Churchill, *In the Balance* (1951), 32–9.
[20] Martin Gilbert, 'From Yalta to Bermuda and Beyond: In Search of Peace with the Soviet Union', in James W. Muller (ed.), *Churchill as Peacemaker* (Cambridge, 1997), 322.

for Western defence.[21] It should also be noted that, as Churchill made clear in another speech some months later, one purpose of a summit would be 'to bring home to the ... Soviet government the gravity of the facts which confront us all'.[22] Thus, even if a nuclear attack were not actually to be threatened by the West, the danger of nuclear war was still seen as the way to induce Stalin to settle his differences with his former allies.

Once again the key to understanding Churchill's thinking was the concept of negotiation from strength. Both elements were generally present in his speeches but the precise balance between them, and the specific proposals that fleshed them out, varied according to the international situation and political needs at home. Despite helping to proclaim the Cold War, Churchill had 'a world view which was quite different to the one the Americans had adopted'; he condemned Communist tyranny and would resist it, but he was also imbued with the British diplomatic tradition that you might have to coexist with those you despised.[23] On returning to Downing Street in 1951 Churchill continued to believe that Communism must be resisted, that the West must be strongly armed – not least with a formidable nuclear arsenal – and that Britain must work closely with America. But he had no desire for a relentless anti-Communist crusade, he wanted to avoid a Soviet nuclear strike on Britain and he hoped to develop diplomatic, personal and trade links as ways of breaching the Iron Curtain.

Despite the Edinburgh speech, and similar calls from Churchill for a summit during the October 1951 election, he returned to power in the wake of taunts from the Labour party that he was a warmonger. These may have reinforced his determination to make his name as a great peacemaker, his reputation as a war leader being secure. His age (he was seventy-six) and his ill health (he had suffered a stroke in 1949) suggested he might not be in power long, but the very arteriosclerosis from which he suffered also made him more set in his ways. Had he been, at heart, an obsessive anti-Communist then it would have been abundantly obvious at this point, given his condition; but in fact he was to focus much of his energy before retirement on a relaxation of tension with the Soviets, undermining their rule through a policy of moderation rather than threat.[24] In early November he sent a message of 'Greetings' to Stalin[25] and told the Commons that there should be

[21] James, *Churchill Speeches*, 7285–93.
[22] *Ibid.*, 8048–50.
[23] Charmley, *Churchill's Grand Alliance*, 265.
[24] On the effect of Churchill's ill health see J. M. Post and R. S. Robins, *When Illness Strikes the Leader* (New Haven, 1993), 18–20, 43–5 and 67–8.
[25] Public Record Office [hereafter PRO], FO 371/94841/134, Churchill to Stalin, 4 Nov. 1951.

'an abatement of the Cold War by negotiation at the highest level.'[26] He was not alone in hoping for such a relaxation. Anthony Eden, also believed in active diplomacy to break down barriers, was prepared to make spheres of influence arrangements with the Soviets and, having returned to the foreign office, devoted his first major international speech, at the UN on 12 November 1951, to a plea for 'a truce to name-calling' in the Cold War.[27] The foreign office drew up a paper late in the year, on fighting the Cold War in the long-term, which seemed to echo Churchill's approach in some ways: the West must first seek an 'equilibrium between the two blocs'; it should then be ready for a 'period of coexistence' in which limited agreements could be possible; and eventually, if there were a 'change in the nature of the ... Soviet regime', there could be a 'genuine settlement.'[28] It soon became clear, however, that even if they shared Churchill's long-term hopes, Eden and the foreign office disliked the idea of an early summit, on a loose agenda, that put the ageing, ailing prime minister in the spotlight. Instead, the professional diplomats preferred talks at foreign ministers' level, on fixed topics, with careful preparation.

His own poor health and the scepticism of the foreign office were not the only problems to face the prime minister. Far more difficult to overcome was the negative attitude of the Truman administration. For Churchill the American alliance was essential to negotiation from strength, and he wanted an early visit to Washington in to establish a close working relationship with the White House. But Cold War fears were at their height in America, where McCarthyism was gathering pace. US planners saw little chance of fruitful talks with the USSR at present and they ruled out a summit meeting, at least until a settlement was achieved to the Korean War, which had been raging for over a year. They were also concerned that any relaxation of tension would undermine efforts to rearm the West, and especially the process of rearming West Germany. The US had proposed West German rearmament in late 1950 and had thereby stirred up a major controversy in the Atlantic alliance. France and other European countries eventually agreed to proceed only on the condition that German troops were securely lodged in a supranational European Army. Negotiations for a 'European Defence Community' (EDC) got underway in 1951 but any sign that the Cold War was ending could lead the French, in particular, to argue that the whole effort should be abandoned.[29]

Given the American position, it is unsurprising that Churchill's visit

[26] James, *Churchill Speeches*, 8296–7.
[27] Young, *Last Campaign*, 44–6 and 49–52.
[28] FO 371/125002/4, PUSC(51)16 (17 Jan. 1952).
[29] Based on Young, *Last Campaign*, 53–62 and 67–72.

to Washington in January 1952 saw no progress towards talks with Stalin. When Churchill suggested that a tough Western policy towards the USSR merely helped to solidify the Stalinist system, the US secretary of state, Dean Acheson, dismissed the argument.[30] The Soviet issue, originally placed first on the agenda, was not actually discussed until the end of the visit, when Truman was quick to set out his doubts about an early summit. He did reassure Churchill that America was not planning a 'showdown' with Moscow, however, and in return the prime minister said that, with regard to a Summit 'he would not do anything ... to make things more difficult for the President'. This meeting was noteworthy for making clear, once more, that Churchill's desire for a summit was part of a broader campaign to undermine Soviet power: the British record shows that time was devoted to the issue of a 'psychological warfare' campaign to provoke division inside the Eastern bloc.[31] After his North American visit, Churchill was well aware that, with the start of the US election campaign, little progress was possible on a summit. In March 1952 therefore he barely expressed interest in the 'Stalin note', a Soviet proposal to sign a German peace treaty on condition that a reunited Germany was neutralised between East and West. In any case, the Stalin note seemed no more than a last-ditch attempt to prevent the EDC Treaty being signed (an event that occurred in May).[32] His enthusiasm for a summit revived over summer, however, when it became obvious that the next American president might be his old wartime colleague, Dwight Eisenhower. In August, Churchill contemplated a summit with Eisenhower and Stalin, where the Potsdam conference – still unfinished business for the prime minister – 'would be reopened'.[33] But the signs from the American election did not necessarily favour détente. The campaign was over-shadowed by the bloody deadlock in Korea, McCarthyism was at its most intense and John Foster Dulles (Eisenhower's chief spokesman on foreign policy) emphasised the need to 'liberate' those living under Soviet rule.[34]

[30] *Foreign Relations of the United States* [hereafter *FRUS*], *1952–4, vol. VI* (Washington, 1986), 530–42; Dean Acheson, *Present at the Creation* (1970), 597–9.

[31] PRO, CAB 134/3058, minutes of fifth plenary meeting (18 Jan. 1952); *FRUS, 1952–4, VI*, 846–9.

[32] See Rolf Steininger, *The German Question: the Stalin Note of 1952 and the problem of reunification* (New York, 1990).

[33] J. Colville (edited by J. Charmley), *The Fringes of Power: 10 Downing Street diaries* (1985), 650 and see 654.

[34] But Eisenhower did moderate his own line as the election approached: see Robert A. Divine, *Foreign Policy and US Presidential Elections, 1952–60* (New York, 1974), 50–56.

Stalin's death and the call for a summit, 1953

In January 1953 Churchill arrived in New York to see Eisenhower, now president-elect. As in the meetings with Truman, the prime minister's purpose was both to establish a close working relationship and explore US views on détente. But again he left disappointed: for, while Eisenhower had expressed a readiness to hold a summit, he also suggested it need not involve the British![35] In late February the president spoke in public of a possible meeting with Stalin, without mentioning Britain: this led Churchill to tell the Commons, on 3 March, 'I should be quite ready at any time to meet President Eisenhower and Marshal Stalin ...'[36] Ironically, however, it was the death of Stalin, only three days later, which really opened the way for Churchill's campaign for a summit. The new 'collective leadership' in Moscow was keen to install itself in power without any external complications and, within a week, made several statements that it wanted to settle international problems peacefully.[37] Churchill wasted little time in suggesting to Eisenhower that a summit should now be proposed but was rebuffed, the president arguing that the 'collective leadership' would merely use such an occasion for propaganda purposes.[38] In Washington, Dulles, now secretary of state, championed the view that now was the time to put pressure on the Soviets, not relax it; and this view tended to win out over the president's more positive approach. It took six weeks before Eisenhower made a public statement – the 'Chance for Peace' speech – welcoming the Kremlin's desire for peace but demanding hard evidence of its good intentions. Specifically, the US wanted to see an end to the Korean War, peace in Vietnam (where France was engaged in a colonial war with Communist-led nationalists) and the signature of an Austrian peace treaty.[39]

In London the foreign office, too, was sceptical about any real change in Soviet policy.[40] But Churchill continued to hope for détente, writing to Eisenhower on 11 April that 'there is a change of heart in Russia'

[35] PREM 11/422, record of meeting (8 January 1953); *FRUS, 1952–4, Secretary of State's Memoranda of Conversations* (microfilm, Washington, 1952); and see Colville, *Fringes,* 662–3.

[36] *Public Papers of the Presidents of the United States: Dwight D. Eisenhower, 1952* (Washington, 1960), 69–70; Hansard, *House of Commons Debates, Volume 512,* cols. 17–19.

[37] Denise Folliot (ed.), *Documents on International Affairs, 1953* (1956), 1–2, 8–9 and 11–13.

[38] Peter Boyle, *The Churchill–Eisenhower Correspondence, 1953–5* (Chapel Hill, NC, 1990), 31–2.

[39] Folliot (ed.), *Documents,* 45–51; and on the debates that preceded the speech see especially Walter W. Rostow, *Europe after Stalin* (Austin, Texas, 1982).

[40] But Eden did consider the possibility of meeting the Soviets at foreign minister's level. See Young, *Last Campaign,* 135–6 and 142–9.

and objecting to parts of the 'Chance for Peace' speech.[41] Only a few days later the prime minister's ability to shape British policy was strengthened when Eden was forced into hospital for a gallstones operation that went terribly wrong, forcing him into temporary retirement for several months. Churchill then took control of the foreign office himself and used a speech in Scotland on 17 April to speak of a 'new breeze blowing on the tormented world'.[42] He sent a number of messages to Eisenhower over the following weeks, suggesting either a summit or 'a personal contact' with Moscow. But the president was opposed to both these ideas.[43] So, on 11 May an exasperated Churchill used a speech on foreign affairs in the Commons to call for 'a conference on the highest level ... between the leading powers without long delay'. The details of what the summit would discuss were left deliberately vague, Churchill preferring to work to an open agenda. Junior ministers from the foreign office were only shown the speech a few hours before it was delivered. Eisenhower was not consulted at all.[44]

It has been claimed that Churchill 'did *not* have in view' any 'concrete agreements' between East and West in the 1950s; and that he did not 'advocate that the West should make any concessions ... on any of the great issues of the day ...'[45] This is simply mistaken. In fact, Churchill did seek concrete advances, not least a relaxation of East–West trade limits (discussed below). He was also ready to concede the creation of a Communist regime in North Vietnam in 1954, telling a US official that it made no sense to clash with the Soviets on 'the fringes' of the world.[46] But, most controversially of all, in the 11 May speech he advocated a 'new Locarno' pact for Europe, which would relax tensions in Central Europe and give the USSR a sense of security, not least by removing the danger of German irredentism. 'Russia has a right to feel assured that ... the ... Hitler invasion will never be repeated ...' This was not a one-sided concession, for his hope was that, under the new system, 'Poland will remain a friendly power ... though not a puppet state' of the Soviet Union. But the idea caused a furore in West Germany, where the Adenauer administration was within six months of an election. The problem for Adenauer was that the 'new Locarno' proposal, however it was pursued, spelt political danger. If it were to involve mutual recognition of Germany's existing borders, that would also mean acknowledging East Germany's existence and put off German

[41] Boyle, *Correspondence*, 41–2.
[42] James, *Churchill Speeches*, 8465–70.
[43] Boyle, *Correspondence*, 46–55.
[44] *House of Commons Debates, Volume 515*, cols. 883–98; Anthony Nutting, *Europe Will Not Wait*, 50.
[45] Carlton, *Soviet Union*, 203.
[46] PREM 11/645, record of conversation with Radford, 26 April 1954.

reunification for the foreseeable future: steps which Bonn – and Washington – were unwilling to take and which would alienate German voters. But if Germany had to be reunified before the 'new Locarno', then that threw open the whole issue of a German peace treaty.[47] For at least one German historian, the proposal suggested that Churchill was ready to sacrifice West Germany's alliance with the West in order to achieve stability in Europe.[48] After discussions with Adenauer later in May, Churchill avoided further public debate over the 'new Locarno' idea but continued to urge it in private meetings.[49]

Adenauer was not the only Western leader to be dismayed by the 11 May speech and it was soon clear that Churchill could not 'bounce' his allies into a summit. In Paris there was grave concern, not only that talk of a relaxation of Cold War tensions would undermine the government's attempts to ratify the EDC treaty, but also that Churchill intended to exclude France from a summit. As a result the French asked Eisenhower to arrange a three-power Western summit to try to control the British leader's ambitions. The president, equally concerned at the situation, agreed to do so. He won Churchill over to the idea partly by agreeing to hold the 'Western summit' on the British territory of Bermuda. Arranging this conference then proved difficult because the French government almost immediately fell from office, plunging France into weeks of political crisis.[50] The conference had still not met when, on 23 June, Churchill suffered an even more grievous blow, a crippling stroke, which forced him to avoid public appearances. Yet even without these problems, the idea of a summit might have come to nothing. Evidence from the Soviet archives suggests that, while ready to improve bilateral relations with Britain, the 'collective leadership' was cautious in its dealings with Churchill. The 11 May speech made little impact in Moscow, mainly because it was felt he would be unable to force a change of policy on Washington.[51]

Soviet policy was itself thrown into confusion in mid-June by the so-called 'Berlin rising'. It is now clear that this event, which in fact affected much of East Germany, was partly triggered by hopes of some Soviet leaders for a radical change of policy. In particular, Lavrenti

[47] Konrad Adenauer, *Errinerungen, 1953–5* (Stuttgart, 1966), 204–9.

[48] Klaus Larres, *Politik der Illusionen: Churchill, Eisenhower und die deutsche Frage* (Gottingen, 1995), 127–33; also Klaus Larres, 'Integrating Europe or ending the Cold War? Churchill's Post-War Foreign Policy', *Journal of European Integration History*, 2 (1996), 34–9. Other discussions of the 'New Locarno' proposal include Anthony Glees, 'Churchill's Last Gambit', *Encounter*, 64 (April 1985), 27–35; and Jurgen Foschepoth, 'Churchill, Adenauer und die Neutralisierung Deutschlands', *Deutschland Archiv*, 12 (1984), 1286–1301.

[49] Young, *Last Campaign*, 164–6 and 193.

[50] Based on Young, *Last Campaign*, 166–76.

[51] Uri Bar-Noi, 'The Soviet Union and Churchill's Appeals for High-Level Talks, 1953–4,' *Diplomacy and Statecraft*, 9 (1998), 112–18.

Beria, chief of the secret police, was ready to contemplate the reunification and neutralisation of Germany.[52] Churchill's reaction to the
rising – which occurred just before his stroke – was astonishing, but
very revealing of the extent to which he wanted to pursue détente: he
complained when allied representatives in Berlin condemned the Red
Army's crushing of the rising; he even told one British general that the
Soviets had the right to enforce martial law 'in order to prevent anarchy
. . .'[53] As it was the rising proved a further blow to any hopes of a 'thaw'
in the Cold War. Following Churchill's stroke, the Bermuda conference
had to be postponed. Instead, Lord Salisbury became acting foreign
secretary and went to Washington to discuss the international situation
with Dulles and the French foreign minister, Georges Bidault. With the
last two opposed to a summit with the Soviets, it was agreed instead
to seek an East–West foreign ministers' meeting on a precise agenda,
including the German problem. But, in the wake of the Berlin rising
the Soviets were keen to stabilise their position in East Germany before
opening the German question for debate with the West. As a result,
they stalled on the idea of a foreign ministers' meeting for several
months.[54]

The renewed campaign and a Cabinet crisis, 1953–4

As Churchill recovered from his stroke, the drive to obtain what he
now called 'easement', linked to the idea of a summit, became one of
the very few issues that interested him. To the despair of his fellow
ministers, the hope of achieving an improved international atmosphere
became the prime motive for the leader's refusal, despite his deteriorating health, to hand over to Eden – who had himself recovered
from illness by October 1953. Some might argue that détente became
a mere rationalisation of Churchill's desire to cling to office; and in
such a character the mix of selfish and idealistic motives was doubtless
complex. But his commitment to détente, and particularly his wish for
a summit, was already obvious *before* his stroke and the tenacity with
which he pursued his aim, especially in mid-1954, shows that it
motivated him strongly. As he explained to Eisenhower (who remained
unmoved by the argument), there was no question 'of being fooled by
the Russians'; Churchill was all too aware of the military threat they
posed to Western Europe; but he believed that the Western alliance
was solid enough to negotiate from a position of strength now, and

[52] See Amy Knight, *Beria* (Princeton, 1994), 191–4.
[53] PRO, FO 800/822, Churchill to Coleman, 22 June.
[54] Based on Young, *Last Campaign*, 184–202.

that time would lead to 'the ebb of Communist philosophy . . .'[55] Some hope of progress was given by the end of the Korean War in July and Churchill told the party conference on 10 October – the occasion that marked his return to active political life – that he was staying in office 'not because of love of power' but because of his hopes of 'sure and lasting peace'.[56] Soon after that he succeeded in reviving the proposal for a 'Western summit' and a date of early December was set for the Bermuda conference.

Any hope that Churchill had of persuading the US and French governments to accept the specific idea of a summit with the Russians was undermined in late November when Moscow finally accepted the proposal for a four-power foreign ministers' meeting. This was arranged for Berlin in late January. The claim, that Churchill 'spent a large portion' of the Bermuda meeting, arguing for a summit.[57] With any diplomatic talks now destined to occur between foreign ministers, what Churchill did focus on was general arguments for a détente policy: the fact that the West was strong enough to pursue this; the desirability of testing whether there was a real change of policy in the Kremlin; the wisdom of providing Moscow with security guarantees in Europe; and his belief that trade and personal contacts could be used to 'infiltrate' the Iron Curtain and undermine Communism from within. But Eisenhower stated that the Kremlin was a 'whore' who had done no more than change her appearance in recent months and the French made it quite clear that signs of a 'thaw' were weakening the Western alliance, by undermining support in the French parliament for the EDC.[58] Churchill, though never enthusiastic about the EDC, reluctantly recognised that it must be passed if Western unity were to be preserved and 'peace through strength' pursued. If it were not passed, then the US could fall back on a 'peripheral' defence strategy, leaving continental Europe open to Communist advances.[59] This would undermine the very Western position of strength that he saw as essential to successful dealings with Moscow.

Churchill complained that the Bermuda communiqué showed not 'the slightest desire for the success of the (Berlin) conference . . .'[60] Sure enough the foreign ministers' gathering quickly became deadlocked on the future of Germany. But Churchill urged Eden to avoid a complete

[55] Boyle, *Correspondence*, 82–6.
[56] James, *Churchill Speeches*, 8494–7.
[57] M. Steven Fish, 'After Stalin's Death: the Anglo-American Debate over a New Cold War', *Diplomatic History*, 10 (1986), 352.
[58] Based on Young, *Last Campaign*, 222–9.
[59] PREM 11/618, Churchill to Eden, 6 Dec.
[60] PREM 11/418, Churchill to Eden, 7 Dec.

breakdown and bid the Soviets 'au revoir and not goodbye'.[61] He got
his wish. Before Berlin closed on 18 February, it was agreed that there
should be another foreign ministers' conference a few months later in
Geneva, to discuss Far Eastern problems. Before this conference met,
Churchill's hopes of moving the negotiations to leaders' level received
encouragement from an unexpected source: the Kremlin. There were
now signs that elements in Moscow realised Churchill might genuinely
be aiming at a relaxation of tension the prime minister, Georgi
Malenkov, wanted to exploit and, in March, a member of the Soviet
embassy approached Churchill's son-in-law, Christopher Soames, saying
a meeting between the two premiers was possible.[62] This was welcome
to Churchill, but he felt he should visit Eisenhower first, in order to
win him over.[63] Before looking at how the proposal developed, however,
it is important to note that Churchill's efforts to improve East–West
relations in another area, that of trade, also reached their height at this
time.

Apart from advocating a summit meeting and a 'new Locarno',
Churchill's campaign for détente included one other main proposal: a
reduction of East–West trade limits. In 1950, Western countries had
created the Co-ordinating Committee (COCOM), which agreed on
lists of goods that would be banned or subjected to quantitative limits
in trade with the Communist bloc. The issue had become a source of
US-European disagreement, with the Americans pressing for tougher
limits than European governments felt necessary.[64] Eisenhower's election
seemed to promise a fresh approach and there has been considerable
debate about how successful the President was in pushing a new policy.
Eisenhower, like Churchill, saw détente in the trade field as a way to
create 'centrifugal' forces in the Soviet bloc: freer trade would create
ties between Eastern European counties and the West. But he met
strong opposition in Washington and, in October 1953, merely proposed
to cut 'peripheral' items from COCOM lists.[65] For Churchill this was

---

[61] PREM 11/664, Churchill to Eden, 15 Feb.

[62] Bar-Noi, 'Soviet Union', 122–4.

[63] See especially Moran, *Struggle for Survival*, diary entry of 8 April 1954.

[64] On the background to this issue see especially: A. Dobson, *The Politics of the Anglo-
American Economic Special Relationship* (Brighton, 1988), 125–34; V. Sorenson, 'Economic
Recovery Versus Containment: the Anglo-American Controversy over East–West trade,
1947–51', *Co-operation and Conflict*, 24 (1989), 69–97; and F. M. Cain, 'Exporting the Cold
War: British Responses to the USA's Establishment of COCOM, 1947–51', *Journal of
Contemporary History*, 29 (1994), 501–22.

[65] For praise of Eisenhower on trade see: P. Funigiello, *American-Soviet Trade in the Cold
War* (Chapel Hill, NC, 1988), 77; and R. M. Spaulding, 'A Gradual and Moderate
Relaxation of Tension: Eisenhower and the Revision of American Export Control Policy',
Diplomatic History, 17 (1993), 224. But for a critical view: T. E. Forland, ' "Selling Firearms
to the Indians": Eisenhower's Export Control Policy', *Diplomatic History*, 15 (1991), 226–
33.

not enough. In January he told the Cabinet that 'increased trade with the Soviet bloc would mean, not only assistance to our exports, but greater possibilities for infiltration behind the iron curtain'.[66] Then, on 25 February (despite pressure from Dulles to avoid such a step[67]) he pressed for a reduction of COCOM lists in a speech to the Commons. The speech is widely accepted as a turning point in the story of East–West trade.[68] It allowed Eisenhower to push his own administration towards compromise and by August COCOM lists had been almost halved. 'The main impetus behind the revisions, though, came not from Eisenhower, but from Winston Churchill.'[69] Once again he had proved ready to speak out publicly on East–West contacts, risking an argument with the US; and trade relaxations were to prove the only concrete success of his pressures for détente.

Churchill's hopes of a two-power summit with Malenkov came to nothing in mid-1954, largely because of the same problems he had faced before: opposition from within his own government and from the US, and suspicion from the Soviets. But in the process he demonstrated the extraordinary lengths to which he was prepared to go in order to achieve his last political dream. He faced an initial delay because of the difficulty in timetabling his visit to Eisenhower. This did not take place until late June, largely because it needed to be dovetailed with a recess in the Geneva conference, so that Eden and Dulles could also be in Washington. Once he saw Eisenhower, Churchill won a remarkable *coup*. The American leader agreed there could be a bilateral meeting.[70] The exact reason for this fateful concession is unclear; but of course Eisenhower had earlier reserved his own right to meet the Soviets on a bilateral basis. On the sea-voyage home Churchill, armed with Eisenhower's approval, drafted a message to Moscow, enquiring whether they would welcome a visit from him. Despite some doubts from Eden, the message was sent off immediately, without the cabinet or foreign office being consulted. But such devious methods only ensured that, when Churchill arrived home in July, there was a cabinet crisis. Some ministers, already exasperated with their chief's declining mental state, his inefficient leadership of government and personal

---

[66] CAB 128/27, CC(54)3rd (18 Jan.).

[67] FO371/111207/29, Berlin to FO, reporting Dulles-Eden conversation, 18 February.

[68] James, *Churchill Speeches*, 8535–6; G. Adler-Karlsson, *Western Economic Warfare* (Stockholm, 1968), 91; Forland, 'Selling Firearms', 223; Spaulding, 'Moderate Relaxation', 241–2.

[69] Ian Jackson, 'The Eisenhower Administration, East–West Trade and the Cold War', *Diplomacy and Statecraft*, 11 (2000), 135; and see 129–35 on the 1954 talks. In general see also John W. Young, 'Winston Churchill's Peacetime Administration and the Relaxation of East-West Trade Controls', *Diplomacy and Statecraft*, 7 (1996), 125–40.

[70] FO371/125143/59, record of meeting, 25 June; *FRUS, 1952–4, VI*, 1079–80.

obsessions were determined to resist his latest attempt to circumvent cabinet government.

The opposition was led by Salisbury, who threatened to resign, but Eisenhower also helped the prime minister's critics by expressing surprise at the speed of his approach to Moscow. After some bitter clashes the cabinet agreed, on 9 July, to await the outcome of the Geneva conference before deciding how to proceed. But this simply put off the hour of decision: Geneva, though it resulted in a settlement of the Indo-China war, did nothing to shift Churchill and Salisbury from their positions vis-à-vis a summit. A cabinet meeting on 23 July was as acrimonious as any earlier in the month and it still seemed as though the government could fall apart. Churchill's behaviour at this time, his determination to seek a bilateral meeting and his willingness to offend so many key ministers, argues against those who question the sincerity of his interest in détente.[71] What eventually saved cabinet unity, and ended Churchill's hopes of a Moscow visit, was the behaviour of the Kremlin. The Soviet foreign minister, Vyacheslav Molotov was especially sceptical about a bilateral meeting, partly because the Soviets still harboured doubts about Churchill's intentions, but also, it seems, because any summit would strengthen the hand of Malenkov within the collective leadership. By 24 July Molotov had persuaded his fellow ministers to sidestep the issue and call instead for four-power talks on a European-wide security system.[72] It was this initiative that allowed the embattled Churchill to back away from a bilateral summit and end the mounting criticism within his own ranks. He now wrote to Molotov arguing that the Soviet proposals were at odds with a bilateral meeting and withdrew the suggestion of one.[73]

End of office

Despite his defeat Churchill, was unapologetic about his search for détente. On 3 August he circulated a cabinet paper, arguing that two decades of peace would bring profound changes within the Communist bloc On 18 August came another, suggesting he might initiate a bilateral meeting again, once EDC was approved.[74] But it was at this point that the Achilles heal of the Atlantic alliance was fully exposed. On 31 August the French assembly refused to ratify the EDC treaty and threw the Western alliance into confusion. Hopes of a negotiation with Moscow from a position of strength were lost and Churchill's remaining

[71] Based on Young, *Last Campaign*, 270–84.
[72] Bar-Noi, 'Soviet Union', 124–7.
[73] PREM 11/670, Churchill to Molotov, 26 July.
[74] CAB 129/70, C(54)263 (3 Aug.) and 271 (18 Aug.).

months as premier were dominated by the results of the action. Only in late December did the national assembly approve a plan for German entry into NATO, but the French senate did not follow suit until March. By then Churchill's summit hopes had suffered another blow, with the fall from power of Malenkov. In the wake of this, and with a general election looming, the British premier, too, agreed to set a date for his departure. In mid-March he did think again about a summit, but this time Eden showed forceful opposition, and Churchill finally retired on 7 April.[75] His most famous public statement about East–West relations during these months was his erroneous claim, in a short speech at Woodford in November, that he ordered the stockpiling of weapons in Germany in 1945 for use against the Soviets. The theme of Woodford was actually negotiation from strength, the basis on which he always planned his march to the summit. But his plea for 'closer contact with Russia' was drowned out in the ensuing press furore over the German weapons.[76]

Ironically, Churchill resigned only months before the first East–West summit since Potsdam, ten years before. The solution of the problem of German rearmament put the West in the position of strength for negotiations that he had sought. At the same time the Kremlin saw advantages in a meeting: the new predominant figure, Nikita Khruschev, believed this would solidify his hold on power; and, by signing a treaty in May that neutralised Austria, the Soviets hoped to demonstrate that a similar solution was possible for Germany. In concluding the Austrian State Treaty, Moscow fulfilled the last of the conditions that Eisenhower set for a summit in the 'Chance for Peace' speech. But the US was not keen on a conference and it was Eden who pressed most for one. Facing a general election, the new premier saw this as one way of ensuring a Conservative victory. 'How much more attractive a top-level meeting seems when one has reached the top', remarked Churchill.[77] The summit, held in Geneva in mid-July, seemed to improve the international atmosphere – there was much talk of 'the spirit of Geneva' – but produced no concrete breakthrough.[78] The problems of German reunification, European security, disarmament and East–West contacts were only discussed there in outline. Detailed talks were held at a separate foreign ministers' conference three months later and, as Churchill had always predicted, such a conference produced only

---

[75] Based on Young, *Last Campaign*, chapter 12.

[76] James, *Churchill Speeches*, 8598, and see 8609–22 for a subsequent exchange with Labour critics in the Commons.

[77] Harold Macmillan, *Tides of Fortune* (1969), 587.

[78] See Gunter Bischof and Saki Dockrill (eds.), *Cold War Respite: the Geneva Summit of 1955* (Baton Rouge, 2000).

deadlock.[79] Undismayed, Churchill continued to urge détente for a time, notably in a 1956 speech in Aachen, where he wanted to break down 'bloc politics' and work for a new 'Unity of Europe', in which the Eastern countries would regain their independence.[80]

Conclusion

Michael Howard has described Churchill as a 'prophet of détente', someone who 'looked beyond the hostile ideology of the Soviet state to the evolution of the Russian people themselves' and who recognised 'their growing restiveness at the deprivation enforced by the regime, a restiveness only likely to increase as their contacts with the West multiplied ...'[81] Howard's short essay does not look in detail at Churchill's ideas beyond his calls for a summit and it would be unhistorical to draw too close a parallel between the Cold War in the 1950s and the situation two decades later, when East–West relations were dominated by the effects of mutually assured destruction and the Vietnam War. But it is certainly possible to see Churchill as an early representative of those, more numerous in later decades, who argued that the safest way to fight Soviet Communism was to engage in contact with it and try to break down the hold it had on the peoples of the Eastern bloc. The specific subjects that Churchill emphasised in his campaign for détente – the need to avoid nuclear war, the desirability of a recognised dividing line in Europe (the 'new Locarno') and an expansion of trade between the two blocs – were paralleled in the 1970s by the SALT negotiations, the talks on security and co-operation in Europe and the relaxation of trade limits. Henry Kissinger, a prime architect of 1970s détente took some interest in the British statesman's ideas, seeing them as far-sighted, if somewhat incoherent.[82] Yet Churchill also seems to have had the main attributes of a particularly *European* approach to détente, later identified with Charles de Gaulle or Willy Brandt: a desire to restrain the US from extreme action, to avoid a crusading form of anti-Communism and to mediate between Washington and Moscow; a readiness to engage in trade and talks with the Eastern bloc, to respect the other side's sphere of influence and to develop an ordered relationship with them; and an acceptance of the

[79] John W. Young, 'The Geneva Conference of Foreign Ministers, October–November 1955: Acid Test of Détente', in Bischof and Dockrill (eds.) *Cold War Respite*, 271–91.

[80] James, *Churchill Speeches*, 8674–6.

[81] Michael Howard, 'Churchill: Prophet of Détente', in R. Crosby Kemper III (ed.), *Winston Churchill* (Columbia, 1996), 177–88, quote from 188.

[82] Henry Kissinger, *Diplomacy* (1994), 506–14.

reality of European division in the short term whilst hoping for the breakdown of Communism in the long term.[83]

It is easy to list the main reasons why, notwithstanding his formidable international reputation, Churchill's attempts to initiate détente resulted only in a relaxation of certain trade controls. His own ill health was one factor, particularly his stroke in 1953. Increasingly, his worsening health, his lack of energy and tendency to become obsessed with one issue, made cabinet ministers anxious both to end his hopes of a summit and to be rid of him. In any case, the foreign office never liked the idea of an East–West summit with an open agenda and neither did the Americans. Churchill vastly overestimated his own influence, and the power of his country, when he felt he could act as the Cold War's mediator. US opposition was highly significant, because Churchill wanted to negotiate with the Soviets from a position of strength and that demanded a united Western alliance. But France (because of its desire to secure a European Army) and West Germany (because of Adenauer's opposition to reunification on the basis of neutralisation) were also fearful of Churchill's aims. Even the USSR showed little interest in his schemes. Indeed, Uri Bar-Noi's work in the Soviet archives provides 'proof that Churchill's attempts to bring about a relaxation of the Cold War were greeted with distrust and scepticism' in Moscow. Malenkov did consider meeting the British premier, but Molotov and others were 'neither interested in a three-power summit, nor ... inclined to hold ... Anglo-Soviet talks ... They were mistrustful of Churchill's intentions and had doubts as to whether he had the ability to persuade his American allies to modify their Cold War diplomacy'.[84]

In a sense, Molotov's position was quite justified. Churchill's anti-Communism cannot be doubted, nor can his deep commitment to the American alliance. However, he was a highly complex character whose personal ambition, approach to international relations and understanding of British national interests led him to dedicate the last few years of his active political career to reducing Cold War tensions. There was an *apparent* paradox here but not an actual one. For it was only his belief in the strength of the Anglo-American position, including the position of a superior nuclear capability that allowed him to contemplate negotiations with Moscow: these had to be pursued from a position of strength. And his hope was that détente, through allowing peaceful penetration of the Soviet bloc, would eventually contribute to its withering away. Thus, while he might want to lower the dangers of an East–West conflict in which Britain would be a prime nuclear target,

[83] See the definition in Kenneth Dyson (ed.), *European Détente* (1986), 2–5.
[84] Bar-Noi, 'Soviet Union', 111–12.

he was actually still *fighting* Soviet totalitarianism, a point that some historians of the subject even now fail to grasp.[85] Trade, personal contacts and security arrangements like a 'new Locarno', might mean the survival of Communism in the short-term; but in the long-term Churchill believed that it was a doctrine that could not survive. In December 1952 he even told his private secretary, John Colville, that the latter, if he lived his normal span, would see the collapse of Communism in Eastern Europe.[86] It was not a bad estimate: Colville died in 1987.

---

[85] For example, Carlton, *Soviet Union*, 162–96 and 202–4.
[86] Colville, *Fringes of Power*, 657–8.

CHURCHILL AND THE PREMIERSHIP
By Peter Hennessy

A POLITICAL and literary life of such extraordinary longevity, variety and richness of vocabulary leaves anyone seeking a consistent theme among any of Winston Churchill's verbal puddings with a bowlful of paradox. The conduct of the premiership and the management of cabinet government are no exceptions. Among the papers his no. 10 private office produced for Harold Macmillan in the summer of 1960 when his appointment of a peer (Alec Home) to the foreign secretaryship led to accusations of excessive prime ministerialism,[1] is a Hansard extract for 1938 in which Churchill defends the appointment by Chamberlain of Lord Halifax to the same post on the grounds that the prime minister sat in the House of Commons. 'What is the point of crying out for the moon', Churchill inquired of the Lower House, 'when you have the sun and you have that bright orb of day from whose effulgent beams the lesser luminaries drive their radiance?'[2] And his most famous characterisation of the premiership seems to treat it as a post of licensed overmightiness. 'The loyalties', he declared in his war memoirs, 'which centre upon number one are enormous. If he trips he must be sustained. If he makes mistakes they must be covered. If he sleeps he must not be wantonly disturbed. If he is no good he must be pole-axed'[3] – a case, to adopt a phrase of John Ramsden's, of 'autocracy tempered by assassination'.[4]

Yet Churchill was a considerable romantic about the linked notions of collective discussion and cabinet government. During his last, early 1950s premiership, he told his doctor, Lord Moran, that: 'I am a great believer in bringing things before the Cabinet. If a minister has got anything on his mind and has the sense to get it argued by Cabinet he will have the machine behind him.'[5] As we shall see, he was attempting

---

[1] Among Macmillan's critics, interestingly enough, was the man who had cuckolded him and served as Churchill's Parliamentary Private Secretary in the 1920s, Robert Boothby. Lord Boothby, 'Parliamentary Decline: Way to Bring Back Members' Power,' *Daily Telegraph*, 4 August 1960.

[2] Public Record Office, PREM 5/233, Bligh to Macmillan, 22 July 1960. Churchill had developed his sun-and-stars metaphor during a Commons debate on Halifax's appointment on 28 February 1938.

[3] Winston S. Churchill, *The Second World War, Vol. 2, Their Finest Hour*, (1949), 15.

[4] Conversation with Professor John Ramsden, 2 January 2001.

[5] Lord Moran, *Winston Churchill: The Struggle for Survival 1940/1965*, (1968), diary entry for 28 April 1953.

in his peacetime premiership at least, to bring even the most sensitive issues such as nuclear weapons policy, to the full cabinet for proper discussion before decision in a manner unmatched by most other prime ministers since Britain became (or aspired to become) an atomic power.

But, as with most premiers, one must not lose sight of the irritation that easily arises when the prime ministerial will is not allowed to triumph. As he wrote in another passage of his war memoirs: 'All I wanted was compliance with my wishes after reasonable discussion.'[6] And of that same war cabinet of whom he declared tearfully on its dissolution in May 1945 that 'The light of history will shine on every helmet',[7] he had earlier opined to one of his military aides (on his way back from the Casablanca Conference early in 1942) that: 'It [the war] was now so straightforward that even the Cabinet could handle it.'[8]

Churchill's conduct of his wartime premiership has been hugely researched, exhaustively written-up and widely read about and absorbed. His peacetime premiership rather less so, for understandable reasons, and it is upon the 1951 to 1955 occupancy of no. 10 Downing Street that I wish to concentrate in this paper though much of it will be couched in a running comparison with his style and approach to the job during the Second World War (not least because he was very prone to this himself during his 'recidivist' premiership, to borrow Roy Jenkins' phrase[9]).

It is too simple, however, to juxtapose the 1940–5 and 1951–5 Churchill premierships in terms of a straight contrast between war and peace. However absorbed he was by the task of licking Hitler and Hirohito, Churchill had to devote at least some of his time and nervous energy to thinking about domestic reconstruction as well as a new postwar global geopolitics, increasingly so from the spring of 1943 when the Beveridge debate began to make the political weather at home. Equally, the nature of the east–west conflict (and the exchange of shot and shell in Korea until the armistice of July 1953) meant that his 'Indian Summer'[10] premiership was conducted against the backdrop of a Cold War which might tip catastrophically not just back into the kind of total war with which Churchill was only too familiar but into what Arthur Koestler called 'total war's successor Absolute War'.[11]

[6] Winston S. Churchill, *The Second World War*, IV (1951).

[7] Ben Pimlott (ed.), *The Second World War Diary of Hugh Dalton, 1940–1945* (1986), p. 865, diary entry for 28 May 1945.

[8] Sir Ian Jacob quoted in the *Calgary Herald*, 20 May 1971. I am grateful to Professor John Ramsden for this gem.

[9] Roy Jenkins, 'Churchill: The Government of 1951–1955', in Robert Blake and Wm Roger Louis (eds.), *Churchill: A Major New Assessment of his Life in Peace and War* (Oxford, 1993), p. 491.

[10] Anthony Seldon, *Churchill's Indian Summer: The Conservative Government, 1951–55* (1981).

[11] Arthur Koestler, *The Yogi and the Commissar and Other Essays* (1945), 256.

For Churchill lived his life after July 1945 in the shadow of a mushroom cloud in a sense that was true of no other of the king's (and from February 1952) the queen's subjects. He remains the only British prime minister to have authorised the use of a nuclear weapon against a human target. For under the terms of the 1943 Quebec Agreement, the concurrence of the British prime minister was required before atomic bombs could be dropped on Japan. By the time they exploded above Hiroshima and Nagasaki in August 1945, Mr Attlee was in Downing Street, but it was Churchill who initialled the minute on 1 July 1945, without consulting the cabinet or ministers collectively, which gave British approval for the weapon to be used if the Alamagordo test proved successful.[12] As is well known, the best of his failing energies were devoted in his last premiership to an attempt to ease the Cold War before the atomic weapon's immensely more destructive successor – the hydrogen bomb – brought what Churchill called an 'equality of ruin'[13] to both east and west.

This uneasy limboland between war and peace crops up often in his no. 10 files. Sometimes it appears among his machinery of government papers. For example, when finally accepting the force of argument deployed against the idea of peacetime 'overlord' ministers by both his cabinet secretary, Sir Norman Brook,[14] and the leader of the opposition, Clement Attlee,[15] Churchill told the House of Commons in the autumn of 1953 that he 'had no experience of being Prime Minister in time of peace and I attached more importance to the grouping of Departments so that the responsible head of the Government [i.e. himself as PM] would be able to deal with a comparatively smaller number of heads than actually exists in peacetime.'[16] Yet in a letter to Lord Woolton, one of the 'supervising' ministers whose 'overlordship' (of food and agriculture) he terminated in September 1953, Churchill said: 'I am myself convinced that the system which the Opposition describes as "the rule of the Overlords" is not necessary now that the *war emergency* [my italics] has receded and the [Korean War-related] Armament programme is spread.'[17]

Churchill's last term can best be seen, I think, as a premiership conducted in the shade of four overlapping shadows: he lived it and

[12] PRO, PREM 11/565, 'Record of Events Leading to Dropping Bombs on Hiroshima and Nagasaki', Cherwell to Churchill, 29 January 1953.
[13] PRO, PREM 11/669, draft Cabinet paper on 'Two-Power meeting with the Soviet Government.'
[14] PRO, CAB 21/2804, 'Supervising Ministers,' Brook to Churchill.
[15] House of Commons, *Official Report*, 3 November 1953, col. 15.
[16] *Ibid.*, col. 20.
[17] PRO, PREM 5/225, 'Ministerial Appointments. Ministry of Sir Winston Churchill (Conservative)', Part 3, Churchill to Woolton, 2 September 1953.

operated it in the long shadow cast by his Second World War experience (the 'overlords' were but one manifestation of this); the lengthening and deepening effect of Britain's waning relative power, of which he was acutely conscious, was the second ('You cannot ignore the facts for they glare upon you', he told Anthony Montague Browne, one of his private secretaries[18]); the potentially devastating shadow of the hydrogen bomb, the third; and, finally, his own growing physical infirmity marred many a working day and night especially after his stroke in July 1953.

Prime ministerial recidivism must be the sweetest of sensations, not least because of its rarity (a catharsis shared in the postwar period only by Churchill and Harold Wilson). And part of the joy of Churchill's restoration in October 1951 was the pleasure he took in reconstructing as far as he could both the honorary extended family notion of no. 10 (having those officials around him bonded by shared and past experience) and his peculiar working methods of both the twilight kind (failing to distinguish between night and day) and direction by the vividly worded philippic of a prime minister's minute (though he did not resume the use of those famous red 'Action This Day' labels which the no. 10 messengers had lovingly exhumed for him[19]). As Jock Colville, the only one of the wartime private secretaries who did return to no. 10 (as joint principal private secretary with the incumbent, David Pitblado), put it, ' "Auld Lang Syne" was ringing out along the Whitehall corridors.'[20]

In addition to Colville, Churchill was consoled by another familiar face of wartime officialdom in the autumn of 1951 in the person of Norman Brook, the cabinet secretary. It was Brook who had to bear the brunt of a good deal of nonsense from his prime ministerially born-again chief who had taken it into his head that both the machinery of government and its minders had been progressively blighted by some kind of Attleean virus in the years and months since his eviction from no. 10 on 26 July 1945.

As Colville expressed it many years later:

When Churchill returned as Prime Minister in 1951, he had long since reached the age [he was a month short of his 77th birthday] at which new faces are palatable. He inherited Mr Attlee's Private Secretaries. Arriving at 10 Downing Street with Sir Norman Brook he flung open the door connecting the Cabinet Room to the Private Secretaries' Offices ... He gazed at them, closed the door without

[18] Peter Hennessy, *Muddling Through: Power, Politics and the Quality of Government since 1945* (1996), 202.
[19] John Colville, *The Fringes of Power: Downing Street Diaries 1939–1955* (1985), 634.
[20] *Ibid.*, 633.

saying a word, shook his head and proclaimed to Norman Brook: 'Drenched in socialism'.[21]

It did not stop there. He badgered Brook for weeks to shrink what he seemed to regard as the Whitehall equivalent of feather-bedded nationalised industries – a bloated cabinet committee system.[22] There was some justification for this, but Brook had to make the case *for* cabinet committees as the best way of co-ordinating government business in peacetime – a development of Second World War practice for postwar purposes as described and advocated in the Anderson Report produced by a coalition cabinet committee and presented to Churchill himself in May 1945.[23]

Brook's attempts to sell the virtues of the Andersonian system were complicated by Churchill's determination to revive the wartime practice of 'overlords' as a way of both co-ordinating swathes of government activity and reducing the burden on himself as head of government with the added bonus of allowing a smaller cabinet to be constructed. This 'overlord' question continues to resonate half-a-century later. As I write in the run-up to the general election of 2001, thought is being given in no. 10 and the cabinet office to the *break-up* of John Prescott's 'overlordship' of environment, transport and the regions and to the possible *creation* of overlordships on 'social exclusion' and other areas. Brook's successor-but-five as cabinet secretary, Sir Richard Wilson, is known to have found the paper Sir Norman had waiting for Churchill on the subject in October 1951 of particular interest.[24]

Brook's objections to the idea of peacetime 'supervising ministers', as they were termed at the time, was very similar to those expressed by John Anderson in the last days of the wartime coalition government. The idea, Brook told Churchill in late of October 1951, was 'fraught with serious difficulties both constitutional and practical' because it was difficult to reconcile with individual ministerial responsibility, it was inconsistent with the principle that policy should be formulated by those with the responsibility for carrying it out. Furthermore, the 'supervising minister' concept rested on the assumption that policy could be divorced from administration and it was contrary to the traditions of cabinet government that one cabinet minister should be subordinate to another.[25]

There was a Whitehall complication, too. 'Supervising ministers'

[21] John Colville, *The Churchillians* (1981), 64.
[22] The toing and froing between Churchill and Brook is vividly preserved in PRO, PREM 11/174, 'Request by Prime Minister for List of all Committees in Whitehall...'
[23] PRO, PREM 4/6/9, 'Cabinet Organization. Report of the Machinery of Government Committee', May 1945.
[24] Private information.
[25] PRO, CAB 21/2804, Brook to Churchill.

would be served by officials whose knowledge of the subject matter was less than that possessed by civil servants working to subordinate ministers. Outside bodies, too, would be influenced by the new dispensation seeking to sway the overlords rather than the overlorded. It would be better, Brook advised his new boss, to seek co-ordination through standing cabinet committees of a kind Churchill himself had developed during the war and Mr Attlee had continued in the years since 1945.[26]

Unusually for Brook, his machinery-of-government advice was disregarded. But for the opposition of Anderson himself (offered what Anderson – by this time, Lord Waverley – thought a nonsensical overlordship of the treasury, the board of trade and the ministry of supply[27]), Rab Butler as chancellor would have been reduced to what Robert Hall of the cabinet office's economic section called the status of 'a tax collector'.[28]

Churchill's tenure at the exchequer in the 1920s had left remarkably little trace on him and not just in his failure to appreciate the impossibility of reviving in peacetime the economic and industrial overlordship Anderson himself had operated as Wartime lord president of the council – when a kind of prime minister-for-the-Home front (the 'automatic pilot,' Churchill had called him[29]) – through the lord president's committee, a powerful instrument with a vast reach over virtually all aspects of a siege economy Britain within which the Treasury found itself in unaccustomed eclipse.[30]

During his twilight premiership, Churchill almost matched his opposite number, Attlee, in being 'tone deaf'[31] to the resonances of modern economic policy and its making. Appointing John Boyd-Carpenter financial secretary to the treasury in October 1951, he confessed: 'I was Chancellor of the Exchequer ... for five years and ... I never understood it.'[32] He was quite incapable, for example, of judging on its merits the huge row over 'Operation Robot' during the run-up to the 1952 budget, the eventually abandoned scheme for a 'dirty float' of the pound as a way of easing the chronic pressure on the balance of payments. And how he must have hated being asked to distinguish between production

[26] *Ibid.*

[27] John. W. Wheeler-Bennett, *John Anderson, Viscount Waverley* (1962), 352.

[28] Alec Cairncross (ed.), *The Robert Hall Diaries, 1947–1953* (1989), 176, diary entry for 29 October 1951.

[29] C.R. Attlee, *As It Happened* (1954), 14.

[30] Lord Robbins, *Autobiography of an Economist* (1971), 172; D.N. Chester, 'The Central Machinery for Economic Policy' in D.N. Chester (ed.), *Lessons of the British War Economy (1951)*, 23.

[31] This was the description of Attlee used by his President of the Board of Trade, Harold Wilson. Harold Wilson, *A Prime Minister on Prime Ministers* (1977), 297.

[32] Hennessy, *Muddling Through*, 188.

and productivity at an election meeting in North-East London by a local grammar schoolboy, the future Labour MP, John Garrett.[33] But what of the 'overlordships' which *were* created? It is possible to discern no fewer than five if one includes Field Marshal Lord Alexander brought back from the governor-generalship of Canada to preside over the service ministries as minister of defence, Lord Swinton as minister of materials and Lord Cherwell as overseer of atomic energy, both civil and military. Only two, however, feature in both the declassified files and the parliamentary debates as carriers of the label – Lord Woolton, the Lord President, and Lord Leathers who carried the grand title of secretary of state for the co-ordination of transport, fuel and power. Both were businessmen and both had been engaged in wartime overlording, Leathers as minister of war transport and Woolton, with considerable success, as minister of food.

Neither relished the non-jobs their 1951–3 incarnations turned out to be[34] and it is plain that Churchill never understood either what they were up to (or were supposed to be up to). In one of the most engagingly frank pieces of archive in his No. 10 files for 1951–5, Churchill, as late as August 1953 in a 'SECRET AND PERSONAL (Not to be shown to anyone else)' minute for Brook and the head of the civil service, Sir Edward Bridges made two requests:

1. Please find out the exact relation of the functions of the Secretary of State for the Co-ordination of Transport, Fuel and Power with the work of the respective Ministers concerned. Let me have if possible a diagram.

2. Let me have a short report, one page, on how in practice these are working and what would be the consequences of abolishing, as is my intention, the new office we created when the Government was formed. What arrangements for the co-ordination of business of these Departments are needed as part of the ordinary mechanism of the Cabinet and its Committees.

The minute is capped by a wonderfully wittily ironic extra plea to the two grand technicians-of-state: 'A statement should also be prepared showing how wise and necessary this was and how what has been achieved justifies me (a) in having created, and (b) in now abolishing the post in question. This might extend to 500 words.'[35]

[33] For details of 'Robot' see Alec Cairncross, *Years of Recovery: British Economic Policy 1945–51* (1985), 234–71. For Garrett and his question at the meeting in Woodford, I am grateful to Mr Garrett for sending me his unpublished article, 'My Life with Labour', in December 2000.

[34] Peter Hennessy, *The Prime Minister: the Office and its Holders since 1945* (Harmondsworth, 2000), 194.

[35] PRO, PREM 5/225. Churchill to Bridges and Brook, 9 August 1953.

Why did Churchill, as it were, persist with his 'overlord' experiment over the first two years of the 1951–5 premiership despite Brook's counsel? A sense of failing powers, as Paul Addison has suggested,[36] and a lack of personal touch on home front problems which presented him from doing overmuch co-ordinating himself plus, maybe, a mistaken belief that Leathers' patch could somehow make sense of the nationalisations of the 1945–8 period. The unhappy outcome has, in general terms, deposited 'overlords' alongside 'inner cabinets' in the 'failed attempts' file of those who have sought to streamline cabinet government in more recent times – perhaps wrongly.

The failing personal powers were painfully and frequently apparent to those on the inner circle even before the stroke of the summer of 1953. Though there is an ever-present danger of portraying Churchill in his premiership-of-shadows incarnation in parody terms as a kind of walking (or tottering) off-licence-cum-pharmacy, it was quite inevitable that a great trencherman and bottleman in his late seventies would find a 1950s workload pretty unsustainable. As he admitted to Harold Macmillan, 'at every cabinet today there are discussed at least two or three problems which would have filled a whole session before the first war'.[37] And as Colville confided to Lord Salisbury a few months before Churchill's stroke: 'I hate to be disloyal, but the PM is not doing his work. A document of five sheets has to be submitted to him as one paragraph, so that many points of the argument are lost.'[38]

For all the scattergun nature of the memos he fired off to ministers, often over-reacting madly to what he read in the newspapers,[39] Churchill was surely right, having decided it was his 'duty' to resume the premiership despite living 'most of the day in bed',[40] to focus his remaining energies on the Cold War and Britain's role, ever harder to sustain, as both an easer of east-west tensions (especially after the death of Stalin in March 1953 when he felt powerfully aware of his being the sole survivor of the wartime 'Big Three' of Yalta[41]) and as a potential restrainer of the United States (particularly with John Foster Dulles at the state department from January 1953[42]).

The Cold War was the most powerful single shaper of the style of his final premiership in a number of interrelated ways. Firstly, and this is often overlooked, he had to direct one last British contribution to a

[36] Hennessy, *Muddling Through*, 189.
[37] Macmillan Diary, Western Manuscripts Department, Bodleian Library, University of Oxford. D.25. entry for 22 February 1953.
[38] Moran, *Struggle for Survival*, 401, diary entry for 22 February 1953.
[39] Hennessy, *The Prime Minister*, 183.
[40] Moran, *Struggle for Survival*, 366, diary entry for 20 September 1951.
[41] Hennessy, *The Prime Minister*, 203.
[42] PRO, PREM 11/669.

substantial war – Korea. Here he operated a mixture of personal diplomacy, individual direction and attention to detail which caught his eye that was very much a micro version of the great days of 1940 to 1945.[43] For example, he was deeply ill at ease with the use of napalm in Korea informing Alexander in August 1952 that: 'We should make a great mistake to commit ourselves to approval of a very cruel form of warfare affecting the civilian population.'[44]

A similar, and striking, outburst of fastidiousness affected him when he was reminded that the old wartime deception organisation, the London controlling section, under its new covername of the directorate of forward plans, had engaged in a dash of disinformation ahead of the first British atomic test off the Australian coast in the autumn of 1952 using *The Sunday Express* as its willing (and knowing) instrument. He threw a fit of constitutionalism about it (as he had when he discovered Attlee had managed to conceal £100m of expenditure on developing the bomb from parliament[45]). He recoiled from the deception as:

> The idea of stimulating, through an inspired article, information both true and false, so mixed up as to be deceptive, to any particular newspaper, [as it] is not one hitherto entertained in time of peace. Certainly no departure from the principle that tells the truth or nothing should be made except upon direct ministerial responsibility as an exception in the public interest.[46]

Churchill became the first British prime minister to have a nuclear weapon at his sole disposal when a 'Blue Danube' atomic bomb was delivered to RAF Wittering in November 1953.[47] But it was the over one thousand times more powerful hydrogen bomb (America's Russia's and, when ready, Britain's) that truly preoccupied him during his last years in no. 10. He fully appreciated the degree to which the nuclear question was a prime ministerial one.

[43] On this theme, I am indebted to my former student, Tom Dibble. Tom Dibble, 'The Importance of Being Winston: A Study of the Churchill Government and the Korean War October 1951–July 1953,' unpublished undergraduate thesis, Department of History, QMW, 1996.

[44] PRO, PREM 11/115, Churchill to Alexander, Prime Minister's Personal Minute, M 444/52, 8 December 1952.

[45] PRO, CAB 21/2281B, Churchill to Bridges, Prime Minister's Personal Minute M140c/51, 8 December 1951.

[46] PRO, PREM 11/257, 'Request by Prime Minister for Report from Minister of Defence on Organisation which is Maintained for Misleading Enemy about Our Future Plans and Intentions' Prime Minister's Personal Minure, M 439/52, Churchill to Brook, 16 August 1952. The article appeared as John L. Garbutt, 'Tactical atom bomb exercise planned', *Sunday Express*, 17 August 1952.

[47] Brian Cathcart, *Test of Greatness: Britain's Struggle for the Atomic Bomb* (1994), 273.

Yet, he subjected the making of a British H bomb decision to full cabinet discussion no less than three times in the summer of 1954,[48] and kept the queen fully informed of developments.[49] The horrifying potential of the nuclear age was made plain in a pair of cabinet papers which went to all cabinet ministers. The first of these reached them in the weeks spanning the decision to manufacture a British H Bomb and took the form of a paper from the chiefs of staff pulling together the implications for future defence policy of recent changes in both international politics and military technology on each side of the Iron Curtain.[50] The second was a bone-chilling report on the consequences for both the survivability of government and the UK's civilian population after a thermonuclear war which Churchill and his defence minister, Macmillan, commissioned in December 1954 from a highly secret Whitehall group chaired by William Strath of the cabinet office.[51] Its findings were circulated 'for their personal information' to cabinet ministers during Churchill's very last days in Downing Street.[52]

Churchill, building on the chiefs of staff argument that 'Our scientific skill and technological capacity to produce the hydrogen weapon puts within our grasp the ability to be on terms with the United States and Russia',[53] sold the indispensability of a *British* H Bomb to the cabinet with the argument 'that we could not expect to maintain our influence as a World Power unless we possessed the most up-to-date nuclear weapons'.[54] The minutes suggest that it was restraining an over-adventurous United States in the Far East (these were the years of the stand-off over Formosa, Quemoy and Matsu) as much as deterring the Soviet Union[55] that drove Churchill to insist on this means of ensuring Britain paid the price of sitting at what he called 'the top table'.[56]

Clearly here the 'glaring facts' of Britain's decline from super-powerdom could be – and were – ignored by Churchill as, in his mind, the H Bomb, at one bound, gave Britain the capacity to narrow the gap between London and both Washington and Moscow thereby

[48] PRO, CAB 128/27, CC (54) 47th Conclusions, 7 July 1954; CC (54) 48th Conclusions, 8 July 1954; CC (54) 53rd Conclusions, 26 July 1954.

[49] PRO, PREM 11/747, 'Churchill to HM Queen', 16 July 1954.

[50] This paper was retained by the Cabinet Office until 1999. PRO, CAB 129/69, C (54) 249, 'United Kingdom Defence Policy', 22 July 1954.

[51] PRO, DEFE 13/45, 'The Defence Implications of Fall-Out from a Hydrogen Bomb, Macmillan to Churchill, 13 December 1954.

[52] *Ibid.*, Lloyd to Eden, 21 April 1955.

[53] PRO, CAB 129/69, C (54) 249.

[54] PRO, CAB 128/27, CC (54) 47th conclusions.

[55] *Ibid.*, CC (54) 48th conclusions.

[56] He used these words to Sir Edwin Plowden on being told by Plowden that the UK had the capacity to make the thermonuclear weapon. Hennessy, *Muddling Through*, 105–6.

creating the continuing possibility of the UK being the skilful resolver of the great confrontation between the USA and the USSR. This latter element of the gilt-edged possibility the cabinet failed to buy. For in that same nuclear-tinged summer of 1954, Churchill received probably his roughest ever treatment at the hands of his full cabinet over his attempts at personal diplomacy with both Eisenhower and the post-Stalin leadership while out of the cabinet's restraining reach on the *Cunarder* returning home with his doubting foreign secretary, Anthony Eden, from his Washington discussions.[57]

In the end it was the Russians who snatched the summit prize from Churchill.[58] But, until the very last hours of his premiership, he behaved as if it still might be there for the grasping. For what was there left by way of honours for Churchill to crave? The Nobel Peace Prize. The Nobel Prize for Literature (which he *did* receive for the war memoirs) was no compensation.[59]

It is almost inconceivable now that a man or woman in their late seventies could fill the British prime ministership, however titanic their prior achievements. Nor could the country be run from a bed. For me the element of the Churchill style of premiership which will linger in my own mind when senescence comes to call will be the bedroom scenes of 1951–5 which, between them, throw into relief all four of the shadows in which, by this time, the grand old man lived and toiled. For there in no. 10 he would work, unless the chairmanship of cabinet or a committee intruded, until shortly before lunch, an unlit Havana in his mouth, the bed covered in papers with a secretary from the 'garden room' beside it to take dictation. Also in attendance would be a member of the private office, Rufus, the halitosis-afflicted poodle at the PM's feet and his beloved budgerigar, Toby, performing aerobatics above.[60]

Toby, like his master, was plainly agitated at the prospect of getting his mind round the frailties of the British economy and would become noticeably more excited when the chancellor, Rab Butler, came to brief the recumbent Churchill. He would zoom round the room while opening his bowels in mid-flight in such a fashion that he could lay a deposit on Rab's bald head. On one occasion, the private secretary, Anthony Montague Browne, saw the chancellor out as he mopped his head with a silk handkerchief emitting an accompanying sigh of, 'The things I do for England...'[61]

[57] Martin Gilbert, *Never Despair: Winston S. Churchill, 1945–1965* (1988), 1018–36.
[58] *Ibid.*, 1036.
[59] Hennessy, *Muddling Through*, 194.
[60] *Ibid.*, 1036.
[61] Anthony Montague Brown, *Long Sunset: Memoirs of Churchill's Last Private Secretary* (1995), 14.

In the last months of the premiership, Harold Macmillan was summoned to the bedroom to discuss the horrors of thermonuclear war. That night in his diary he recorded an extraordinary scene in which Toby managed to upstage even the H Bomb. The bird began the meeting sitting on top of Churchill's head. Occasionally he would drop down to take sips from the whisky and soda beside the PM's bed. 'Really', wrote Macmillan,

> he is a unique dear man with all his qualities and faults . . . The bird flew about the room; perched on my shoulder and pecked (or kissed my neck) . . . while all the sonorous 'Gibbonesque' sentences were rolling out of the maestro's mouth on the most destructive and terrible engine of mass warfare yet known to mankind. The bird says a few words in a husky voice like an American actress. . .[62]

Never again will no. 10 be enlivened by such grand and glorious eccentricity or by such appealing furred and feathered friends.

[62] Macmillan diary. D. 19, diary entry for 26 January 1955.

EPILOGUE: CHURCHILL REMEMBERED
Recollections by Tony Benn, Lord Carrington, Lord Deedes and Lady Soames

[The following is a transcription of a panel discussion chaired by Professor David Cannadine in the Chancellor's Hall, Senate House, University of London, on Thursday 11 January 2001].

TONY BENN: Time does funny things to your memory. For the whole of my childhood Winston Churchill was a political giant, but my grandfathers always referred to him as 'young Winston', because one of them was born in 1850 (I never knew him) and the other in 1863, eleven years before Winston was born. All three of them, both my grandfathers and my father, sat with Winston when he was a Liberal before the First World War, and although it may sound impertinent, in our family we always referred to him as Winston, never Churchill, it was just Winston: 'What did Winston say', 'Young Winston' and so on. I had the honour of sitting with him for fourteen years in the House of Commons and have recollections of that time.

Churchill's early politics, the politics of before the First World War, were of course quite radical Liberal politics. The historians will correct me if I am wrong, but I think he set up the labour exchanges, and therefore had an idea that labour had rights. Was he involved in the troops going to the Rhondda? In Wales there is still a recollection of that. But I quoted him regularly in the House of Commons, because in 1914, as first lord of the admiralty, at the time the navy was shifting from having coal-fired ships to oil-fired, he nationalised British Petroleum, and when I did the same with the British National Oil Corporation I used to entertain the House of Commons with the exact words that Winston used in 1914. He bought the Anglo-Iranian Oil Company for £2 million (BP) and he used the most powerful language about how multi-national trusts were squeezing the government of the day and so on. He was well to the left of New Labour, but that covers a very wide range of opinion!

My mother in 1914, it must have been just after the outbreak of the First World War (her father was a member of course at the time) was in the gallery of the House of Commons when Churchill, as first lord of the admiralty, made a statement about some naval engagement. I have never checked it in Hansard and many stories are not true, but I think this one must be. She used to repeat as best she could the phrase he used. He said, 'And I hope the whole Housh will be glad to hear that the German shubmarine wash purshued and shunk' – and that was her recollection of young Winston.

Of course in the 1920s Churchill, as chancellor of the exchequer, followed a policy now being followed by the present chancellor: then it was called the gold standard, now it is called prudence. But he followed a policy which undoubtedly did him an enormous amount of damage among his contemporaries, because it was thought that that absolute purity of economic policy contributed to the difficulties that came in 1929, and I have often thought that if Winston had died in 1931 the recollection of him would have been probably as a failure, even though it would have been quite untrue, whereas of course he lived to achieve far greater things.

Winston was of course a Liberal Imperialist. My father, who was secretary for India 1929–31, had a number of clashes with Winston in the House of Commons. I was introduced to Mr Gandhi in 1931, when I was six years old, I was taken by my father to see him – I have no recollection of what he said or anything I said, which would not have mattered – but I was much impressed by the way in which he took an interest in children. I think I am right that Churchill described him as 'the naked fakir loping up the steps of the viceregal lodge to parley on equal terms with the representative of the King-Emperor'. And I have a video of Winston from the 1930s, in which he talks about 600 million poor benighted Indians, who depended on the empire to preserve their society. That was his position and although it is easy now to dismiss imperialism, it was part of the whole philosophy that illuminated the thinking not just of Conservatives but of many Liberals as well.

The first time I ever heard him speak was in 1937, when my father, who had been defeated in 1931, was re-elected and he took me to the House of Commons as a twelve-year-old boy, introduced me to Lloyd George, and I sat in the gallery and I heard Winston warn about the Nazis. In our household the hostility to Neville Chamberlain and appeasement was enormous and the admiration for Winston was very, very great. When he went back to the admiralty in 1939, before he became prime minister, a message was sent out 'Winston is back', so the navy knew he was there, and then, of course, when he took over after the famous Norway debate, he provided absolute inspiration to everybody. I lived in London during the blitz and I remember it very well indeed. The speeches that he made really did inspire us. On his eightieth birthday when he made a speech, which I attended, at Westminster Hall, you were probably there Mary Soames (was that when the picture was given to him which subsequently came to an unfortunate end?), he dismissed his role. He said: 'People say I was the lion. The British people were the lion and I was privileged to give the roar.' I remember that very modest account of his interpretation of his role as a political leader.

There is a family story here you will allow me perhaps to tell. In the summer of 1940, when the war was really going very, very badly, there was a big discussion in the press as to whether children should be sent to America. My brother David, who was then twelve, wrote a letter to my mother saying 'I would rather be bombed to fragments than leave this country'. My mother wrote to *The Times* about it. Brendan Bracken drew this to Winston's attention and in the middle of this period of war Winston, in his own hand, wrote a letter to my mother about it. My brother has this letter, the copy is in the Churchill Library in Churchill College, Cambridge, and he sent my brother a copy of *My Early Life*. Now you think of a prime minister having time to write a manuscript letter at that period in history! It is just an indication of the extraordinary qualities of the man.

About a year later, when Winston and Clem [Attlee] were in coalition, Winston said to Clem 'We need a few more Labour peers' and so Clem said to my dad 'Would you like a peerage?' My dad was then sixty-four or something, he had rejoined the air force because he felt during the war you had to fight and not be a parliamentarian – he ended up as an air gunner before they caught up with him, because he had been a pilot in the First World War. He took the peerage, he didn't consult me, which made me very angry, but he asked my elder brother, because of course in those days there were no life peerages, and my elder brother didn't care one way or the other. Then my brother was killed in 1944, so by the time I got into Parliament in 1950 as a member of the House of Commons my father was already seventy-three, but the local Labour constituency association very sweetly never raised the matter of the peerage at the selection conference, though I did tell them.

Dingle Foot once told me a marvellous story about the difference between a cabinet that Winston presided over and a cabinet presided over by Clem. Dingle was parliamentary secretary at the ministry of economic warfare, a very junior job, and he was occasionally brought into the cabinet with some issue that had to be clarified. He said when Winston was in the chair, which was most of the time, he had the opportunity of hearing the most brilliant historical summary of the whole history of the human race, culminating in the period they had reached, and he said 'I left the Cabinet without knowing what I had to do.' When Clem was in the chair he would say 'Right minister, what is it', 'Right, agreed, right', and he said 'I left the Cabinet about two minutes later, knowing exactly what I had to do.' Churchill's quality of historical analysis is difficult if you want a quick decision, but it is the only thing which makes politics tolerable.

The other thing I remember about the war was Winston's attitude to the alliance with the Soviet Union, because he had been a bitter critic of the Russian Revolution. But as soon as Hitler attacked Stalin in 1941 Winston came out one hundred per cent for the Anglo-Soviet alliance. I have copies of the magazine *British Ally*, which was published in English here and in Russian in the Soviet Union, and his support for the Soviet Union when they were bearing the brunt of the war was one of the factors that interested me.

Now we come to the end of the war. I was on a troopship coming back in 1945 and I heard his broadcast saying 'If Labour was elected a Gestapo would be introduced.' Clem, whatever his weaknesses, wouldn't harm a fly, but it was an indication that Winston in campaigning mode was capable of using fairly strong language. Actually he and Clem got on very well together. I think they had the same nanny at one time or another.

When I was elected an MP Clem was prime minister, but a year later Winston became prime minister again. In those days you could actually ask the prime minister a question and get an answer, a thing that is inconceivable nowadays, and I remember asking him a question about atomic weapons and I got a perfectly straightforward answer about the nature of our relationship with the United States. Clem Attlee came up to me afterwards and said 'You had *no* right to ask that question without consulting me. I am the only one who knows what the arrangements were', which was probably true. I think almost a couple of days after I was elected was the famous occasion when Winston pursued Clem over the question of an American admiral. Under the arrangements, before NATO I suppose, an American admiral was put in charge of the Atlantic fleet and Winston absolutely tore Clem into shreds at prime minister's question time. That was the day Mrs Attlee had asked the new MPs to tea, so I went to Number 10, very excited as a new MP, and Vi Attlee turned on Clem with absolute brutality and said 'You made a fool of yourself, why didn't you know the answer to the question that Winston was putting', and Clem scuttled out like a mouse, because he was so frightened of Vi!

In 1951, when Winston got back into power, he appointed Walter Monckton as Minister of Labour. Now Walter was a member of parliament for Bristol and I travelled down on the train with him at one stage and he gave a marvellous account of the occasion when Winston appointed him. 'All he said to me was "Walter, I want you to look after the home front" ', and that phrase, to deal with the whole of labour in terms of 'the home front' during a war, seemed to me very characteristic. Lady Violet [Bonham Carter], who I knew of course, adored Winston. I think he went to speak for her in the 1951 election and she said at the meeting 'A cat may look at a king.' She was a Liberal and he was a Conservative, but those were the early days of 'the third way'.

When it was clear I was going to be thrown out of the Commons when my dad died, I wrote to Winston: 'Dear Prime Minister, you refused a peerage, can you help me with my problem' and so on. And he wrote me a lovely letter back, saying 'I think yours is a very hard case, I think people *should* be able to give up their peerages.' He did add 'and resume them later', because coming from aristocratic stock the idea of giving them up forever would be a bit much! So I wrote to him and thanked him and said 'Can I publish your letter' and he said 'I can't, because it has to be confidential because I am Prime Minister.' But the day he resigned I wrote to him again and I said, 'Dear Sir Winston, now you are not in office, could I publish your letter' and do you know, within twenty-four hours of retiring, when he must have had ten million letters, he arranged to send me the same letter for publication. And when I was thrown out of the Commons and I fought a by-election, I must have been the only Labour candidate, I circulated 25,000 copies of a photocopy of Winston's letter, which played some part in getting me re-elected – and then of course thrown out again. The only time I ever spoke to him personally, I went up to thank him at the end of a vote at 10 o'clock and he said to me 'You must carry on' and I owe a lot of the victory that ultimately came to that.

I am very proud that my sons Stephen and Hilary, who is now a member of parliament, saw him from the gallery in the House of Commons. And of course I remember the 1945 election, which I forgot to mention, when we canvassed Number 10, before the Thatcher gates were up, and Jeremy Hutchinson, the Labour candidate, with me driving the loudspeaker van (which is much harder than flying a plane) went to Number 10, to the front door. Jeremy Hutchinson said 'I am the Labour candidate and I have got the electoral register here and there is a Mr Churchill I want to canvass', and the whole domestic staff were brought out, it was like *Upstairs, Downstairs*. The butler in the front said 'We are all Conservative in this house' and a maid at the back with a little bonnet, I give her full marks, said 'And we would lose our jobs if we weren't!'

I am very, very proud to have been a contemporary of Winston and to have known him. His memory will remain as an example of someone who believed what he said, said what he believed, did what he said he would do if he got there, even if you didn't agree with any of it.

LORD CARRINGTON: I think it was a very great pity that Tony Benn was encouraged by Winston Churchill to leave the House of Lords: we could have done with him, after that splendid speech he had made. I think that Bill Deedes and I are the only surviving members of the last Churchill administration. I must tell you that I was there in a very humble capacity, as parliamentary secretary to the Ministry of Agriculture and Fisheries and I can't say that I spent much time at that time in the cabinet room seeing the prime minister. In fact I think I only went into the cabinet room twice during that particular time and so you must forgive the inadequacy of what I have to say.

I would just like to say one or two things about what Winston Churchill meant to my generation, those of us who were growing up in the 1930s. Of course he was a very controversial figure. He was a hero in my home, partly because of his policy against appeasement, partly because my family were also Liberal Imperialists and they agreed with him about India. But of course in a way what he was saying at that time was against the mainstream feeling in the Conservative Party and in the Labour party, generally speaking, and I think that there were great doubts amongst ordinary people about his judgement, which I suppose in a way was reinforced when he supported the duke of Windsor at the time of the abdication crisis. He was I think to some extent mistrusted in the country, and even when he became prime minister, though most of us were rather pleased that a real leader was going to be prime minister rather than Neville Chamberlain.

My first cousin, Jock Colville, who was private secretary to Neville Chamberlain and so to speak inherited Winston Churchill at Number 10, in his diaries (which he should never have written) really made it quite clear what trepidation those at Number 10 felt when Winston Churchill arrived as prime minister. The diaries are very frank and I know they are true, because he used to talk to me about it. It didn't take him very long to realise what a mistake he had made.

For me and my generation, my fellow officers, it was a very great relief that we felt that we then had (I was in the army at the time) a man who was a leader, a fighter, with a soldier's reputation and with the power to inspire our partners. Those of us who were alive at that particular time will never forget the debt that we owe him. I mean, his voice on the radio, his unmistakable figure, that wonderful billycock hat that he wore, the boiler suit, the formidable face, the personification of resistance – it was impossible to believe in defeat when he was there.

At the time, in 1940, I was commanding a very great military outfit, the demonstration platoon at the Small Arms School in Hythe, and when we were not doing demonstrations and teaching people how to fire weapons we spent every night on the beaches at Hythe, which was a place where the Germans might have landed. In my platoon I had forty-eight men, three bren guns, forty-five rifles and my pistol, and we had three-and-a-half miles of beach. You won't believe this, but it simply never occurred to me that we were going to be defeated. I was really in a way rather sorry for the Germans if they arrived on my beach! I am quite sure that that spirit was very largely due to Winston Churchill: the feeling that we had a leader who inspired us and was determined that we weren't going to be beaten. Of course we didn't understand the problem, but it seemed to me then and it seems to me now that we were in good hands and that those now who are very critical about what happened simply weren't alive at the time and don't know what we who were there felt about him.

After the war I took my seat in the House of Lords, rather against my wishes, but I didn't have the guts of Tony Benn. I remember that when I first took my seat I decided to go and look down at the House of Commons from the peers' gallery at all these extraordinary figures whom one had known about during the war, who seemed larger than life, because there they had been headlines in the paper. I was quite convinced that they were going to look quite different from ordinary human beings, that they had bigger heads and haloes and were grander in every respect than ordinary people. I was deeply disappointed when I looked down from the Peers' Gallery to find that they were very ordinary people – with two exceptions. One (sitting on the opposition benches) was Winston Churchill, who looked quite different from everybody else in his bow tie and his black short coat and the pinstripe trousers and that extraordinary head and the sort of bulldog expression. He looked quite different from anybody else on the Conservative benches. And on the Labour government benches, there was Ernest Bevin, who also looked quite different from anybody else. He looked like some gigantic benign frog, but he looked a big man. Those were the two who, in my judgement, stood out.

Looking back on that, what a very difficult time that must have been for Winston Churchill. He must have felt how ungrateful the British public were to him when, after five or six years of war, he was defeated at the [1945] election. Whatever the reasons were, he behaved with remarkable generosity at that time.

About a year later, I became a whip in the House of Lords and there was a custom that the leader of the Conservative party came and had lunch once a year with the chief whip and the whips. Winston Churchill came along and we sat in the dining room of the House of Lords, and of course we looked at him with great awe because of his reputation. He was obviously either bored or in a very bad temper, or both, and for the first course and the meat course he never really spoke at all, he just sat there looking thoroughly bored and disagreeable. We were getting more and more uncomfortable and shifting about in our seats, when in through the door of the House of Lords dining room came Bessie Braddock, who, as some of you may remember, was rather large and had a considerable reputation. Winston Churchill looked at her as she went by and then she disappeared. He said 'Ah, there goes that constipated Britannia', and he was so pleased with this comment that he then became absolutely a different person and we saw something of the magic and the fascination of his personality.

Then when he became prime minister again in 1951, I must say it never occurred to me that anybody was going to offer me a job. So on the day after the election I was not waiting at the end of a telephone for Randolph Churchill to pretend that he was the prime minister and offer me a job. But I was, if one can be so politically incorrect, out shooting partridges at home. About 3 o'clock in the afternoon somebody came running up from the house and said to me 'Number 10 wants you on the telephone.' I was a bit surprised, so I hurried back and rang up Number 10 and I was put through and waited, and there was the prime minister on the end of the telephone. He said 'I hear you have been shooting partridges' and I said 'Yes, prime minister'. He said 'Would you like to join my shoot?' And there I was, appointed as parliamentary secretary to the ministry of agriculture and food. Now can you imagine the prime minister today ringing up the most humble parliamentary secretary to ask him if he would take a job in his government? I thought it was the most extraordinary thing to do, and something which I shall never forget.

About a couple of years later, there was a terrible scene, a terrible crisis, in Critchell Down. This was a situation in which the lines of the graph had crossed between the rights of the private owners of property and the need to produce maximum production of food. The ministry of agriculture, and I indeed, had taken the view that maximum production of food, because we still had rationing, was more important than the rights of the owners. But now the rights of the owners became more important than the production of food. There was a terrible scandal and everybody was blamed and Tom Dugdale, my boss, resigned. I thought since I had been wrong too I had better resign as well, so I put in my resignation. I was sent for by the prime minister to the cabinet room and he said to me 'You put in your resignation.' I said 'Yes prime minister'. 'Do you want to resign from my government?', he said. I said 'Well no, of course I don't.' He said 'Well, then you'd better not.' So that was that! And when he said that to you you certainly didn't contradict him.

Parliamentary secretaries didn't very often go to the cabinet, but when Tommy Dugdale or someone was away, I remember going to a cabinet meeting in which there was a discussion about whether or not we were going to take rationing off sweets or off meat, I can't remember which it was. Gwyl Lloyd George, who was the minister of food, said that he felt that it was not possible to remove rationing, because we didn't have enough supplies and it was impossible to do it. But I remember the prime minister saying 'We said we were going to do it and we *will* do it, so that's that.' Of course it was done and it was perfectly alright, but it was an example of the conviction and the courage that he had. He was determined to get rid of the bureaucracy and constraints and regulations and all those things that were inevitable in a time of war and which hung on after the war.

I suppose you could say that he stayed on too long as prime minister, but then, who doesn't? I mean, they all do. I suppose the only one who didn't really was Harold Wilson, I think probably he was the only one. I don't know whether he regretted it, but certainly in my Australian days, when I was in Australia, Bob Menzies resigned and he regretted it forever afterwards, because he disliked all his successors so much. I think there is a compulsion on people in high places not to like their possible successors and to stay as long as they can. So I think that that was probably true, and anyway, my party has a great history of disloyalty to its leaders. Everyone, from Winston Churchill downward, has been stuck in the back by a knife. Eden, Alec Home, Ted Heath, Margaret Thatcher, John Major, they have all been, so I suppose to some extent the prime minister of the day has to ignore that.

Just one final thought. There is a fashion now to judge people of a different generation by the standards and customs and thoughts of the present generation. Now I think that is a very difficult and wrong thing to do. How can you really judge what people felt like when they were born 130 or 140 years ago and were brought up in totally different circumstances and totally different customs than those which you find today. I think those critics of Winston Churchill sometimes seem to ignore that. That is certainly so about his feelings about Liberal imperialism and all the rest of it, people now don't understand. One example of this relates to Churchill's views on Europe. When I was at NATO I had to go to Zürich and make a speech and I thought it would be quite a good idea to read that famous speech Churchill made in Zürich, in which most people now think that he was advocating British membership of the European Union. If you read the speech, of course, he wasn't doing anything of the kind. What he was saying was that people should be magnanimous in Europe, Europe must get together and forget what happened. But Britain was quite removed from that: we were not part of Europe, we were part of an alliance which had won the war with the Americans, the Europeans had not really been enormously successful in the war, we defeated the Germans, the French had been defeated, the Italians had been rather ambivalent one way or the other, and there wasn't a particular reason why he felt that we should join Europe. We had an empire; Churchill was brought up in the days when a quarter of the land surface of the world was coloured red and was British. That is the sort of thing that people nowadays seem to me not to understand about people of his generation.

What an extraordinary man Churchill must have been. Of all the people that I have ever met in my life I think that I admire him most of all, and I think he did more than anybody I know to enable all of us to live the sort of lives that we live now. For me it was a privilege to have known him as distantly as I did and I am very happy I did.

LORD DEEDES: I did have a certain amount to do with Winston in the 1930s, mainly over India, because *The Morning Post*, the newspaper I was on, worked together with Winston against self-government for India. But I don't want to dwell on that so much, what I want go dwell on is a quality in Winston, one single quality which I have come greatly to admire and which I think is very much underrated. It came into my mind very forcibly the other day when I was looking through a volume which has just appeared, Martin Gilbert's volume *1941, The Churchill Papers*. It is an enormously thick book and it carries all the papers connected with Winston in 1941. It put in my mind, reading through these papers in 1941, something that Field Marshal Wavell once said. Wavell said he thought that the prime requirement for any general was mental robustness. Now in my view that was a quality which Winston had abundantly and in my belief that mental robustness was an enormous factor in his getting through the war and getting us through as well. I want to dwell on this, because I think it is a much rarer quality in politics now than most people believe.

I want to dwell on the year 1941, not at all a cheerful year. In fact if you think about it, between Winston taking over in 1940 and the Battle of Alamein in October 1942, which is roughly twenty-eight months, there weren't really many happy days in the course of those two-and-a-half years. And throughout that period, Winston had to run the war and govern the country, with a stream of bad news, much of which we knew nothing about. I can remember (I was a soldier at the time like Peter Carrington) getting pretty depressed at various times during that period. But for Churchill, who was privy to countless setbacks, difficulties, disasters of which the rest of the world knew nothing, it must have been a supreme test of mental robustness.

Let's just go through some of the factors that weighed on his mind. First of all, I think hardest to bear of all, was the bombing that began almost as soon as he took office, the lives lost and the destruction it created. There is a passage in the 1941 papers of a visit by Winston to Plymouth after it had been bombed four nights out of five. Winston was appalled by what he saw and at the same time got a warning from various people that the country would not be able to put up with much more of it. Imagine that weight of thought on the mind. When he left Plymouth he kept saying to Jock Colville and others with him 'I never saw the like', he really was profoundly upset.

After the bombing, factor two, the sinking at sea by U-boats, with which Churchill was amply familiar because he knew all about it from the First World War. He knew quite well that the U-boat campaign against the ships bringing supplies to this country could ditch us. There was the position in France, this is the third factor. How to deal with Vichy; what to do about the French navy; what, above all, to do with General De Gaulle who, for all his great patriotism, was extremely tiresome through a great part of the war to Winston. Then there loomed, this is the fourth factor, over much of this period the threat of invasion, which was acute in 1940, slightly relieved in 1941 and when Russia was attacked by Germany probably faded into the background. But that was a factor constantly to be borne in mind. There was the need to rebuild our army after the defeat at Dunkirk, not simply for war in the desert, which was to take place, but ultimately for a return to Europe. Then after Russia was attacked by Germany in 1942, constant pressure from Stalin for more support and eventually a call for a second front long before we were ready for it. Churchill was under constant pressure from Stalin to open up the second front.

There was also a critical House of Commons, with many of the loyalists, remember, in those days absent in uniform. Those loyal to Churchill, many of them were away from the House, they were in uniform and they were involved in the war. There is this passage, I think in June 1941, from Chips Channon's diary: 'On all sides one hears increasing criticism of Churchill, he is undergoing a noticeable slump in popularity and many of his enemies, long silenced by his personal popularity, are once more vocal.' Crete had been a great blow there. That is another factor to weigh on the mind and keep somebody from sleep. There was the ever urgent problem of keeping American on our side, until Pearl Harbor, and giving us as much neutral aid, pseudo-neutral aid, as they could be persuaded to do.

Now my list is not complete, but there are nine constant anxieties, any one of which really would be enough to absorb the human mind, constantly nagging, constantly nagging at Churchill's mind. And from this flood of anxiety, if you think about it, really no relief at all. I can't think of any time in our history when a prime minister was subjected to such an unrelieved burden. In the First World War, you may remember, the duty in a sense was shared – Asquith in a sense did the first half of the war, Lloyd George did the latter part. In the Second World War Winston bore responsibility from 1940 until the finish. Although he had the wit to devise recreation of his own sort, it wasn't much to live on. What he really enjoyed at Chequers was a good film and probably his favourite film was a film about Nelson and Lady Hamilton made by Alexander Korda, whom he knighted in 1942. Churchill really enjoyed a thoroughly sentimental film, but that was about the only recreation he got. He enjoyed his meals, he enjoyed good company, his sleeping hours were eccentric but then they were what he needed.

George VI found the burden of the war very heavy indeed and got very depressed. Churchill and the king used to have lunch once a week at Buckingham Palace – rather a frugal lunch I may say. But anyway, that weekly talk, in the presence of Queen Elizabeth the Queen Mother, was mutually supporting.

Winston's life before 1940 was very much a preparation for what really amounted to a tremendous threat to his sanity. He began his career as a subaltern, he fought in a number of wars, he was at Omdurman (I have been there at that battlefield, I know exactly how he was involved in the Lancers charge), he had big setbacks at the Dardanelles when he was first lord of the admiralty, he left the government to go into the front line. There is a very good story about why Winston went into the front line. He was with the Grenadier Guards, who were dry at battalion headquarters. They very much liked tea and condensed milk, which had no great appeal to Winston, but alcohol was permitted in the front line, in the trenches. So he suggested to the colonel that he really ought to see more of the war and get into the front line. This was highly commended by the colonel, who thought it was a very good thing to do.

Churchill's mental robustness was also much tested during what is called his wilderness years: he was out of office 1929 to 1939, quite a long time for a man with his abilities. There was the battle over India, which I was faintly involved in, and the battle over rearmament just before the war. Now some will argue that when I talk about mental robustness I am talking about courage, which of course is not in question. But not quite, because few men, no matter how courageous, could have sustained the constant adversity of the first twenty-eight months of that war and emerge from it as triumphantly as he did. There were men in history who showed the same quality, but most of them were altogether more roughly hewn than Winston. There were plenty of men who were less sensitive, they didn't have a cat sleeping on their bed, they didn't keep a pet canary like Winston. There was a very gentle side to Winston, which is rarely matched with people of such resolution. And the men who were in a sense as mentally robust as Winston, they weren't given as readily to tears as Winston, who cried very easily, showing a side of his nature which many people didn't suspect was there. That seems to me the amazing feature of this mental robustness: the fact that it was a nature which had an altogether softer side, an altogether kindlier, more thoughtful side than anyone might suppose. It was not a ruthless temperament, it was not a brutal temperament, it was a sensitive temperament mixed with mental robustness. And in my judgement, no one has ever really assessed sufficiently what that mental robustment meant for this country at the most critical time in its life. That fact alone has led me, the more I think about it, very close to believing in destiny.

LADY SOAMES: I have to say it has been a great thrill for me and very moving to sit here with former colleagues and friends of my father and to hear their different approaches to him. Given the distinguished audience we have got here I feel rather nervous, but I would like just to pick out two aspects of my father's life – one about his character and the other which is a slight sort of fancy on my part about him.

I want to talk about my father's quality of naturalness, which as a matter of fact has been brought out very much, both by Tony Benn and by Peter Carrington. This quality was apparent principally of course to his family, colleagues and friends. He was extremely natural and almost, I would say, entirely lacking in hypocrisy. I can truthfully say that he was the least pompous person I have ever met in my life. Even as his standing and fame grew, his public and private persona remained very much the same and many of those who knew him, both in private and public, have testified to what I can only call the sort of oneness of his character. His engaging, almost uninhibited frankness of expression and candour often I think quite surprised people, who were accustomed to more guarded and more circumspect public figures.

I remember an occasion when this was strongly demonstrated. I was accompanying my father after the war, during his second prime ministership. He was going somewhere tremendously important to be received, I am not sure it wasn't to have a freedom or perhaps a degree or something. I think my mother must have been away and I was in charge, and I was appalled to realise that we were going to be extremely late, so I was much embarrassed, and my father even seemed a little bit fussed, the way he kept looking at the turnip (which he called his watch) – 'we are going to be very late'. So when we got there I thought 'oh dear, glum faces'. Not at all. Charming people on the doorstep, mayors in robes and gold chains, and everybody saying 'Oh prime minister of course we quite understand'. My father got out and said 'I am so sorry I am late', 'Oh no prime minister, we quite understand, we quite understand last minute matters of state held you.' So I thought how wonderful, how divine they are, they have held him out this excuse without him having to say anything, feeling much relieved. To my horror I saw papa going rather pink, which was always a sort of sign that he was going to say something very truthful. He went very pink and he said 'Well, that is most kind of you, but I have to say I started late.' It was so unnecessary, I was quite cross with him!

But it was this very characteristic of an often unguarded spontaneity which he was aware of himself, and I think in his later life, when, particularly at mealtimes, he liked to feel that he could talk in an unguarded way, it caused him very much to prefer small groups of what came to be known as the golden circle, which was the group of his family and closest colleagues and friends. He was always wary, until he got to know them, of strangers. He preferred a small company, which did not include strangers with ears avidly pricked up for quotes, watchful eyes and wagging tongues.

He was blessed in that for him the boundary line between work and recreation was smudged. His life's main work was a natural expression of his gifts for heroic action, oratory and writing. And his naturalness and zest for life were among his most attractive characteristics, of which those of us who were fortunate enough to be close to him were the lucky beneficiaries. As a child at Chartwell I was one of these, although of course for a long time I took my luck for granted. But he was such fun to be with and Chartwell was his playground: landscaping, creating waterfalls and lakes, bricklaying, though I have to say that the charms of being a bricklayer's mate palled fairly soon for me, because moments of boredom caused inattention, which caused dropping of heavy bricks on small toes. So I used to retreat howling to the house quite often.

My father's love and concern for animals, whether farm, wild or domestic, was particularly appealing to a child. My vivid and happy memories are of a man whose zest for life made quite ordinary things exciting, and who despite all other preoccupations and heavy burdens never quite gave up his toys. Among my fondest adult memories of my father in extreme old age is of him on high summer days at Chartwell, sitting for long periods in front of the buddleia bushes, which he had caused to be planted for their delectation, watching the butterflies quivering and hovering, and keeping delighted tally of the red admirals, the tortoiseshells and the painted ladies, which he recognised and knew quite clearly.

The other thing I want to talk about is of how most of us probably envisage my father. For none of us here, or indeed anywhere, can recall Winston Churchill other than as a middle-aged or very old man. Our instant image of him is of a formidable and now legendary war leader, a venerable statesman crowned with honours, the hero of our finest hour. But I like sometimes to try to imagine my father as he must have been as a young man and to try to recapture the sheer dash and dare and determination of the young Winston. Although at Harrow he had not distinguished himself at games, or indeed at anything else very much, he won the public schools' fencing competition – no mean feat. And he must have been superbly fit after his training at Sandhurst as a cavalry officer. He was a brilliant polo player; long days in the saddle on the North-West Frontier; several brushes with death, and in the Sudan the cavalry charge at Omdurman. Then in South Africa the Boer War, the armoured train, his imprisonment and escape, which rang throughout the world, putting him on the front pages where he would remain for the rest of his life. All these adventures were also grist to his emerging skill as writer: pen and sword. Of course to a number of people, particularly senior officers in the field, young Churchill was insufferably bumptious, a medal hunter with an overplus of vitamin I.

But I want to end my contribution by just reminding myself and, if I may, you, of the effect the younger Winston Churchill could have on people. His army days over, the emerging politician soon to be controversial, jumping ship from Tory to Liberal, but already the star quality shone in him obviously, and was recognised by for instance at least one sophisticated observer: Lady Violet Asquith, who met him for the first time at a party in 1906. She was 19, a young woman quite accustomed to the company of brilliant people. He was 32, in his first ministerial office in her father's government. She would write: 'Until the end of dinner I listened to him spellbound. I can remember thinking this is what people mean when they talk about seeing stars. I was transfixed, transported, into a new element. I knew only that I had seen a great light. I recognised it as the light of genius.'

At the time of Winston and Clementine's engagement, his prospective mother-in-law, Lady Blanche Hozier, wrote to an old friend, the poet Wilfred Scawen Blunt: 'He is so like Lord Randolph, he has some of his faults and all of his qualities. He is gentle and tender and affectionate to those he loves, much hated by those who have not come under his personal charm.' And Sir Edward Grey took a charitable view of Winston after colleagues in 1908 had complained that he talked too loudly and too much at cabinets. Similar complaints, I may say, would emerge and are recorded on other occasions down the years. But Sir Edward took the long view and amicably ironic wrote: 'Winston very soon will become incapable from sheer activity of mind of being anything in a Cabinet but Prime Minister.' He also thought young Churchill was a genius, and forecast that his faults and mistakes would be forgotten in his achievements. I think that that long-ago prophecy has largely come true.

CHAIRMAN (DAVID CANNADINE) I thank all our speakers for such a marvellously varied and yet consistent set of memoirs of Churchill.

Question: I was very interested by Lord Carrington's remarks about the disloyalty of Conservatives to their leaders. I don't know whether the story is true, of Churchill sitting on the government benches after the war when a young Conservative MP came up and sat next to him and said 'Mr Churchill, isn't it wonderful to be here amongst all our friends, and across the floor are the enemy', and Churchill growled back 'No my boy, across the floor are the opposition, the enemy is all around you.' My question is to Tony Benn: would that apply today to Tony Blair?

TONY BENN: I think the difference between the Labour and Conservative parties is that the Labour party elects a leader, argues with them from the day they are elected and keeps them until they want to go. The Tory party worship their leader and put a knife between their shoulderblades just as soon as they fail. Now that is the difference. Tony Blair could go on until he is 95, we have never got rid of a leader, but we make life very difficult for them while they are there. But the Conservative party's loyalty, I mean six minutes' standing ovations for Mrs Thatcher, and then we knew that Michael Heseltine was sharpening his penknife. We have never got rid of a leader to the best of my knowledge. Ramsay went, thank God, but that was a different consideration. I met him in 1930 at Number 10 and he offered me a chocolate biscuit, and since then I have looked at Labour leaders with chocolate biscuits very suspiciously and I am getting a lot of them at the moment!

Question: Can I tempt Bill Deedes into saying something about Churchill, *The Morning Post* and India in the mid-1930s?

LORD DEEDES: What happened was, the government determined upon self-government for India quite early on and this came to fruition in the early 1930s. Winston was convinced that it was a false step, not only provincial autonomy would go wrong, but the centre would go wrong, and with I suppose about twenty-five Conservative members on his side and the backing of *The Morning Post* and occasionally *The Daily Mail*, we had this campaign that ran for a couple of years whether or not India should be granted self-government. In fact the Government of India Bill, 356 clauses, was seen through by Sam Hoare and Rab Butler as his number two while all this was going on. In defiance of Winston's wishes, self-government for India was postponed because of the war but was in a sense statutorily arranged before the war broke out.

I of course had sympathy with Winston. I was at the Wavertree by-election where Randolph fought and worked with the Churchill family up there, and I had developed sympathy with the whole thing. But I have since come to see that it was probably a mistake to think that India should not have self-government. It was a misjudgement, you can't alter that fact. Baldwin in a sense was right about it. I think it came out of Winston's great affection for India, his early days on the North-West Frontier, it was from the best motives. But I have to say in all honesty, although I supported the campaign – I was India correspondent for *The Morning Post* for a while – I do think it was a misjudgement.

LORD CARRINGTON: This has got not much to do with Churchill, but I think it is quite interesting about India. In 1947, when the India Independence Bill was going through parliament, it arrived in the House of Lords. The House of Lords was then opposed to independence for India, very largely I think because so many of them had been influenced by Winston Churchill, and this rather derided character Halifax got up to speak and it is almost the only occasion in all the time that I have been sitting in the House of Lords when one speech turned the whole debate. Because of that speech the House of Lords passed the second reading of the India Bill, and it was really rather a notable occasion. He did make the most magnificent speech.

TONY BENN: Halifax, as Lord Irwin, was viceroy of India from 1929–31 when my father was secretary of state. I got from the India Office library the full correspondence between Halifax, this very High-Church Conservative, and my dad, who was a radical man, and the account of India at the time is absolutely fascinating. Irwin was respected in India, because when he arrived it was Good Friday and he wouldn't meet anybody for religious reasons, and the Indians said 'here must be an Englishman who believes in his religion', which surprised them very much indeed. Irwin arranged for Gandhi to come to London for the round-table conference, which is when I met him. I was in the House of Lord when the royal assent was given to the India Independence Act, at the moment when the title emperor of India jumped into the dustbin of history, because after that of course no king of England was emperor of India. As for what Peter Carrington says about Halifax, I must go and read it because sometimes one speech *does* make a difference and if he says that influenced such a reactionary body as the House of Lords it must have been quite a speech.

Question: Mr Benn, you were in the House when the Conservatives came back in 1951. One of the first acts of Churchill was to get rid of everything that was on the Festival of Britain site. Can you comment on what you felt about that at the time?

TONY BENN: I remember the Festival of Britain very well. It was an attempt of course to boost our morale after the war. I think the first exhibition we had was 1946, called Britain Can Make It, and then there was the Festival of Britain, which was as controversial as the Dome. It was actually very successful. I went to the opening and I enjoyed it very much – the skylon, the dome and so on. But Churchill had it cleared. I daresay he wanted the South Bank free of memories. What he would have done with the wheel (the London Eye) now I do not know. But can I just add one thing that came out of Mary Soames's account: what a tremendous sense of fun he had. At Chequers, when I stayed there, a Dutch painting was pointed out to me, in the corner of which Winston had painted a mouse. Another occasion I remember was when he got up at a very critical moment of a debate, it must have been as leader of the opposition, and Attlee was very worried that Winston rose. And Winston said 'If the Right Honourable gentleman wonders about me, I am looking for my zuzubes', he had lost them, and he took one and dragged it down towards him. An enormous sense of fun he had. On one occasion a Labour member had one of these enormously elaborate question – 'Does the Right Honourable gentleman, recognising and remembering and take into account' and so on and so on – it went on about two minutes, and Winston said 'Yes sir' and sat down and he completely deflated the questioner. I think his sense of fun was something that did make him enormously attractive and free of pomposity, and these are the things you remember about people after you have forgotten the political arguments.

Question: One of the greatest blows that Churchill suffered from was of course the defeat in the 1945 election. Lord Deedes, Lord Carrington and Mr Benn had served in the forces during the war, and Churchill believed that the forces voted largely against him. Do you believe that was so, and if so, why was it so?

LORD DEEDES: I would very much like to answer that question. In my view in 1945 Winston was a victim of the between-the-wars government, the National Government that came into office in 1931 on the resignation of a Labour government, a government in which he had no part at all. What the country remembered in 1945 was the best part of three million unemployed during the 1930s – I am not blaming the government, but it happened – that was a major, major factor; laxity over rearmament; Munich, all of which Winston opposed. And I have always believed that the verdict in 1945 had more to do with the record of the government in the 1930s of which Winston was not part, than any kind of comment upon Winston himself.

TONY BENN: Can I confirm that. I was coming back in a troopship in the summer of 1945 and we had a political debate on board the troopship and I was the Labour candidate. There is no doubt whatever that all the troops on board that ship, including people who had served with General Slim in Burma and so on, were undoubtedly in favour of a change. But they weren't anti-Winston, and I think what Bill Deedes says is absolutely right: people said 'never again, we are never going back to the means test, we are never going back to unemployment, we are never going back to fascism, we are never going back to that, we want a new Britain'. And remember this, war does funny things. I think somebody said it is 99 per cent boredom and 1 per cent moments of real danger, so you had masses of time to talk. I learned much more as an aircraftsman second class in Rhodesia and in Egypt than ever I learned at university, because you met people, you talked and talked, and a lot of the discussion during the war was political – what is the war about, what are we going to do afterwards, what is the postwar world going to be like.

I remember on the troopship going out, this was earlier, going to the officer commanding troops and I said 'We want to have a discussion on War Aims.' The colonel said to me, I was the most junior, an aircraftman second class was probably known as a private, 'Well Benn, if you have a discussion on War Aims, I hope there will be no politics'. I said 'Oh no sir, certainly not!'

I have a funny feeling, and this is the difference between the left and the right. I think the right in Britain was fighting the Germans and the left was fighting fascism. That is quite an important difference. We were fighting to see that the ideas of fascism never came, whereas for some people this was teaching the Hun another lesson because they wouldn't learn from the defeat of 1918. I don't know that others will agree, but that was certainly the way that I saw it and my family saw it, and I would be interested to know whether Bill Deedes would go along with that second part.

LORD DEEDES: Good point.

LORD CARRINGTON: If I may just say, in my squadron in France in 1945 there was not one single man who would vote for the Conservative party, not one. This was partly due, as Bill Deedes and Tony Benn have said, to the fact that quite a large number of them were unemployed before the war and had had a pretty awful time, and they remembered it. It was also a fact, which perhaps is not particularly creditable, that quite a number of them thought that if they voted Labour they would still get Winston Churchill as the prime minister. Thirdly, there was an appalling publication called *ABCA*, which was edited by Dick Crossman and which was pure Labour party propaganda, and which we had to go and tell our squadron was the be-all and end-all and the absolute truth in the future. It was the most wonderful Labour party propaganda there has ever been.

LORD DEEDES: As we are reminiscing, they offered me the editorship of *ABCA*, but I turned it down.

TONY BENN: Mind you, we never thought we'd win the election. During the whole campaign in 1945, when I was driving a loudspeaker van in Westminster when I got back from Egypt, not one of us thought we'd win. There were no opinion polls to mislead us, there were no spin doctors to confuse us, and we all thought we had lost. I was at Transport House when the results came out, it was two weeks if you remember after polling day, and I was sitting there in the dark watching the results on an epidiascope, and we couldn't believe it. And out of the bright light into the room came Clem, who had flown back from the meeting at Potsdam, and I saw his face when he heard he was prime minister. The BBC man came up to me and said 'Will you say "three cheers to the prime minister"', for which I was too shy, but Clem was astonished that he had won. So in a sense that confirmed that it wasn't an anti-Winston vote in any way at all.

Question: I want to put a trivial question and a very serious one. I was inspired by Mary Soames' account of the young Winston to ask a question about the very young Winston. Perhaps you can only answer by checking backwards from what you know. If I recall rightly one of the great stories of his early life is that when he was a very young officer the London County Council had put up screens in the music hall to try to cut down the competition and make them somewhat more respectable places, and as a very young officer Churchill was said to have led a gang of young officers and men to knock down these screens. I wonder if this was just a sign of pluck and dash, that he'd like to be at the head of an exciting escapade, or whether there was a more or less conscious and principled gesture against sexual puritanism going on.

LADY SOAMES: No, I am sure you are reading too much into it. I think it was just unseemly larkiness on the part of a lot of perhaps young officers out for an evening. I really refuse to have political correctness cast on my father as long ago as that! I can't throw any light on it, it was before even my time.

D.C. WATT: Coming back to the 1945 general election, if there hadn't been a party truce during the war the results of the 1945 election would be much clearer. The whole country's revulsion was not against Winston Churchill at all, but against the Tory party, the Tory party organisation and the kind of candidates they preferred in the 1930s and during the war.

Question: Churchill believed in a Liberal and Conservative axis, now we have a Labour and Liberal axis. Do you think the Conservative party should try and get back to the Churchillian position and ally more with the Liberals?

LORD DEEDES: This relates to something that Lord Carrington said. One cannot compare the mood, the attitude, the thinking of the Liberal party of Winston's day with the party of today, it is simply not comparing like with like. The Liberal party of Winston's time and the Liberal party of today are two totally different handkerchiefs. People stick to their names and change their views. That is why Winston Churchill changed his own view and joined the Conservative party. The past is no guide whatsoever as to what might happen now, that is the point I want to make.

LORD CARRINGTON: Without being party political, if I were a member of the Liberal party I would be very anxious about what their leadership is doing, because it seems to me that they lay themselves open really to 'what is the point of voting Liberal, you might as well vote Labour'.

TONY BENN: Well, that raises a very big question. If I were a Conservative I would say that, of course, I fully understand that. But I think of Churchill and Macmillan, and to some extent Ted Heath, as One Nation Tories, who would have a lot in common with the Liberal party. Even Clem Attlee, it used to be said he was a typical major from the First World War: it was the horses first, the men second and the officers last. That was the way he saw it, a very responsible view. Macmillan's view was much influenced by the fact that he fought in the First World War and then saw the people with whom he had fought being thrown into unemployment in the interwar years. Harold Macmillan's book *The Middle Way* would lead to expulsion from the Labour party of today, because he said we have to plan our economy. So the politics are very complicated. Of course there always were Simonite Liberals. You know what they said about John Simon – he sat on the fence so long, the iron had entered into his soul. But he was a man who was really a natural Conservative, and ended up of course as Conservative lord chancellor, but he had been a Liberal in the old days and then the Simonites moved over with MacDonald in 1931. It is very complex. Normally, the more progressive of the two parties is destroyed by any coalition, which is why Lloyd George destroyed the Liberal party by going into coalition after the First World War and why my dad would never touch a coalition with a bargepole. He didn't believe in that type of politics, designed to get power and not to do anything.

LORD CARRINGTON: You are coming round to my point of view!

TONY BENN: We might agree about the rapid reaction force as a force undermining NATO, but I won't go into that either.

CHAIRMAN: I think there is a danger that agreement is going to break out and we should probably stop at that point. But before we do so, let me ask each member of our panel if they have a final brief thought.

TONY BENN: The wonderful use of language. It came home to me very much, because of the famous speech he made about the RAF – 'Never in the field of human conflict has so much been owed by so many to so few.' Shortly after that, the BBC had the week's good cause and a Labour MP called Geoff Muff, who later became Lord Calverly, gave the broadcast, and I have never forgotten the words with which he finished. He said 'I cannot put our debt to the Royal Air Force better than the words used by our own Prime Minister. Never since wars began have such a relatively large number of people been indebted to such a relatively small number!'

LORD DEEDES: I will end up by offering you a bit of advice that Winston once gave a very timid Conservative candidate. I was not at the lunch, but the candidate took a sip of Winston's claret and said 'A very nice wine, sir'. And Winston turned to him and said 'Sip burgundy, swill claret.' Keep it in mind!

CHAIRMAN: It has been a great pleasure for me to find myself, wholly by association, sitting in such an illustrious and anecdotally memorable company this evening. We have all been informed, moved, amused and entertained in spectacular style. I ask you to join with me in thanking Tony Benn, Lord Carrington, Lord Deedes and Mary Soames for their marvellous memories of Winston Churchill.

INDEX